THE
INTERLINEAR PSALMS

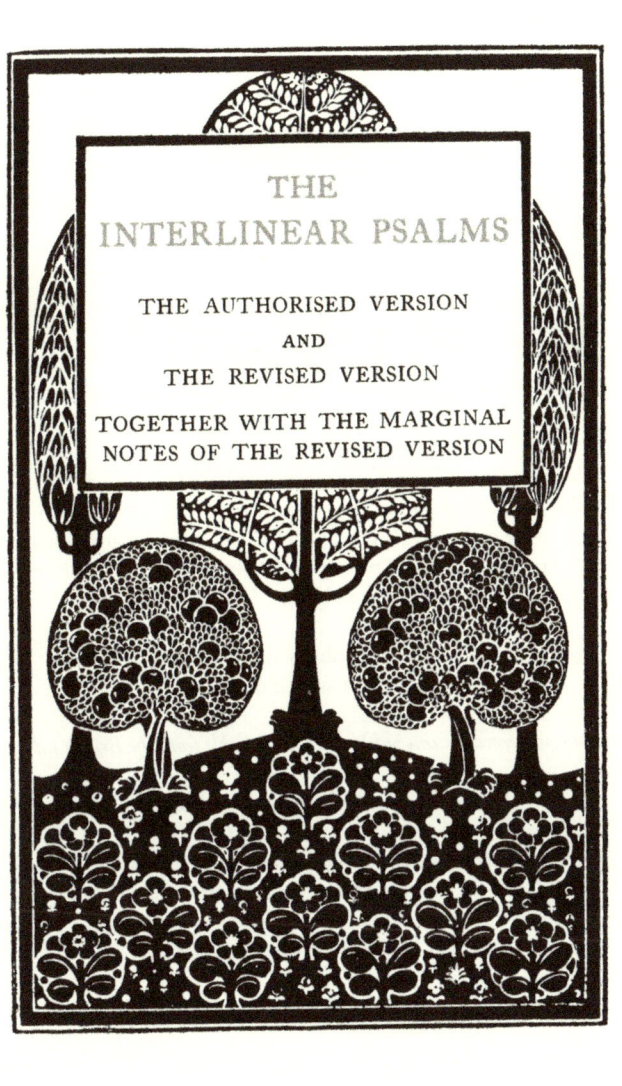

THE
INTERLINEAR PSALMS

THE AUTHORISED VERSION
AND
THE REVISED VERSION
TOGETHER WITH THE MARGINAL
NOTES OF THE REVISED VERSION

CAMBRIDGE UNIVERSITY PRESS
Cambridge, New York, Melbourne, Madrid, Cape Town,
Singapore, São Paulo, Delhi, Mexico City

Cambridge University Press
The Edinburgh Building, Cambridge CB2 8RU, UK

Published in the United States of America by Cambridge University Press, New York

www.cambridge.org
Information on this title: www.cambridge.org/9781107615021

First published 1908
First paperback edition 2013

A catalogue record for this publication is available from the British Library

ISBN 978-1-107-61502-1 Paperback

THE PSALMS

BOOK I

I [1] [1]Blessed is the man that walketh not in the counsel of the ^{wicked,}ungodly,
Nor standeth in the way of sinners,
Nor sitteth in the seat of the scornful.

2 But his delight is in the law of the Lord;
And in his law doth he meditate day and night.

3 And he shall be like a tree planted by the ^{streams}rivers of water,
That bringeth forth ^{its}his fruit in ^{its season,}his season;
^{Whose}his leaf also ^{doth}shall not wither;
And [2]whatsoever he doeth shall prosper.

4 The ^{wicked}ungodly are not ^{so;}so:
But are like the chaff which the wind driveth away.

5 Therefore the ^{wicked}ungodly shall not stand in the ^{judgement,}judgment,
Nor sinners in the congregation of the righteous.

R.V. [1] Or, *Happy*   [2] Or, *in whatsoever he doeth he shall prosper*

⁶ For the LORD knoweth the way of the righteous :
But the way of the _{ungodly} wicked shall perish.

2 ¹ Why do the nations heathen ¹rage,
       And the peoples people ²imagine a vain thing?
   ² The kings of the earth set themselves,
   And the rulers take counsel together,
   Against the LORD, and against his anointed,
       saying,
   ³ Let us break their bands asunder,
   And cast away their cords from us.

⁴ He that sitteth in the heavens shall laugh :
   The Lord shall have them in derision.
⁵ Then shall he speak unto them in his wrath,
   And ³vex them in his sore displeasure:
⁶ Yet I have have I set my king
   Upon my holy hill of Zion.

⁷ I will tell of declare the decree :
   The LORD hath said unto me, Thou art my son Son;
   This day have I begotten thee.
⁸ Ask of me, and I will shall give *thee* the nations heathen for
   thine inheritance,
   And the uttermost parts of the earth for thy
   possession.
⁹ Thou shalt break them with a rod of iron;

R.V.   ¹ Or, *tumultuously assemble*   ² Or, *meditate*   ³ Or,
trouble

Thou shalt dash them in pieces like a potter's vessel.

10 ^{Now therefore be wise,}/_{Be wise now therefore,} O ye kings :
Be instructed, ye judges of the earth.

11 Serve the LORD with fear,
And rejoice with trembling.

12 ¹Kiss the ^{son,}/_{Son,} lest he be angry, and ye perish ⁱⁿ/_{*from*} the way,
For/when his wrath ²will soon be kindled./is kindled but a little.
³Blessed are all they that ⁴put their trust in him.

3

A Psalm of David, when he fled from Absalom his son.

1 LORD, how are ^{mine adversaries increased}/_{they increased that trouble me} !
Many are they that rise up against me.

2 Many there be which say ⁵of my soul,
There is no ⁶help for him in God. Selah.   [Selah

3 But thou, O LORD, art a shield ^{about}/_{*for*} me ;
My glory, and the lifter up of mine head.

4 I ^{cry}/_{cried} unto the LORD with my voice,
And he ^{answereth}/_{heard} me out of his holy hill. Selah. [Selah

5 I laid me down and slept ;
I awaked ; for the LORD ^{sustaineth}/_{sustained} me.

6 I will not be afraid of ten thousands of ^{the} people,

R.V. ¹ Some ancient versions render, *Lay hold of* (or, *Receive*) *instruction* others, *Worship in purity.* ² Or, *may* ³ Or, *Happy* ⁴ Or, *take refuge* ⁵ Or, *to* ⁶ Or, *salvation*

3   A 2

That have set themselves against me round
  about.
7 Arise, O Lord; save me, O my God:
For thou hast smitten all mine enemies upon
  the cheek bone;
Thou hast broken the teeth of the wicked.

correction: wicked. / ungodly.

8 1Salvation belongeth unto the Lord:
Thy blessing be is upon thy people.   Selah.   [Selah

4 For the Chief Musician; on stringed instruments. A Psalm of David.
To the chief Musician on Neginoth,

1 Answer me when I call, O God of my righteousness;

Answer / Hear ... righteousness; / righteousness:

Thou hast set me at large *when I was* in distress:

set me at large / enlarged me ... distress: / distress;

2Have mercy upon me, and hear my prayer.
2 O ye sons of men, how long shall my glory be turned
  into dishonour?

shall my glory be turned / will ye turn my glory ... dishonour? / shame?

How long will ye love vanity, and seek after
falsehood?   Selah.   [Selah

falsehood? / leasing?

3 But know that the Lord hath set apart 3him
  that is godly for himself:
The Lord will hear when I call unto him.
4 4Stand in awe, and sin not:
Commune with your own heart upon your bed,
  and be still.   Selah.   [Selah
5 Offer the sacrifices of righteousness,
And put your trust in the Lord.
6 Many there be that say, Who will shew us *any* good?

Many there be / There be many

4

LORD, lift thou up the light of thy countenance upon us.

⁷ Thou hast put gladness in my heart,
More than _they have_ _when_ in the time _that_ their corn and their wine ᵃʳᵉ increased.

⁸ In peace will I will I both lay me down in peace, and sleep:
For thou, LORD, ¹alone only makest me dwell in safety.

5 For the Chief Musician; with the ²Nehiloth. A Psalm of David.
To the chief Musician upon Nehiloth,

¹ Give ear to my words, O LORD,
Consider my meditation.

² Hearken unto the voice of my cry, my King, and my God:
For unto thee do will I pray.

3 O LORD, in the morning shalt thou hear my voice ;
My voice shalt thou hear in the morning, O LORD ;
In the morning will I order direct _my prayer_ unto thee, and will keep watch. look up.

⁴ For thou art not a God that hath pleasure in wickedness:
³Evil neither shall not sojourn evil dwell with thee.

⁵ ⁴'The arrogant foolish shall not stand in thy sight:
Thou hatest all workers of iniquity.

⁶ Thou shalt destroy them that speak lies leasing :
The LORD abhorreth will abhor the bloodthirsty bloody and deceitful man.

R.V.   ¹ Or, _in solitude_   ² Or, _wind instruments_   ³ Or, _The evil man_   ⁴ Or, _Fools_

7 But as for me, ^{in the multitude of thy lovingkindness will I come} ^{I will come *into* thy house in the multitude of} into thy house , thy mercy :
_{In} _{and} in thy fear will I worship toward thy holy temple.

8 Lead me, O LORD, in thy righteousness because of ¹mine enemies;
Make thy way _{straight} ^{plain} before my face.

9 For there is no ²faithfulness in their mouth;
Their inward part is ³very ^{wickedness:}_{wickedness;}
Their throat is an open sepulchre;
They ⁴flatter with their tongue.

10 ^{Hold them guilty,}_{Destroy thou them,} O God;
Let them fall ⁵by their own ^{counsels:}_{counsels;}
_{Thrust}_{cast} them out in the multitude of their transgressions;
For they have rebelled against thee.

11 ⁶But let all those that put their trust in thee _{rejoice,}_{rejoice:}
Let them ever shout for joy, because thou defendest them:
Let them also that love thy name be joyful in thee.

12 For _{thou}_{thou, LORD,} wilt bless the righteous;
_{O LORD, thou wilt}_{with favour wilt thou} compass him ^{with favour} as with a shield.

R.V.   ¹ Or, *them that lie in wait for me*   ² Or, *stedfastness*
³ Or, *a yawning gulf*   ⁴ Heb. *make smooth their tongue.*
⁵ Or, *from their counsels*   ⁶ Or, *So shall all those...rejoice, they shall ever shout...and thou shalt defend them: they also...shall be joyful in thee*

6

6 For the Chief Musician; on stringed instruments, set to [1] the Sheminith.
To the chief Musician   Neginoth upon Sheminith,
                A Psalm of David.

[1] O LORD, rebuke me not in thine anger,
Neither chasten me in thy hot displeasure.

[2] Have mercy upon me, O LORD; for I am
withered away :
weak
O LORD, heal me; for my bones are vexed.

[3] My soul also is sore vexed :
is also
And thou, O LORD, how long?
but

[4] Return, O LORD, deliver my soul :
Save me for thy lovingkindness' sake.
oh save   mercies'

[5] For in death there is no remembrance of
thee :
In Sheol who shall give thee thanks?
the grave

[6] I am weary with my groaning ;
Every night make I my bed to swim ;
all the
I water my couch with my tears.

[7] Mine eye wasteth away because of grief ;
is consumed
It waxeth old because of all mine adversaries.
enemies.

[8] Depart from me, all ye workers of iniquity ;
For the LORD hath heard the voice of my
weeping.

[9] The LORD hath heard my supplication ;
The LORD will receive my prayer.

[10] Let all mine enemies shall be ashamed and sore
All
vexed :
They shall turn back, they shall be ashamed suddenly.
let them return *and*

7 Shiggaion of David, which he sang unto the LORD, concerning the words of Cush ^athe Benjamite.

1 O LORD my God, in thee do I ¹put my
trust:
Save me from all them that _{persecute}pursue me, and
deliver me:

2 Lest he tear my soul like a lion,
Rending it in pieces, while there is none to
deliver.

3 O LORD my God, if I have done this;
If there be iniquity in my hands;

4 If I have rewarded evil unto him that was at
peace with me;
(Yea, I have delivered him that without cause
_{is}was mine _{enemy}adversary :)

5 Let the enemy _{persecute}pursue my soul, and _{take}overtake
it;
Yea, let him tread _{down my life upon}my life down to the earth,
And lay _{mine honour}my glory in the dust.　Selah.　　[Selah

6 Arise, O LORD, in thine anger,
Lift up thyself _{because of}against the rage of mine
adversaries
enemies ·
And awake for _{me to}me; thou hast commanded judgement. the judgment *that* thou hast commanded.

7 ²_{So shall}And let the congregation of the _{people}peoples compass
thee about:
^{And over them}for their sakes therefore return thou on high.

8 The LORD _{shall judge}ministereth judgement to the _{people}peoples :

R.V.　¹ Or, *take refuge*　　² Or, *So shall*

8

Judge me, O Lord, according to my righteous-
ness, and _{according} to mine integrity ¹that is
in me.

⁹ Oh let the wickedness of the wicked come to
an _{end;}^{end;} but establish ^{thou} the ^{righteous}_{just} :

For the righteous God trieth the hearts and
reins.

¹⁰ My ^{shield}_{defence} is ^{with}_{of} God,
Which saveth the upright in heart.

¹¹ God _{is a righteous judge,}_{judgeth the righteous,}
^{Yea, a}_{and} God ^{that hath indignation}_{is angry with the wicked} every day.

¹² ²If ^a_{he} ^{man} turn not, he will whet his sword ;
He hath bent his bow, and made it ready.

¹³ He hath also prepared for him the instruments
of death ;
He ^{maketh}_{ordaineth} his arrows ^{fiery shafts.}_{against the persecutors.}

¹⁴ Behold, he travaileth with ^{iniquity;}_{iniquity,}
^{Yea, he}_{and} hath conceived mischief, and brought
forth falsehood.

¹⁵ He ^{hath} made a pit, and digged it,
And is fallen into the ditch which he made.

¹⁶ His mischief shall return upon his own head,
And his ^{violence}_{violent dealing} shall come down upon his
own pate.

¹⁷ I will ^{give thanks unto}_{praise} the Lord according to his
righteousness :
And will sing praise to the name of the Lord
^{Most High.}_{most high.}

R.V. ¹ Or, *be it unto me*   ² Or, *Surely he will again whet*

8   For the Chief Musician; set to the Gittith. A Psalm of David.
       To the chief Musician upon Gittith,

1 O LORD, our Lord,
   How excellent is thy name in all the earth !
   Who [1]hast set thy glory [2]upon the heavens.
                                 above
2 Out of the mouth of babes and sucklings hast
   thou established strength,
         ordained strength
   Because of thine adversaries,
                     enemies,
   That thou mightest still the enemy and the
     avenger.
3 When I consider thy heavens, the work of thy
     fingers,
   The moon and the stars, which thou hast
     ordained ;
4 What is man, that thou art mindful of him ?
   And the son of man, that thou visitest him ?
5 For thou hast made him but little lower than
                           a
     [3]God,
     the angels,
   And crownest him with glory and honour.
        hast crowned
6 Thou madest him to have dominion over the
     works of thy hands ;
   Thou hast put all things under his feet :
7 All sheep and oxen,
   Yea, and the beasts of the field ;
8 The fowl of the air, and the fish of the
     sea,

R.V. [1] So some ancient versions. The Hebrew is obscure.
[2] Or, *above*   [3] Or, *the angels* Heb. *Elohim.*

_{Whatsoever}
_{and whatsoever} passeth through the paths of the
seas.

9 O _{LORD,} our Lord,
   _{LORD}
How excellent is thy name in all the earth !

9 For the Chief Musician; set to Muth-labben. A Psalm of David.
      To the chief Musician upon Muth-labben,

1 I will _{give thanks unto the LORD} with my whole heart ;
         _{praise thee, O LORD,}
  I will shew forth all thy marvellous works.
2 I will be glad and _{exult} in thee :
                      _{rejoice}
  I will sing praise to thy name, O thou _{1 Most}
                                         _{most}
  High.
3 When mine enemies _{are turned} back,
  They _{stumble} and perish at thy presence.
       _{shall fall}
4 For thou hast maintained my right and my
  cause ;
  Thou satest in the throne judging _{righteously.}
                                    _{right.}
5 Thou hast rebuked the _{2 nations,} thou hast de-
                        _{heathen,}
  stroyed the wicked,
  Thou hast _{blotted} out their name for ever and
             _{put}
  ever.
6 ³ The enemy are come to an end, they are desolate for ever:
  O thou enemy, destructions are come to a perpetual end:
    ⁴ And _{the cities which} thou hast _{5 overthrown,}
                                          _{destroyed cities:}
  Their _{very memorial is perished.}
         _{memorial is perished with them.}
7 But the LORD _{sitteth as king} for ever :
                _{shall endure}
  He hath prepared his throne for _{judgement.}
                                   _{judgment.}
8 And he shall judge the world in righteousness,

R.V. ¹ Or, *Most High; because mine &c.*   ² Or, *heathen*
³ Or, *O thou enemy, desolations are come to a perpetual end*   ⁴ Or,
And their *cities thou hast overthrown*   ⁵ Heb. *plucked up.*

He shall minister ^judgement/judgment to the ^1 peoples/people in uprightness.

9 The LORD also will be a ^high tower/refuge for the oppressed,

A ^high tower/refuge in times of ^trouble;/trouble.

10 And they that know thy name will put their trust in ^thee;/thee:

For thou, LORD, hast not forsaken them that seek thee.

11 Sing praises to the LORD, which dwelleth in Zion:

Declare among the ^2 people his doings.

12 ^3 For he that/When he maketh inquisition for ^blood/blood, he remembereth them:

He forgetteth not the cry of the ^4 poor./humble.

13 Have mercy upon me, O LORD;

^Behold/consider my ^affliction/trouble *which I suffer* of them that hate me,

Thou that liftest me up from the gates of ^death;/death:

14 That I may shew forth all thy ^praise:/praise:

In the gates of the daughter of ^Zion,/Zion:

I will rejoice in thy ^5 salvation.

15 The ^nations/heathen are sunk down in the pit that they made:

In the net which they hid is their own foot taken.

16 The LORD ^hath made himself known, he hath executed judgement./is known *by* the judgment *which* he executeth ·

R.V. ^1 Or, *people*　　^2 Or, *peoples*　　^3 Or, *For when he maketh ...he remembereth*　　^4 Or, *meek*　　^5 Or, *saving help*

¹The wicked is snared in the work of his own
hands. Higgaion. Selah. [Higgaion. Selah

¹⁷ The wicked shall ᵣₑₜᵤᵣₙ ₜₒ Sₕₑₒₗ,
      be turned into hell,
      Even all the nations that forget God.
      and

¹⁸ For the needy shall not alway be forgotten,
                                        forgotten:
      Nor the expectation of the ²poor shall not perish
      for ever.

¹⁹ Arise, O LORD; let not man prevail:
      Let the nations be judged in thy sight.
              heathen

²⁰ Put them in fear, O LORD:
      Let the nations may know themselves to be but
      that
      men. Selah. [Selah

      ¹ Why standest thou afar off, O LORD?

10　Why hidest thou thyself in times of
      trouble?

2 In the pride of the wicked ³the poor ⁴is hotly pursued;
      The wicked in *his* pride doth persecute the poor:
      ⁵Let them be taken in the devices that they
      have imagined.

³ For the wicked boasteth of his heart's desire,
      And ⁶the covetous renounceth, *yea*, ⁷contemneth the LORD.
          blesseth the covetous, *whom* the LORD abhorreth.

⁴ The wicked, in the pride of his counten-
                  through
      ance, *saith*, He will not require it.
                              seek *after God*:
      All his thoughts are, There is no God.
          God *is* not in all his thoughts.

⁵ His ways are ⁸firm at all times.
                  always grievous;
      Thy judgements are far above out of his sight:
          judgments

R.V. ¹ Or, *He snareth the wicked*　　² Or, *meek*　　³ Or, *he
doth hotly pursue the poor*　⁴ Heb. *is set on fire.*　⁵ Or, *They
are taken*　　⁶ Or, *blesseth the covetous*, but *contemneth &c.*
⁷ Or, *revileth*　　⁸ Or, *grievous*

As for all his ^{adversaries,}/_{enemies,} he puffeth at them.

6 He ^{saith}/_{hath said} in his heart, I shall not be moved:
To all generations I shall not be / for *I shall* never *be* in adversity.

7 His mouth is full of cursing and deceit and
¹oppression/fraud :
Under his tongue is mischief and ^{iniquity.}/_{vanity.}

8 He sitteth in the lurking places of the villages:
In the ^{covert}/_{secret} places doth he murder the in-
nocent:
His eyes are privily set against the ²helpless./poor.

9 He ^{lurketh}/_{lieth} in ^{the covert}/_{wait secretly} as a lion in his den :
He lieth in wait to catch the poor :
He doth catch the poor, when he draweth him
ⁱⁿ/_{into} his net.

10 ³He croucheth, ^{he boweth down,}/_{*and* humbleth himself,}
^{And}/_{that} the ²helpless/_{poor may} fall by his strong ones.

11 He ^{saith}/_{hath said} in his heart, God hath forgotten :
He hideth his face; he will never see it.

12 Arise, O Lord; O God, lift up thine hand :
Forget not the ⁴poor./humble.

13 Wherefore doth the wicked contemn ^{God,}/_{God?}
^{And say}/_{he hath said} in his heart, Thou wilt not require ^{*it*}/_{*it.*}

14 Thou hast seen *it*; for thou beholdest ⁵mis-
chief and spite, to ^{take}/_{requite} it ^{into}/_{with} thy hand :
The ²helpless/poor committeth *himself* unto thee;
Thou ^{hast been}/_{art} the helper of the fatherless.

15 Break thou the arm of the ^{wicked;}/_{wicked}

R.V. ¹ Or, *fraud*   ² Or, *hapless*   ³ Another reading is, *And being crushed.*   ⁴ Or, *meek*   ⁵ Or, *travail and grief*

14

And as for the evil man, seek out his wickedness
till thou find none.

¹⁶ The LORD is King for ever and ever:
The ¹nations are perished out of his land.

¹⁷ LORD, thou hast heard the desire of the
meek:
Thou wilt ²prepare their heart, thou wilt cause
thine ear to hear:

¹⁸ To judge the fatherless and the oppressed,
That man which is of the earth may be terrible no more.

II   For the Chief Musician.   *A Psalm* of David.

¹ In the LORD put I my trust:
How say ye to my soul,
Flee ³*as* a bird to your mountain?

² For, lo, the wicked bend the bow,
They make ready their arrow upon the string,
That they may shoot in darkness at the upright in
heart.

³ ⁴If the foundations be destroyed,
What can the righteous do?

⁴ The LORD is in his holy temple,
The LORD, his throne is in heaven:
His eyes behold, his eyelids try, the children
of men.

⁵ The LORD trieth the righteous:

R.V. ¹ Or, *heathen*   ² Or, *establish*   ³ Or, *ye birds*
⁴ Or, *For the foundations are destroyed; what hath the righteous
wrought?*

15

But the wicked and him that loveth violence
his soul hateth.

6 Upon the wicked he shall rain ^{snares;}
Fire and ^{brimstone} and ^{burning wind shall be} the
portion of their cup.

7 For the ^{LORD is righteous; he} loveth ^{1righteousness:}
^{2The upright shall} behold ^{his face.}

12 ^{For the Chief Musician; set to 3the Sheminith.}   A Psalm of David.

1 Help, LORD; for the godly man ceaseth;
For ⁴the faithful fail from among the children
of men.

2 They speak vanity every one with his neighbour:
With flattering ^{lip,} and with a double ^{heart,} do
they speak.

3 The LORD shall cut off all flattering lips,
^{The} tongue that speaketh ^{great} things:

4 Who have said, With our tongue will we
prevail;
Our lips ^{are} ⁵our own: who is lord over us?

5 For the ^{spoiling} of the poor, for the sighing of
the needy,
Now will I arise, saith the LORD;
I will set him ⁶in safety ^{at whom they puff.}

6 The words of the LORD are pure ^{words;}

R.V. 1 Or, *righteous deeds*   2 Or, *His countenance doth behold*
the upright   3 Or, *the eighth*   4 Or, *faithfulness faileth*
5 Heb. *with us.*   6 Or, *in the safety he panteth for*

16

As silver tried in a furnace ^{on the}_{of} earth,
Purified seven times.
⁷ Thou shalt keep them, O Lord,
Thou shalt preserve them from this generation
for ever.
⁸ The wicked walk on every side,
When ^{vileness is exalted among the sons of men.}_{the vilest men are exalted.}

13   For the Chief Musician.
To the chief Musician,   A Psalm of David.

¹ How ^{long, O Lord,}_{long} wilt thou forget _{me, O Lord?} for
ever?
How long wilt thou hide thy face from
me?
² How long shall I take counsel in my
soul,
Having sorrow in my heart ^{all the day}_{daily}?
How long shall mine enemy be exalted over
me?
³ Consider *and* ^{answer}_{hear} me, O Lord my God:
Lighten mine eyes, lest I sleep the *sleep of*
death;
⁴ Lest mine enemy say, I have prevailed against
him;
^{*Lest* mine adversaries}_{*and* those that trouble me} rejoice when I am moved.
⁵ But I have trusted in thy mercy;
My heart shall rejoice in thy ^{salvation:}_{salvation.}
⁶ I will sing unto the Lord,
Because he hath dealt bountifully with me.

14

For the Chief Musician.
To the chief Musician,   *A Psalm* of David.

¹ The fool hath said in his heart, There is no
   God.
   They are corrupt, they have done abominable
      works;
      works,
   There is none that doeth good.
² The Lord looked down from heaven upon the
   children of men,
   To see if there were any that did ¹understand,
      That did seek after God.
      and
³ They are all gone aside; they are *all* together
      aside,
   become filthy;
      filthy:
   There is none that doeth good, no, not one.
⁴ Have all the workers of iniquity no knowledge?
   Who eat up my people *as* they eat bread,
   And call not upon the Lord.
⁵ There were they in great fear:
   For God is in the generation of the righteous.
⁶ Ye put to shame the counsel of the poor,
      have shamed
   ²Because the Lord is his refuge.
⁷ Oh that the salvation of Israel were come out
   of Zion !
   When the Lord ³bringeth back the captivity
   of his people,
      Then shall Jacob rejoice, *and* Israel shall be glad.
      Jacob shall

R.V.   ¹ Or, *deal wisely*   ² Or, *But*   ³ Or, *returneth to*

15

A Psalm of David.

¹ LORD, who shall _{abide}^{sojourn} in thy ¹tabernacle ?
Who shall dwell in thy holy hill ?
² He that walketh uprightly, and worketh righteousness,
And speaketh _{the} truth in his heart.
³ ²He that _{backbiteth}^{slandereth} not with his tongue,
Nor doeth evil to his _{neighbour,}^{friend,}
Nor taketh up a reproach against his neighbour.
⁴ In ³whose eyes a _{vile person}^{reprobate} is _{contemned}^{despised} ;
But he honoureth them that fear the LORD.
⁴He that sweareth ⁵to his own hurt, and
changeth not.
⁵ ⁶He that putteth not out his money to usury,
Nor taketh reward against the innocent.
He that doeth these things shall never be
moved.

16

Michtam of David.

¹ Preserve me, O God : for in thee do I put my
trust.
² _{O my soul, thou hast}^{⁷I have} said unto the LORD, Thou art
⁸my Lord :
I have no good beyond thee.
my goodness *extendeth* not to thee;

R.V.   ¹ Heb. *tent.*   ² Or, *He slandereth*   ⁸ Or, *his*
⁴ Or, *He sweareth*   ⁵ Some ancient versions have, *to his friend.*
⁶ Or, *He putteth*   ⁷ So the Sept., Vulg. and Syr. The Hebrew
text as pointed reads, *Thou hast said*, O my soul.   ⁸ Or, *the Lord*

3 ¹*As for*
But to the saints that are in the earth,,
²*They are*
and to the ^{excellent}_{excellent,} in whom is all my delight.

4 Their sorrows shall be multiplied that ³^{exchange}_{hasten}
the Lord for
after another *god* :
Their drink offerings of blood will I not offer,
Nor take _{up} their names ^{upon}_{into} my lips.

5 The Lord is the portion of mine inheritance
and of my cup :
Thou maintainest my lot.

6 The lines are fallen unto me in pleasant places;
Yea, I have a goodly heritage.

7 I will bless the Lord, who hath given me
counsel :
^{Yea, my reins}_{my reins also} instruct me in the night seasons.

8 I have set the Lord always before me :
Because he is at my right hand, I shall not be
moved.

9 Therefore my heart is glad, and my glory
rejoiceth :
My flesh also shall ^{dwell}_{rest} ⁴in ^{safety.}_{hope.}

10 For thou wilt not leave my soul ^{to Sheol}_{in hell} ;
Neither wilt thou suffer thine ^{5holy one}_{Holy One} to see
⁶corruption.

11 Thou wilt shew me the path of life :
In thy presence is fulness of joy ;
^{In}_{at} thy right hand there are pleasures for ever-
more.

R.V.   ¹ Or, *Unto*   ² Or, *And the excellent...delight : their &c.*
³ Or, *give gifts for*   ⁴ Or, *confidently*   ⁵ Or, *godly* Or, *beloved*
⁶ Or, *the pit*

20

17

A Prayer of David.

¹ Hear the right, O LORD, attend unto my ᶜʳʸ⁺
ᶜʳʸ,
Give ear unto my prayer, that goeth not out of
feigned lips.

² Let my sentence come forth from thy presence;
¹Let thine eyes ᵇᵉʰᵒˡᵈ ᵗʰᵉ ᵗʰⁱⁿᵍˢ ᵗʰᵃᵗ ᵃʳᵉ ᵉqᵘᵃˡ.ˡᵒᵒᵏ ᵘᵖᵒⁿ ᵉqᵘⁱᵗʸ.

³ Thou hast proved mine heart; thou hast visited
me in the night;
Thou hast tried me, and ˢʰᵃˡᵗ ᶠⁱⁿᵈ ²ᶠⁱⁿᵈᵉˢᵗ nothing;
I am purposed that my mouth shall not transgress.

⁴ ᶜᵒⁿᶜᵉʳⁿⁱⁿᵍᴬˢ ᶠᵒʳ the works of men, by the word of thy
lips
I have kept me from the ᵖᵃᵗʰˢʷᵃʸˢ of the ᵈᵉˢᵗʳᵒʸᵉʳ.ᵛⁱᵒˡᵉⁿᵗ.

⁵ ᴴᵒˡᵈ ᵘᵖ ᵐʸ ᵍᵒⁱⁿᵍˢ ⁱⁿᴹʸ ˢᵗᵉᵖˢ ʰᵃᵛᵉ ʰᵉˡᵈ ᶠᵃˢᵗ ᵗᵒ thy paths,
ᵗʰᵃᵗ ᵐʸ ᶠᵒᵒᵗˢᵗᵉᵖˢ ˢˡⁱᵖ ⁿᵒᵗ.ᴹʸ ᶠᵉᵉᵗ ʰᵃᵛᵉ ⁿᵒᵗ ˢˡⁱᵖᵖᵉᵈ.

⁶ I have called upon thee, for thou wilt ʰᵉᵃʳᵃⁿˢʷᵉʳ me,
O God:
Incline thine ear unto me, *and* hear my speech.

⁷ Shew thy marvellous lovingkindness, O thou
that savest ᵇʸ ᵗʰʸ ʳⁱᵍʰᵗ ʰᵃⁿᵈ them which put their
trust *in thee*
³From those that rise up *against* ᵗʰᵉᵐ, ᵇʸ ᵗʰʸ ʳⁱᵍʰᵗ ʰᵃⁿᵈ.ᵗʰᵉᵐ.

⁸ Keep me as the apple of the eye,
Hide me under the shadow of thy wings,

R.V. ¹ Or, *Thine eyes behold with equity*   ² Or, *findest no
evil purpose in me; my mouth &c.*   ³ Or, *From those that
rise up against thy right hand*

21

⁹ From the wicked that ~spoil~ ₒₚₚᵣₑₛₛ me,
~from my~ ^My^ deadly enemies, ~that~ ᵂʰᵒ compass me about.
¹⁰ ¹They are inclosed in their own fat:
With their mouth they speak proudly.
¹¹ They have now compassed us in our steps:
They ₕₐᵥₑ set their eyes ᵗᵒ ᵤₛ ₑₐᵣₜₕ.
 bowing cast down to the
earth:
¹² ~He is like~ ₗᵢₖₑ ₐₛ a lion that is greedy of his prey,
And as it were a young lion lurking in secret
places.
¹³ Arise, O Lᴏʀᴅ,
²~Confront~ ᵈᵢₛₐₚₚₒᵢₙₜ him, cast him down:
Deliver my soul from ³the ~wicked by~ wᵢcₖₑd, ʷʰⁱᶜʰ ⁱˢ thy
~sword~; ₛwₒᵣd:
¹⁴ From ⁴ₘₑₙ. ᵇʸ ~men which are~ thy hand, O Lᴏʀᴅ,
⁵From men of the world, ~whose portion is~ ʷʰⁱᶜʰ ʰᵃᵛᵉ their portion in
this life,
And whose belly thou fillest with thy ₕᵢd
treasure:
They are ˢᵃᵗⁱˢᶠⁱᵉᵈ ʷⁱᵗʰ ~full of~ children,
And leave the rest of their substance to their
babes.
¹⁵ As for me, ⁶I ˢʰᵃˡˡ ~will~ behold thy face in righteousness:
⁶I shall be satisfied, when I awake, with thy
⁷likeness.

R.V.   ¹ Or, *They have shut up their heart:*   ² Or, *Forestall*
³ Or, *the wicked, which is thy sword*   ⁴ Or, *men which are*
thy hand   ⁵ Or, *From men whose portion in life is of the world*
⁶ Or, *let me*   ⁷ Heb. *form.* See Num. 12. 8.

18 For the Chief Musician. *A Psalm* of David, the servant of the
To the chief Musician,   *A Psalm* of David,
LORD, ¹who spake unto the LORD the words of this song in the
day that the LORD delivered him from the hand of all his enemies,
and from the hand of Saul: and he said,
And

1 I will love thee, O LORD, my strength.
2 The LORD is my rock, and my fortress, and
  my deliverer;
  My God, my strong rock, in him will I trust;
  My shield, buckler, and the horn of my salvation, *and* my
  high tower.
3 I will call upon the LORD, who is worthy to be
  praised:
  So shall I be saved from mine enemies.
4 The cords/sorrows of death compassed me,
  And the floods of ²ungodliness/ungodly men made me afraid.
5 The cords/sorrows of Sheol/hell were round about me,/compassed me about:
  The snares of death came upon/prevented me.
6 In my distress I called upon the LORD,
  And cried unto my God:
  He heard my voice out of his temple,
  And my cry before him came/came before him, *even* into his ears.
7 Then the earth shook and trembled,/trembled;
  The foundations also of the mountains/hills moved
  And were shaken, because he was wroth.
8 There went up a smoke ³out of his nostrils,
  And fire out of his mouth devoured:
  Coals were kindled by it.
9 He bowed the heavens also, and came down:/down:

And ^{thick} darkness was under his feet.

10 And he rode upon a cherub, and did fly:
Yea, he ^{flew swiftly}_{did fly} upon the wings of the wind.

11 He made darkness his ^{hiding place,}_{secret place;} his pavilion
round about ^{him;}_{him}
^{Darkness of waters,}_{were dark waters and} thick clouds of the skies.

12 At the brightness _{that was} before him his thick
clouds passed,
^{Hailstones}_{hail stones} and coals of fire.

13 The LORD also thundered in the heavens,
And the ^{Most High uttered}_{Highest gave} his voice;
^{Hailstones}_{hail stones} and coals of fire.

14 ^{And}_{Yea,} he sent out his arrows, and scattered
them;
^{¹Yea, lightnings manifold,}_{and he shot out lightnings,} and discomfited them.

15 Then the channels of waters ^{appeared,}_{were seen,}
And the foundations of the world were ^{laid bare.}_{discovered}
At thy rebuke, O LORD,
At the blast of the breath of thy nostrils.

16 He sent from ^{on high,}_{above,} he took ^{me;}_{me,}
He drew me out of ²many waters.

17 He delivered me from my strong enemy,
And from them ^{that}_{which} hated ^{me,}_{me:} for they were
too ^{mighty}_{strong} for me.

18 They ^{came upon}_{prevented} me in the day of my calamity:
But the LORD was my stay.

19 He brought me forth also into a large place,
He delivered me, because he delighted in me.

R.V.　¹ Or, *And he shot out lightnings*　　² Or, *great*

²⁰ The LORD rewarded me according to my righteousness;
 According to the cleanness of my hands hath
 he recompensed me.
²¹ For I have kept the ways of the LORD,
 And have not wickedly departed from my God.
²² For all his judgements/judgments were before me,
 And I did not put / put not away his statutes from me.
²³ I was also perfect with / upright before him,
 And I kept myself from mine iniquity.
²⁴ Therefore hath the LORD recompensed me
 according to my righteousness,
 According to the cleanness of my hands in his
 eyesight.
²⁵ With the merciful thou wilt shew thyself
 merciful;
 With the perfect / an upright man thou wilt shew thyself perfect / upright;
²⁶ With the pure thou wilt shew thyself pure;
 And with the perverse / froward thou wilt shew thyself
 froward.
²⁷ For thou wilt save the afflicted people;
 But the haughty eyes thou wilt bring down. / wilt bring down high looks.
²⁸ For thou wilt light my lamp / candle:
 The LORD my God will lighten / enlighten my darkness.
²⁹ For by thee I have run through / run [1]upon a troop;
 And by my God have I leaped / do I leap over a wall.
³⁰ As for God, his way is perfect:
 The word of the LORD is tried: / tried:

R.V.   [1] Or, *through*

25

He is a shield unto buckler to all them those that trust in him.

31 For who is God: God: save the LORD?
And or who is a rock, beside rock save our God?

32 The It is God that girdeth me with strength,
And maketh my way perfect.

33 He maketh my feet like hinds' feet: feet,
And setteth me upon my high places.

34 He teacheth my hands to war: war,
So that mine arms do bend a bow of brass. a bow of steel is broken by mine arms.

35 Thou hast also given me the shield of thy
salvation:
And thy right hand hath holden me up,
And thy [1]gentleness hath made me great.

36 Thou hast enlarged my steps under me,
And that my [2]feet have did not slipped. slip.

37 I will pursue have pursued mine enemies, and overtake overtaken them:
Neither will did I turn again till they are were consumed.

38 I will smite them through have wounded them that they shall not be were not able to
rise:
They shall fall are fallen under my feet.

39 For thou hast girded me with strength unto
the battle:
Thou hast [3]subdued under me those that rose
up against me.

40 Thou hast also made mine enemies turn their backs unto me, given me the necks of mine enemies;
That I might cut off destroy them that hate me.

41 They cried, but there was none to save *them*:

R.V. [1] Or, *condescension*   [2] Heb. *ankles*   [3] Heb. *caused
to bow.*

Even unto the LORD, but he answered them not.

⁴² Then did I beat them small as the dust before the wind:

I did ¹cast them out as the ^{mire of}_{dirt in} the streets.

⁴³ Thou hast delivered me from the strivings of the people;

^{Thou}_{and thou} ²hast made me the head of the ^{nations}_{heathen}:

A people whom I have not known shall serve me.

⁴⁴ As soon as they hear of ^{me}_{me,} they shall obey me:

The strangers shall ³submit themselves unto me.

⁴⁵ The strangers shall fade away,

And ^{shall come trembling}_{be afraid} out of their close places.

⁴⁶ The LORD liveth; and blessed be my rock;

And ^{exalted be}_{let} be the God of my ^{salvation:}_{salvation be exalted.}

⁴⁷ ^{Even the}_{It is} God that ^{executeth vengeance for}_{avengeth} me,

And subdueth ^{peoples}_{the people} under me.

⁴⁸ He ^{rescueth}_{delivereth} me from mine enemies:

Yea, thou liftest me up above ^{them}_{those} that rise up against me:

Thou ^{deliverest}_{hast delivered} me from the violent man.

⁴⁹ Therefore ^{I will}_{will I} give thanks unto thee, O LORD, among the ^{nations.}_{heathen,}

And ^{will} sing praises unto thy name.

R.V. ¹ Heb. *empty.*   ² Or, *wilt make*   ³ Or, *yield feigned obedience* Heb. *lie.*

⁵⁰ Great ¹deliverance giveth he to his king ;
  And sheweth ^lovingkindness_mercy to his anointed,
  To ^David_David, and to his ^seed,_seed for evermore.

19

For the Chief Musician.
To the chief Musician, A Psalm of David.

¹ The heavens declare the glory of God ;
  And the firmament sheweth his handywork.
² Day unto day uttereth speech,
  And night unto night sheweth knowledge.
³ There is no speech nor ^language;_language,
  ^where their ^Their voice ^cannot be_is not heard.
⁴ Their line is gone out through all the earth,
  And their words to the end of the world.
  In them hath he set a ²tabernacle for the sun,
⁵ Which is as a bridegroom coming out of his
    chamber,
  And rejoiceth as a strong man to run ^his course_a race.
⁶ His going forth is from the end of the heaven,
  And his circuit unto the ends of it :
  And there is nothing hid from the heat thereof.

⁷ The law of the LORD is perfect, ^restoring_converting the
    soul :
  The testimony of the LORD is sure, making
    wise the simple.
⁸ The ^precepts_statutes of the LORD are right, rejoicing the
    heart :

R.V.   ¹ Heb. *salvations.*   ² Heb. *tent.*

The commandment of the L<small>ORD</small> is pure, enlightening the eyes.

⁹ The fear of the L<small>ORD</small> is clean, enduring for ever:

The ^{judgements}_{judgments} of the L<small>ORD</small> are ^{true,}_{true.} *and* righteous altogether.

¹⁰ More to be desired are they than gold, yea, than much fine gold:

^{Sweeter}_{sweeter} also than honey and ¹the honeycomb.

¹¹ Moreover by them is thy servant warned:

^{In}_{and} in keeping of them there is great reward.

¹² Who can ^{discern}_{understand} *his* errors?

^{Clear}_{cleanse} thou me from ^{hidden}_{secret} *faults*.

¹³ Keep back thy servant also ²from presumptuous *sins*;

Let them not have dominion over me: then shall I be ^{perfect,}_{upright,}

And I shall be _{innocent}^{clear} from _{the} great transgression.

¹⁴ Let the words of my ^{mouth,}_{mouth,} and the meditation of my ^{heart,}_{heart,} be acceptable in thy sight,

O L<small>ORD</small>, my _{strength,}^{rock,} and my redeemer.

20　　　For the Chief Musician.　A Psalm of David.
　　　　　To the chief Musician,

¹ The L<small>ORD</small> ^{answer}_{hear} thee in the day of trouble;

The name of the God of Jacob ^{set thee up on high}_{defend thee};

R.V.　¹ Heb. *the droppings of the honeycomb.*　² Or, *from the proud*

29

² Send thee help from the sanctuary,
  And ¹strengthen thee out of Zion;
³ Remember all thy ²offerings,
  And ³accept thy burnt sacrifice; Selah.   [Selah
⁴ Grant thee $^{\text{thy heart's desire,}}_{\text{according to thine own heart,}}$
  And fulfil all thy counsel.
⁵ We will $^{\text{triumph}}_{\text{rejoice}}$ in thy ⁴salvation,
  And in the name of our God we will set up
    our banners:
  The Lord fulfil all thy petitions.
⁶ Now know I that the Lord saveth his anointed;
  He will $^{\text{answer}}_{\text{hear}}$ him from his holy heaven
  With the saving strength of his right hand.
⁷ Some *trust* in chariots, and some in horses:
  But we will $^{\text{make mention of}}_{\text{remember}}$ the name of the Lord
    our God.
⁸ They are $^{\text{bowed}}_{\text{brought}}$ down and fallen:
  But we are risen, and stand upright.
⁹ ⁵Save, Lord:
  Let the $^{\text{King answer}}_{\text{king hear}}$ us when we call.

21   For the Chief Musician.   A Psalm of David.
           To the chief Musician,

¹ The king shall joy in thy strength, O Lord;
  And in thy salvation how greatly shall he
    rejoice!

R.V. ¹ Or, *support*   ² Or, *meal offerings*   ³ Heb. *accept
as fat*.   ⁴ Or, *victory*   ⁵ Or, as some ancient versions have,
O Lord, save the king; and answer &c.

² Thou hast given him his heart's desire,
  And hast not withholden the request of his
  lips. Selah.   [Selah

³ For thou preventest him with the blessings of
  ¹goodness:
  Thou settest a crown of fine/pure gold on his head.

⁴ He asked life of thee, *and* thou gavest it him;/him,
  Even length of days for ever and ever.

⁵ His glory is great in thy salvation:
  Honour and majesty dost/hast thou lay/laid upon him.

⁶ For thou ²makest/hast made him most blessed for ever:
  Thou makest/hast made him glad with joy in/exceeding glad with thy presence./countenance.

⁷ For the king trusteth in the LORD,
  And through the lovingkindness/mercy of the Most/most High he
  shall not be moved.

⁸ Thine hand shall find out all thine enemies:
  Thy right hand shall find out those that hate
  thee.

⁹ Thou shalt make them as a fiery furnace/oven in the
  time of thine ³anger./anger:
  The LORD shall swallow them up in his
  wrath,
  And the fire shall devour them.

¹⁰ Their fruit shalt thou destroy from the earth,
  And their seed from among the children of
  men.

¹¹ For they intended evil against thee:

R.V. ¹ Or, *good things*   ² Heb. *settest him to be blessings.*
See Gen. 12. 2.   ³ Or, *presence* Heb. *countenance.*

They imagined a _{mischievous} device, which they are not able to perform.

¹² ^{For thou shalt} Therefore shalt thou make them turn their back,

^{Thou} when thou shalt make ready ^{with thy bowstrings} thine arrows upon thy strings against the face of them.

¹³ Be thou exalted, ^{O LORD,} _{O LORD,} in ^{thy} thine own strength:

So will we sing and praise thy power.

22　　For the Chief Musician; set to ¹Aijeleth ^{hash-Shahar.}
　　　　To the chief Musician upon　　　　_{Shahar,}
　　　　　　　　A Psalm of David.

¹ My God, my God, why hast thou forsaken me?

²*Why art thou so* far from helping me, *and from* the words of my roaring?

² O my God, I cry in the ^{day-time,} _{daytime,} but thou ^{answerest} _{hearest} not;

And in the night season, and am not silent.

³ But thou art holy,

O thou that ⁴inhabitest the praises of Israel.

⁴ Our fathers trusted in thee:

They trusted, and thou didst deliver them.

⁵ They cried unto thee, and were delivered:

They trusted in thee, and were not ^{ashamed.} _{confounded.}

⁶ But I am a worm, and no man;

A reproach of men, and despised of the people.

⁷ All they that see me laugh me to scorn:

R.V. ¹ That is, *The hind of the morning.* ² Or, *Far from my help* are *the words of my roaring.* ³ Or, *but find no rest* ⁴ Or, *art enthroned upon*

They shoot out the lip, they shake the head,
   saying,
8 [1]Commit *thyself* unto the LORD; let him deliver him :
  He trusted on the LORD *that* he would
  Let him deliver him, seeing he delighteth in him.
9 But thou art he that took me out of the womb :
  Thou didst make me trust *when I was* upon my
    mother's breasts.
10 I was cast upon thee from the womb :
  Thou art my God from my mother's belly.
11 Be not far from me ; for trouble is near ;
  For there is none to help.
12 Many bulls have compassed me :
  Strong bulls of Bashan have beset me round.
13 They gape upon me with their mouth,
  As a ravening and a roaring lion.
14 I am poured out like water,
  And all my bones are out of joint :
  My heart is like wax ;
  It is melted in the midst of my bowels.
15 My strength is dried up like a potsherd ;
  And my tongue cleaveth to my jaws ;
  And thou hast brought me into the dust of
    death.
16 For dogs have compassed me :
  The assembly of evil-doers have inclosed me :
  [2]They pierced my hands and my feet.

R.V. 1 Or, *He trusted on the LORD, that he would deliver him*
2 So the Sept., Vulg. and Syr. According to other ancient versions,
They bound. The Hebrew text as pointed reads, *Like a lion.*

¹⁷ I may tell all my ^{bones;}_{bones:}
They look and stare upon ^{me:}_{me.}

¹⁸ They part my garments among them,
And ^{upon my vesture do they cast lots.}_{cast lots upon my vesture.}

¹⁹ But be not thou far ^{off,}_{from me,} O LORD :
O ^{thou} my ^{succour,}_{strength,} haste thee to help me.

²⁰ Deliver my soul from the sword ;
¹ My darling from the power of the dog.

²¹ Save me from the lion's ^{mouth;}_{mouth:}
Yea, from the horns of the wild-oxen thou hast answered me.
for thou hast heard me from the horns of the unicorns.

²² I will declare thy name unto my brethren :
In the midst of the congregation will I praise
thee.

²³ Ye that fear the LORD, praise him ;
All ye the seed of Jacob, glorify him ;
And ^{stand in awe of}_{fear} him, all ye the seed of Israel.

²⁴ For he hath not despised nor abhorred the
affliction of the afflicted ;
Neither hath he hid his face from him ;
But when he cried unto him, he heard.

²⁵ ^{Of thee cometh my praise}_{My praise *shall be* of thee} in the great congregation :
I will pay my vows before them that fear him.

²⁶ The meek shall eat and be satisfied :
They shall praise the LORD that seek ^{after} him :
^{Let your heart}_{your heart shall} live for ever.

²⁷ All the ends of the ^{earth}_{world} shall remember and
turn unto the LORD :

R.V.   ¹ Heb. *My only one.*

And all the kindreds of the nations shall worship before thee.
28 For the kingdom is the LORD's:
And he is the $^{\text{ruler over}}_{\text{governor among}}$ the nations.
29 All $^{\text{the fat ones of the}}_{\textit{they that be}\text{ fat upon}}$ earth shall eat and worship:
All they that go down to the dust shall bow before $^{\text{him,}}_{\text{him:}}$
$^{\text{Even he that cannot}}_{\text{and none can}}$ keep $^{\text{his soul alive.}}_{\text{alive his own soul.}}$
30 A seed shall serve him;
1 It shall be $^{\text{told of}}_{\text{accounted to}}$ the Lord $^{\text{unto the }\textit{next}}_{\text{for a}}$ generation.
31 They shall $^{\text{come}}_{\text{come,}}$ and shall declare his righteousness
Unto a people that shall be born, that he hath done $^{\text{it.}}_{\textit{this.}}$

23 A Psalm of David.

1 The LORD is my shepherd; I shall not want.
2 He maketh me to lie down in green pastures:
He leadeth me beside the 2still waters.
3 He restoreth my soul:
He $^{\text{guideth}}_{\text{leadeth}}$ me in the paths of righteousness for his name's sake.
4 Yea, though I walk through the valley of 3the shadow of death,
I will fear no $^{\text{evil;}}_{\text{evil:}}$ for thou art with $^{\text{me:}}_{\text{me;}}$
Thy rod and thy $^{\text{staff,}}_{\text{staff,}}$ they comfort me.

R.V. 1 Or, *It shall be counted unto the Lord for* his *generation*
2 Heb. *waters of rest.* 3 Or, *deep darkness* (and so elsewhere)

⁵ Thou preparest a table before me in the
  presence of mine enemies :
 Thou ^{hast anointed}_{anointest} my head with oil; my cup
  runneth over.
⁶ ¹Surely goodness and mercy shall follow me
  all the days of my life :
 And I will dwell in the house of the Lord
  ²for ever.

24   A Psalm of David.

¹ The earth is the Lord's, and the fulness
  thereof;
 The world, and they that dwell therein.
² For he hath founded it upon the seas,
 And established it upon the floods.
³ Who shall ascend into the hill of the Lord?
 ^{And}_{or} who shall stand in his holy place?
⁴ He that hath clean hands, and a pure heart ;
 Who hath not lifted up his soul unto vanity,
 ^{And hath not}_{nor} sworn deceitfully.
⁵ He shall receive _{the}^a blessing from the Lord,
 And righteousness from the God of his salva-
  tion.
⁶ This is the generation of them that seek ^{after} him,
 That seek thy face, ³O ⁴*God of* Jacob. _{Selah.} [Selah

⁷ Lift up your heads, O ye gates ;

R.V. ¹ Or, *Only*   ² Heb. *for length of days.*   ³ Or, even *Jacob*
⁴ So some ancient versions.

And be ye lift up, ye ¹everlasting ^{doors:} doors;
And the King of glory shall come in.
⁸ Who is ^{the} this King of glory?
The LORD strong and mighty,
The LORD mighty in battle.
⁹ Lift up your heads, O ye gates;
Yea, even lift them up, ye ¹everlasting doors:
And the King of glory shall come in.
¹⁰ Who is this King of glory?
The LORD of hosts,
He is the King of glory.   Selah.   [Selah

25   *A Psalm* of David.

¹ Unto thee, O LORD, do I lift up my soul.
² O my God, in thee have I trusted, I trust in thee:
Let me not be ashamed;
Let not mine enemies triumph over me.
³ Yea, let none that wait on thee shall be ashamed:
They shall let them be ashamed that deal treacherously which transgress without
cause.
⁴ Shew me thy ways, O LORD;
Teach me thy paths.
⁵ Guide Lead me in thy truth, and teach me;
For thou art the God of my salvation;
On thee do I wait all the day.
⁶ Remember, O LORD, thy tender mercies and
thy lovingkindnesses;

R.V.   ¹ Or, *ancient*

For they have been ever of old.
[7] Remember not the sins of my youth, nor my
transgressions:
According to thy ^lovingkindness_mercy remember thou ^me,_me
For thy goodness' sake, O Lord.
[8] Good and upright is the Lord:
Therefore will he ^instruct_teach sinners in the way.
[9] The meek will he guide in ^Judgement:_judgment:
And the meek will he teach his way.
[10] All the paths of the Lord are ^lovingkindness_mercy and
truth
Unto such as keep his covenant and his
testimonies.
[11] For thy name's sake, O Lord,
Pardon mine ^iniquity,_iniquity; for it is great.
[12] What man is he that feareth the Lord?
Him shall he ^instruct_teach in the way that he shall
choose.
[13] His soul shall dwell at ease;
And his seed shall inherit the ^land._earth.
[14] The [1]secret of the Lord is with them that
fear him;
[2]And he will shew them his covenant.
[15] Mine eyes are ever toward the Lord;
For he shall pluck my feet out of the net.
[16] Turn thee unto me, and have mercy upon me;
For I am desolate and afflicted.

R.V. [1] Or, *counsel* Or, *friendship*   [2] Or, *And his covenant,
to make them know it*

38

17 The troubles of my heart ¹are enlarged :
O bring thou me out of my distresses.

18 ^{Consider}_{Look upon} mine affliction and my ^{travail}_{pain} ;
And forgive all my sins.

19 Consider mine ^{enemies,}_{enemies;} for they are many ;
And they hate me with cruel hatred.

20 O keep my soul, and deliver me :
Let me not be ^{ashamed;}_{ashamed;} for I put my trust in
thee.

21 Let integrity and uprightness preserve ^{me;}_{me;}
For I wait on thee.

22 Redeem Israel, O God,
Out of all his troubles.

26   *A Psalm* of David.

1 Judge me, O ^{LORD,}_{LORD;} for I have walked in mine
integrity :
I have trusted also in the _{LORD;} ^{LORD} ²without wavering.
therefore I shall not slide.

2 Examine me, O LORD, and prove me ;
Try my reins and my heart.

3 For thy lovingkindness is before mine ^{eyes;}_{eyes:}
And I have walked in thy truth.

4 I have not sat with vain ^{persons;}_{persons,}
Neither will I go in with dissemblers.

5 I ^{hate}_{have hated} the congregation of ^{evil-doers,}_{evil doers;}
And will not sit with the wicked.

R.V. ¹ Or, as otherwise read, *relieve thou, and bring me &c.*
² Or, *I shall not slide*

⁶ I will wash mine hands in _{innocency:}
    So will I compass thine altar, O LORD :
⁷ That I may _{publish with} the voice of ^{thanksgiving to be heard,}
    And tell of all thy wondrous works.
⁸ LORD, I _{have loved} the habitation of thy house,
    And the place ²where _{thine honour} dwelleth.
⁹ ³Gather not my soul with sinners,
    Nor my life with _{bloody men} :
¹⁰ In whose hands is mischief,
    And their right hand is full of bribes.
¹¹ But as for me, I will walk in mine integrity :
    Redeem me, and be merciful unto me.
¹² My foot standeth in an even place :
    In the congregations will I bless the LORD.

27

A Psalm of David.

¹ The LORD is my light and my salvation ; whom
        shall I fear?
    The LORD is the ⁴strength of my life ; of whom
        shall I be afraid?
² When _{the wicked,} *even* ^{evil-doers} _{mine enemies and my foes,} came upon
        me to eat up my flesh,
    Even mine adversaries and my foes, they stumbled and fell.
³ Though an host should encamp against me,
    My heart shall not fear :

R.V. ¹ Or, *publish with the voice of thanksgiving
of the tabernacle of thy glory.* ³ Or, *Take not away*   ² Heb.
                                                                  ⁴ Or,
strong hold

40

Though war should rise against me,
¹Even then will I be confident.
in this

⁴ One thing have I asked of the Lord, that will
desired
I seek after ;
That I may dwell in the house of the Lord
all the days of my life,
To behold ²the beauty of the Lord, and to
³inquire in his temple.

⁵ For in the day of trouble he shall keep me secretly
time   hide me
in his pavilion :
In the covert of his ⁴tabernacle shall he hide
secret
me ;
He shall lift me up upon a rock.
set

⁶ And now shall mine head be lifted up above
mine enemies round about me:
me;
And I will I offer in his ⁴tabernacle sacrifices of
therefore will
⁵joy ;
I will sing, yea, I will sing praises unto the
Lord.

⁷ Hear, O Lord, when I cry with my voice :
Have mercy also upon me, and answer me.

⁸ *When thou saidst,* Seek ye my face ; my heart
said unto thee,
Thy face, Lord, will I seek.

⁹ Hide not thy face *far* from me ;
Put not thy servant away in anger :
Thou hast been my help ;

R.V. ¹ Or, *In this*   ² Or, *the pleasantness*   ³ Or, *consider
his temple*   ⁴ Heb. *tent.*   ⁵ Or, *shouting* Or, *trumpet-sound*

^{Cast me not off,}_{leave me not,} neither forsake me, O God of my
salvation.

10 ^{1 For}_{When} my father and my mother ^{have forsaken}_{forsake} me,
^{But}_{then} the LORD will take me up.

11 Teach me thy way, O ^{LORD;}_{LORD,}
And lead me in a plain path,
Because of ² mine enemies.

12 Deliver me not over unto the will of mine
^{adversaries}_{enemies} :
For false witnesses are risen up against me,
and such as breathe out cruelty.

13 *I had fainted*, unless I had believed to see the
goodness of the LORD
In the land of the living.

14 Wait on the LORD :
Be ^{strong,}_{of good courage,} and ^{let thine heart take courage;}_{he shall strengthen thine heart:}
^{Yea, wait thou}_{wait, I say,} on the LORD.

28   *A Psalm* of David.

1 Unto ^{thee, O LORD, will I call;}_{thee will I cry, O LORD}
My ^{rock,}_{rock;} be not ^{thou deaf unto}_{silent to} me :
Lest, if thou be silent ^{unto}_{to} me,
I become like them that go down into the
pit.

2 Hear the voice of my supplications, when I cry
unto thee,

R.V. ¹ Or, *When my father and my mother forsake me, the
LORD &c.* ² Or, *them that lie in wait for me*

When I lift up my hands [1]toward thy holy
oracle.

3 Draw me not away with the wicked,
And with the workers of ^{iniquity;}_{iniquity,}
Which speak peace ^{with}_{to} their neighbours,
But mischief is in their hearts.

4 Give them according to their ^{work,}_{deeds,} and accord-
ing to the wickedness of their _{endeavours}^{doings}:
Give them after the ^{operation}_{work} of their hands;
Render to them their desert.

5 Because they regard not the works of the
LORD,
Nor the operation of his hands,
He shall ^{break them down}_{destroy them,} and not build them up.

6 Blessed be the LORD,
Because he hath heard the voice of my supplications.

7 The LORD is my strength and my shield;
My heart ^{hath} trusted in him, and I am
helped:
Therefore my heart greatly rejoiceth;
And with my song will I praise him.

8 The LORD is [2]their strength,
And he is ^{a strong hold of salvation to}_{the saving strength of} his anointed.

9 Save thy people, and bless thine inheritance:
Feed them also, and ^{bear}_{lift} them up for ever.

R.V.   [1] Or, *toward the innermost place of thy sanctuary*   [2] According to some ancient versions, *a strength unto his people.*

29
A Psalm of David.

¹ Give unto the Lord, O ye [1]sons of the [2]mighty,
Give unto the Lord glory and strength.
² Give unto the Lord the glory due unto his
name ;
Worship the Lord [3]in the beauty of holiness.

³ The voice of the Lord is upon the waters :
The God of glory thundereth,
thundereth:
Even the Lord
the Lord *is* upon [4]many waters.
⁴ The voice of the Lord is powerful ;
The voice of the Lord is full of majesty.
⁵ The voice of the Lord breaketh the cedars ;
Yea, the Lord breaketh in pieces the cedars of
Lebanon.
⁶ He maketh them also to skip like a calf ;
Lebanon and Sirion like a young wild-ox.
unicorn.
⁷ The voice of the Lord [5]cleaveth
divideth the flames of
fire.
⁸ The voice of the Lord shaketh the wilderness ;
The Lord shaketh the wilderness of Kadesh.
⁹ The voice of the Lord maketh the hinds to
calve,
And strippeth
discovereth the forests bare :
And in his temple doth every thing saith, Glory.
every one speak of *his* glory.

¹⁰ The Lord sat *as king* at
sitteth upon the Flood
flood ;

R.V. ¹ Or, *sons of God*   ² Or, *gods* See Ex. 15. 11.   ³ Or,
in holy array   ⁴ Or, *great*   ⁵ Or, *heweth out flames of fire*

Yea, the Lord sitteth ^{as king}_{King} for ever.

¹¹ The Lord will give strength unto his people;
The Lord will bless his people with peace.

30 A Psalm; a Song at the Dedication of the House; a Psalm
A Psalm *and* Song at the dedication of the house
of David.

¹ I will extol thee, O Lord; for thou hast ¹_{raised}_{lifted}
me up,
And hast not made my foes to rejoice over me.

² O Lord my God,
I cried unto thee, and thou hast healed me.

³ O Lord, thou hast brought up my soul from
_{Sheol}
the grave:
Thou hast kept me alive, ²that I should not go
down to the pit.

⁴ Sing ^{praise} unto the Lord, O ye saints of his,
And give thanks ^{to his holy ³name.}_{at the remembrance of his holiness.}

⁵ For his anger ^{is but for}_{endureth but} a moment;
⁴In his favour is life:
Weeping ⁵may ^{tarry for the}_{endure for a} night,
But joy *cometh* in the morning.

⁶ As for me, I said in my prosperity,
And in my prosperity I said,
I shall never be moved.

⁷ ^{Thou,} Lord, ^{of}_{by} thy favour ^{hadst}_{thou hast} made my
mountain to stand strong:

R.V. ¹ Or, *drawn*   ² Another reading is, *from among them
that go down to the pit.*   ³ Heb. *memorial.* See Ex. 3. 15.
⁴ Or, *His favour is for a life time*   ⁵ Heb. *may come in to
lodge at even.*

Thou didst hide thy _{face,} ^{face;} _{and} I was troubled.

⁸ I cried to thee, O Lord;
And unto the Lord I made ^{supplication:}_{supplication.}

⁹ What profit is there in my blood, when I go
down to the pit?
Shall the dust praise thee? shall it declare thy
truth?

¹⁰ Hear, O Lord, and have mercy upon me:
Lord, be thou my helper.

¹¹ Thou hast turned for me my mourning into
dancing;
dancing:
Thou hast ^{loosed}_{put off} my sackcloth, and girded me
with ^{gladness:}_{gladness;}

¹² To the end that *my* glory may sing praise to
thee, and not be silent.
O Lord my God, I will give thanks unto thee
for ever.

31

For the Chief Musician.
To the chief Musician,   A Psalm of David.

¹ In thee, O Lord, do I put my trust; let me
never be ashamed:
Deliver me in thy righteousness.

² Bow down thine ear ^{unto}_{to} me; deliver me
speedily:
Be thou ^{to me}_{my} a strong rock, _{for} an house of
¹defence to save me.

³ For thou art my rock and my fortress;

R.V.   ¹ Heb. *fortresses.*

Therefore for thy name's sake lead ^{me}_{me,} and
　　guide me.

4 ^{Pluck}_{Pull} me out of the net that they have laid
　　privily for ^{me}_{me:}
　　For thou art my ^{strong hold.}_{strength.}

5 Into thine hand I ^{commend}_{commit} my spirit :
　　Thou hast redeemed me, O ^{LORD, thou}_{LORD} God of
　　truth.

6 I ^{hate}_{have hated} them that regard lying vanities :
　　But I trust in the LORD.

7 I will be glad and rejoice in thy mercy :
　　For thou hast ^{seen}_{considered} my ^{affliction .}_{trouble ;}
　　Thou hast known ¹my soul in ^{adversities:}_{adversities;}

8 And ^{thou} hast not shut me up into the hand of
　　the ^{enemy;}_{enemy:}
　　Thou hast set my feet in a large ^{place.}_{room.}

9 Have mercy upon me, O LORD, for I am in
　　^{distress .}_{trouble :}
　　Mine eye ^{wasteth away}_{is consumed} with grief, *yea*, my soul and
　　my ^{body.}_{belly.}

10 For my life is spent with ^{sorrow,·}_{grief,} and my years
　　with sighing :
　　My strength faileth because of mine iniquity,
　　and my bones are ^{wasted away.}_{consumed.}

11 Because of all mine adversaries I am become a reproach,
　　I was a reproach among all mine enemies, but
　Yea, unto my neighbours exceedingly,· and a fear to mine
　especially among my neighbours,
　　acquaintance :
　　They that did see me without fled from me.

R.V.　¹ Or, *the adversities of my soul*

¹² I am forgotten as a dead man out of mind :
I am like a broken vessel.

¹³ For I have heard the *defaming slander* of *many, many*:
Terror fear *was* on every side :
While they took counsel together against me,
They devised to take away my life.

¹⁴ But I trusted in thee, O LORD :
I said, Thou art my God.

¹⁵ My times are in thy hand :
Deliver me from the hand of mine enemies,
and from them that persecute me.

¹⁶ Make thy face to shine upon thy servant :
Save me *in for* thy *lovingkindness. mercies' sake.*

¹⁷ Let me not be ashamed, O LORD ; for I have
called upon thee :
Let the wicked be ashamed, *and* let them be
silent in *Sheol. the grave.*

¹⁸ Let the lying lips be *dumb put to silence* ;
Which speak *against the righteous insolently, grievous things proudly*
With pride and contempt.
and contemptuously against the righteous.

¹⁹ Oh how great is thy goodness, which thou hast
laid up for them that fear *thee, thee;*
Which thou hast wrought for them that *put their*
trust in *thee, thee;* before the sons of men !

²⁰ *In the covert of thy presence shalt thou hide them*
Thou shalt hide them in the secret of thy presence from the
plottings pride of man :
Thou shalt keep them secretly in a pavilion
from the strife of tongues.

²¹ Blessed be the LORD :

For he hath shewed me his marvellous ^{lovingkindness}_{kindness}
in a strong city.

22 As _{for me,}_{For} I said in my ¹haste, I am cut off from
before thine eyes:

Nevertheless thou heardest the voice of my
supplications when I cried unto thee.

23 O love the LORD, all ye his saints:
_{for the}_{The} LORD preserveth ²the faithful,
And plentifully rewardeth the proud doer.

24 Be _{of good courage,}_{strong,} and _{he shall strengthen your heart,}_{let your heart take courage,}
All ye that ³hope in the LORD.

32   *A Psalm of* _{David.}_{David,} Maschil.

¹ Blessed is he whose transgression is forgiven,
whose sin is covered.

² Blessed is the man unto whom the LORD im-
puteth not iniquity,
And in whose spirit there is no guile.

³ When I kept silence, my bones waxed old
Through my roaring all the day long.

⁴ For day and night thy hand was heavy upon
me:
My moisture _{is turned into}_{was changed ⁴as with} the drought of
summer. _{Selah.}   [Selah

⁵ I acknowledged my sin unto thee, and mine
iniquity have I not _{hid.}_{hid:}

I said, I will confess my transgressions unto
the LORD;
And thou forgavest the iniquity of my sin.
[Selah.

⁶ For this let shall every one that is godly pray
unto thee ¹in a time when thou mayest be
found:
Surely when the great waters overflow they shall not
in the floods of great waters
reach come nigh unto him.

⁷ Thou art my hiding place; thou wilt shalt preserve
me from trouble;
Thou wilt shalt compass me about with songs of
deliverance. Selah. [Selah

⁸ I will instruct thee and teach thee in the way
which thou shalt go:
I will counsel guide thee with mine eye upon thee. eye.

⁹ Be ye not as the horse, or as the mule, which
have no understanding:
Whose trappings mouth must be bit and bridle to hold them in, held in with bit and bridle,
²Else lest they will not come near unto thee.

¹⁰ Many sorrows shall be to the wicked:
But he that trusteth in the LORD, mercy shall
compass him about.

¹¹ Be glad in the LORD, and rejoice, ye righteous:
And shout for joy, all ye that are upright in
heart.

R.V. ¹ Or, *in the time of finding out* sin   ² Or, *That they
come not near*

50

33 ¹ Rejoice in the LORD, O ye righteous:
_{for praise} ^{Praise} is comely for the upright.
2 ^{Give thanks unto} the LORD with harp:
Sing ^{praises} unto him with the psaltery *and* an
_{instrument} of ten strings.
³ Sing unto him a new song;
Play skilfully with a loud noise.
⁴ For the word of the LORD is right;
And all his _{works} ^{work is} *are* *done* in _{truth.} ^{faithfulness.}
⁵ He loveth righteousness and _{judgment} ^{judgement}:
The earth is full of the _{goodness} ^{lovingkindness} of the LORD.
⁶ By the word of the LORD were the heavens
made;
And all the host of them by the breath of his
mouth.
⁷ He gathereth the waters of the sea together as
an heap:
He layeth up the _{depth} ^{deeps} in storehouses.
⁸ Let all the earth fear the LORD:
Let all the inhabitants of the world stand in
awe of him.
⁹ For he spake, and it was done;
He commanded, and it stood fast.
¹⁰ The LORD bringeth the counsel of the _{heathen} ^{nations}
to nought:
He maketh the _{devices} ^{thoughts} of the _{people} ^{peoples to be} of none
effect.
¹¹ The counsel of the LORD standeth ^{fast} for
ever,

51

The thoughts of his heart to all generations.

12 Blessed is the nation whose God is the LORD;
And the people whom he hath chosen for his own inheritance.

13 The LORD looketh from heaven;
He beholdeth all the sons of men;

14 From the place of his habitation he looketh forth
Upon all the inhabitants of the earth.

15 He that fashioneth the hearts of them all,
That considereth all their works.

16 There is no king saved by ¹the multitude of an host:
A mighty man is not delivered by great strength.

17 An horse is a vain thing for safety:
Neither shall he deliver any by his great power.

18 Behold, the eye of the LORD is upon them that fear him,
Upon them that ²hope in his mercy;

19 To deliver their soul from death,
And to keep them alive in famine.

20 Our soul hath waited for the LORD:
He is our help and our shield.

21 For our heart shall rejoice in him,
Because we have trusted in his holy name.

22 Let thy mercy, O LORD, be upon us,
According as we ²have hoped in thee.

34 *A Psalm of* David;/David, *when he* [1] *changed his behaviour before* Abimelech,/Abimelech; *who drove him away, and he departed.*

[1] I will bless the LORD at all times :
His praise shall continually be in my mouth.

[2] My soul shall make her boast in the LORD :
The meek/humble shall hear thereof, and be glad.

[3] O magnify the LORD with me,
And let us exalt his name together.

[4] I sought the LORD, and he answered/heard me,
And delivered me from all my fears.

[5] They looked unto him, and were lightened :
And their faces shall never be confounded./were not ashamed.

[6] This poor man cried, and the LORD heard him,
And saved him out of all his troubles.

[7] The angel of the LORD encampeth round about them that fear him,
And delivereth them.

[8] O taste and see that the LORD is good :
Blessed is the man that trusteth in him.

[9] O fear the LORD, ye his saints :
For there is no want to them that fear him.

[10] The young lions do lack, and suffer hunger :
But they that seek the LORD shall not want any good thing.

[11] Come, ye children, hearken unto me :
I will teach you the fear of the LORD.

R.V. [1] Or, *feigned madness*

12 What man is he that desireth life,
   And loveth *many* days, that he may see good?
13 Keep thy tongue from evil,
   And thy lips from speaking guile.
14 Depart from evil, and do good;
   Seek peace, and pursue it.
15 The eyes of the Lord are $^{toward}_{upon}$ the righteous,
   And his ears are *open* unto their cry.
16 The face of the Lord is against them that do
   evil,
   To cut off the remembrance of them from the
   earth.
17 *The righteous* $^{cried,}_{cry,}$ and the Lord $^{heard,}_{heareth,}$
   And $^{delivered}_{delivereth}$ them out of all their troubles.
18 The Lord is nigh unto them that are of a
   broken $^{heart,}_{heart;}$
   And saveth such as be of a contrite spirit.
19 Many are the afflictions of the righteous:
   But the Lord delivereth him out of them
   all.
20 He keepeth all his bones:
   Not one of them is broken.
21 Evil shall slay the wicked:
   And they that hate the righteous shall be
   ¹condemned.
   desolate.
22 The Lord redeemeth the soul of his servants:
   And none of them that trust in him shall be
   ¹condemned.
   desolate.

R.V. ¹ Or, *held guilty*

35

A Psalm of David.

1 _{Strive thou,
Plead *my cause*,} O LORD, with them that strive with
me :
Fight ^{thou} against them that fight against me.
2 Take hold of shield and buckler,
And stand up for mine help.
3 Draw out also the spear, ¹and stop the way
against them that _{persecute}^{pursue} me :
Say unto my soul, I am thy salvation.
4 Let them be ^{ashamed}_{confounded} and ^{brought}_{put} to ^{dishonour}_{shame} that
seek after my soul :
Let them be turned back and _{brought to confusion}^{confounded}
that devise my hurt.
5 Let them be as chaff before the _{wind:}^{wind,}
And _{let} the angel of the LORD ^{driving *them* on}_{chase *them*.}
6 Let their way be ²dark and ^{slippery,}_{slippery:}
And _{let} the angel of the LORD ^{pursuing}_{persecute} them.
7 For without cause have they hid for me ³their
net *in* a pit,
_{*which* without}^{Without} cause ^{have they}_{they have} digged ^{*a pit*} for my soul.
8 Let destruction come upon him at unawares ;
And let his net that he hath hid catch himself:
_{into that very}^{*With} destruction let him fall ^{therein}.
9 And my soul shall be joyful in the LORD :
It shall rejoice in his salvation.

R.V. ¹ Or, *and the battle axe against &c.* ² Heb. *darkness
and slippery places.* ³ Or, *the pit of their net* ⁴ Or, *Into
that very destruction let him fall*

¹⁰ All my bones shall say, LORD, who is like unto
      thee,
   Which deliverest the poor from him that is too
      strong for him,
   Yea, the poor and the needy from him that
      spoileth him?

¹¹ ¹_{False}Unrighteous witnesses _{did} rise up;
   They _{laid to my charge}ask me of things that I _{knew}know not.

¹² They _{rewarded}reward me evil for _{good}good,
   To the _{spoiling}bereaving of my soul.

¹³ But as for me, when they were sick, my
      clothing was sackcloth:
   I _{humbled}afflicted my soul with fasting;
   And my prayer ²returned into mine own bosom.

¹⁴ I behaved myself as though _{he}it had been my
      friend or ^{my} brother:
   I bowed down _{heavily,}mourning, as one that _{mourneth for}bewaileth his
      mother.

¹⁵ But _{in mine adversity}when I halted they rejoiced, and gathered
      themselves together:
   _{yea, the}The ³abjects gathered themselves together
      against me, and ⁴I knew *it* not;
   They did tear me, and ceased not:

¹⁶ ⁵_{With hypocritical}Like the profane mockers in feasts,
   They gnashed upon me with their teeth.

¹⁷ Lord, how long wilt thou look on?
   Rescue my soul from their destructions,

R.V. ¹ Or, *Malicious* See Ex. 23. 1.   ² Or, *shall return*
³ Or, *smiters*   ⁴ Or, those whom *I knew not*   ⁵ Or, *Among*

¹My darling from the lions.

¹⁸ I will give thee thanks in the great congregation:

I will praise thee among ²much people.

¹⁹ Let not them that are mine enemies ³wrong-
fully rejoice over me:

Neither let them wink with the eye that hate
me without a cause.

²⁰ For they speak not peace:

But they devise deceitful words/matters against them
that are quiet in the land.

²¹ Yea, they opened their mouth wide against me;/me,

They/and said, Aha, aha, our eye hath seen it.

²² Thou/This thou hast seen it, O LORD;/seen, O LORD: keep not silence:

O Lord, be not far from me.

²³ Stir up thyself, and awake to my judgement,/judgment,

Even unto my cause, my God and my Lord.

²⁴ Judge me, O LORD my God, according to thy
righteousness;

And let them not rejoice over me.

²⁵ Let them not say in their heart,/hearts, ⁴Aha,/Ah, so would
we have it:

Let them not say, We have swallowed him up.

²⁶ Let them be ashamed and brought to confusion/confounded together that rejoice at mine hurt:

Let them be clothed with shame and dishonour
that magnify themselves against me.

R.V. ¹ Heb. *My only one.*   ² Or, *a mighty people*   ³ Heb.
falsely.   ⁴ Heb. *Aha, our desire.*

²⁷ Let them shout for joy, and be glad, that
    ¹favour my righteous cause:
  Yea, let them say continually, _Let the_ LORD be
    magnified,
  Which hath pleasure in the prosperity of his
    servant.
²⁸ And my tongue shall _talk_/speak of thy righteousness,/righteousness
  And of thy praise all the day long.

36 For the Chief Musician./To the chief Musician, _A Psalm_ of David the servant
    of the LORD.

¹ ²The transgression of the wicked ³saith within
    ⁴my heart,
  There is/that there is no fear of God before his eyes.
² For ⁵he flattereth himself in his own eyes,
  ⁶That/until his iniquity _shall not_ be found _out and/to_ be _hated./hateful._
³ The words of his mouth are iniquity and
    deceit:
  He hath left off to be _wise/wise,_ _and_ to do good.
⁴ He deviseth _iniquity/mischief_ upon his bed;
  He setteth himself in a way that is not good;
  He abhorreth not evil.

⁵ Thy _lovingkindness,/mercy,_ O LORD, is in the heavens;
  Thy/and thy faithfulness _reacheth_ unto the _skies./clouds._

R.V. ¹ Heb. _have pleasure in my righteousness._ ² Or, _Trans-_
gression saith to the wicked   ³ Or, _uttereth its oracle_   ⁴ Or,
according to many ancient versions, _his_   ⁵ Or, _it_ (or, _he_) _flattereth_
him in his eyes   ⁶ Or, _Until his iniquity be found and be hated_
Heb. _Concerning the finding out of his iniquity and hating it._

⁶ Thy righteousness is like the ^mountains of God; ^great mountains;
  Thy ^judgements ^judgments are a great deep :
  O Lord, thou preservest man and beast.
⁷ How ^precious ^excellent is thy lovingkindness, O God !
  ^And ^therefore the children of men ^take refuge ^put their trust under the
      shadow of thy wings.
⁸ They shall be ¹abundantly satisfied with the
      fatness of thy house ;
  And thou shalt make them drink of the river
      of thy pleasures.
⁹ For with thee is the fountain of life :
  In thy light shall we see light.
¹⁰ O continue thy lovingkindness unto them that
      know thee ;
  And thy righteousness to the upright in heart.
¹¹ Let not the foot of pride come against me,
  And let not the hand of the wicked ^drive me away. ^remove me.
¹² There are the workers of iniquity fallen :
  They are ^thrust ^cast down, and shall not be able to
      rise.

37   *A Psalm* of David.

¹ Fret not thyself because of ^evil-doers, ^evildoers,
  Neither be thou envious against ^them that work ^the workers
      ^unrighteousness. ^of iniquity.
² For they shall soon be cut down like the grass,
  And wither as the green herb.

R.V.   ¹ Heb. *watered.*

³ Trust in the LORD, and do good;
And ¹Dwell *so shalt thou dwell* in the land, and ²follow after faithfulness. *verily thou shalt be fed.*

⁴ ³Delight thyself also in the LORD;
And he shall give thee the ⁴desires of thine heart.

⁵ ⁵Commit thy way unto the LORD;
Trust also in him, *him*; and he shall bring it to pass.

⁶ And he shall make thy righteousness to go forth *bring forth thy righteousness* as the light,
And thy judgement *judgment* as the noonday.

⁷ ⁶Rest in the LORD, and wait patiently for him:
Fret not thyself because of him who prospereth in his way,
Because of the man who bringeth wicked devices to pass.

⁸ Cease from anger, and forsake wrath:
Fret not thyself, *it tendeth* only *thyself in any wise* to evil-doing. *do evil.*

⁹ For evil-doers *evildoers* shall be cut off:
But those that wait upon the LORD, they shall inherit ⁷the land. *earth.*

¹⁰ For yet a little while, and the wicked shall not be:
Yea, thou shalt diligently consider his place, and ⁸he *it* shall not be.

¹¹ But the meek shall inherit the land; *earth;*

R.V. ¹ Or, *So shalt thou dwell in the land and feed securely*
² Heb. *feed on.*   ³ Or, *So shalt thou have thy delight in &c.*
⁴ Heb. *petitions.*   ⁵ Heb. *Roll thy way upon the LORD.*   ⁶ Or,
Be still before (Heb. *silent to*) *the* LORD   ⁷ Or, *the earth* (and
so in vv. 11, 22, 29, 34)   ⁸ Or, *it*

And shall delight themselves in the abundance
of peace.

¹² The wicked plotteth against the just,
And gnasheth upon him with his teeth.

¹³ The Lord shall laugh at him:
For he seeth that his day is coming.

¹⁴ The wicked have drawn out the sword, and
have bent their bow; bow,
To cast down the poor and needy,
To and to slay such as be of upright in the way: conversation.

¹⁵ Their sword shall enter into their own heart,
And their bows shall be broken.

¹⁶ Better is a little that the a righteous man hath
Than the abundance A
is better than the riches of many wicked.

¹⁷ For the arms of the wicked shall be broken:
But the Lord upholdeth the righteous.

¹⁸ The Lord knoweth the days of the perfect upright:
And their inheritance shall be for ever.

¹⁹ They shall not be ashamed in the time of evil. evil time:
And in the days of famine they shall be
satisfied.

²⁰ But the wicked shall perish,
And the enemies of the Lord shall be as ¹the
excellency of the pastures:
fat lambs
They shall consume; ²in into smoke shall they
consume away.

²¹ The wicked borroweth, and payeth not again:
But the righteous dealeth graciously, sheweth mercy, and giveth.

R.V.   Or, *the fat of lambs*   ² Or, *like smoke*

²² For such as be blessed of him shall inherit the land ;
              earth ;
And they that be cursed of him shall be cut off.

²³ A man's goings are established of the LORD;
The steps of a *good* man are ordered by the LORD:
And he delighteth in his way.

²⁴ Though he fall, he shall not be utterly cast down :
For the LORD ¹upholdeth him with his hand.

²⁵ I have been young, and now am old ;
Yet have I not seen the righteous forsaken,
Nor his seed begging *their* bread.

²⁶ All the day long he dealeth graciously, and lendeth ;
      He is ever merciful,
And his seed is blessed.

²⁷ Depart from evil, and do good ;
And dwell for evermore.

²⁸ For the LORD loveth judgement,
             judgment.
And forsaketh not his saints ;
They are preserved for ever :
But the seed of the wicked shall be cut off.

²⁹ The righteous shall inherit the land,
And dwell therein for ever.

³⁰ The mouth of the righteous talketh of wisdom,
                 speaketh
And his tongue speaketh judgement.
            talketh of judgment.

³¹ The law of his God is in his heart ;
None of his steps shall slide.

³² The wicked watcheth the righteous,
And seeketh to slay him.

R.V. ¹ Or, *upholdeth his hand*

³³ The Lord will not leave him in his hand,
Nor condemn him when he is judged.
³⁴ Wait on the Lord, and keep his way,
And he shall exalt thee to inherit the land:
When the wicked are cut off, thou shalt see it.
³⁵ I have seen the wicked in great power,
And spreading himself life a green ^{tree in its} _{bay}
^{native soil.}
_{tree.}
³⁶ ^{1 But} ^{2 one} passed ^{by,} and, lo, he was not:
_{Yet he} _{away,}
Yea, I sought him, but he could not be found.
³⁷ Mark the perfect man, and behold the up-
right:
For ³the ^{latter} end of *that* man is peace.
³⁸ ^{As for transgressors, they} shall be destroyed together:
_{But the transgressors}
The ^{latter} end of the wicked shall be cut off.
³⁹ But the salvation of the righteous is of the
Lord:
He is their ^{strong hold} in the time of trouble.
_{strength}
⁴⁰ And the Lord ^{helpeth} them, and ^{rescueth} them:
_{shall help} _{deliver}
He ^{rescueth} them from the wicked, and ^{saveth}
_{shall deliver} _{save}
them,
Because they ^{have taken refuge} in him.
_{trust}

38

A Psalm of David, ⁴to bring to remembrance.

¹ O Lord, rebuke me not in thy wrath:
Neither chasten me in thy hot displeasure.

R.V. ¹ Or, *Yet he passed away* ² Or, according to some
ancient versions, *I passed by* ³ Or, *there is a reward* (or, *future*
or, *posterity) for the man of peace* ⁴ Or, *to make memorial*

² For thine arrows ¹stick fast in me,
And thy hand ¹presseth me sore.
³ There is no soundness in my flesh because of
thine ^{indignation}; _{anger}
Neither is there any ²^{health}_{rest} in my bones because
of my sin.
⁴ For mine iniquities are gone over mine head:
As an heavy burden they are too heavy for
me.
⁵ My wounds stink and are ^{corrupt.}_{corrupt}
Because of my foolishness.
⁶ I am ^{³pained and}_{troubled; I am} bowed down greatly;
I go mourning all the day long.
⁷ For my loins are filled with a loathsome ^{burning;}_{disease.}
And there is no soundness in my flesh.
⁸ I am ^{faint}_{feeble} and sore ^{bruised}_{broken}:
I have roared by reason of the disquietness of
my heart.
⁹ Lord, all my desire is before thee;
And my groaning is not hid from thee.
¹⁰ My heart ^{throbbeth,}_{panteth,} my strength faileth me:
As for the light of mine eyes, it also is gone
from me.
¹¹ My lovers and my friends stand aloof from my
^{plague.}_{sore}
And my kinsmen stand afar off.
¹² They also that seek after my life lay snares
for ^{me}_{me}:

R.V. ¹ Heb. *lighted on me.*   ² Or, *rest*   ³ Heb. *bent.*

And they that seek my hurt speak mischievous
  things,
And imagine deceits all the day long.
13 But I, as a deaf man, hear not;
  And I am as a dumb man that openeth not his
    mouth.
14 Yea, I am as a man that heareth not,
  And in whose mouth are no ¹reproofs.
15 For in thee, O LORD, do I hope:
  Thou wilt answer, O Lord my God.
16 For I said, Hear me, lest otherwise they should rejoice
    over me:
  When my foot slippeth, they magnify them-
    selves against me.
17 For I am ready to halt,
  And my sorrow is continually before me.
18 For I will declare mine iniquity;
  I will be sorry for my sin.
19 But mine enemies are lively, and they are strong:
  And they that hate me ²wrongfully are multi-
    plied.
20 They also that render evil for good
  Are adversaries unto me, because I follow the thing
    that is good.
21 Forsake me not, O LORD:
  O my God, be not far from me.
22 Make haste to help me,
  O Lord my salvation.

R.V. ¹ Or, *arguments* ² Heb. *falsely.*

c

39 For the Chief Musician, for Jeduthun. A Psalm of David.
To the chief *even* to Jeduthun,

1 I said, I will take heed to my ways,
That I sin not with my tongue:
I will keep [1] my mouth with a bridle,
While the wicked is before me.

2 I was dumb with silence, I held my peace,
[2] even from good;
And my sorrow was stirred.

3 My heart was hot within me;
While I was musing the fire kindled:
Then spake I with my tongue:

4 LORD, make me to know mine end,
And the measure of my days, what it is;
Let me know how frail I am.

5 Behold, thou hast made my days *as* handbreadths;
And mine age is as nothing before thee:
Surely every man [3] at his best estate is altogether
[4] vanity. Selah. [Selah

6 Surely every man walketh [5] in a vain shew:
Surely they are disquieted [6] in vain:
He heapeth up *riches*, and knoweth not who
shall gather them.

7 And now, Lord, what wait I for?
My hope is in thee.

8 Deliver me from all my transgressions:

R.V. [1] Heb. *a bridle* (or, *muzzle*) *for my mouth*. [2] Or, *and
had no comfort* Heb. *away from good*. [3] Heb. *standing firm.*
[4] Heb. *a breath.* [5] Or, *as a shadow* [6] Or, *for vanity*

Make me not the reproach of the foolish.
9 I was dumb, I opened not my mouth ;
Because thou didst it.
10 Remove thy stroke away from me :
I am consumed by the [1]blow of thine hand.
11 When thou with rebukes dost correct man for
iniquity,
Thou [2]makest his beauty to consume away
like a moth :
Surely every man is [3]vanity.   Selah.   [Selah
12 Hear my prayer, O Lord, and give ear unto
my cry ;
Hold not thy peace at my tears :
For I am a stranger with thee,
$_{and}^{A}$ a sojourner, as all my fathers were.
13 [4]O spare me, that I may [5]recover strength,
Before I go hence, and be no more.

40   For the Chief Musician.
To the chief Musician,   A Psalm of David.

1 I waited patiently for the Lord ;
And he inclined unto me, and heard my
cry.
2 He brought me up also out of [6]an horrible pit,
out of the miry $_{clay,}^{clay;}$
And ^{he} set my feet upon a rock, and established my goings.

R.V. [1] Heb. *conflict.*   [2] Or, *consumest like a moth his delights*
[3] Heb. *a breath.*   [4] Or, *Look away from me*   [5] Heb.
brighten up.   [6] Heb. *a pit of tumult* or *destruction.*

³ And he hath put a new song in my mouth,
   even praise unto our God:
   Many shall see it, and fear,
   And shall trust in the LORD.
⁴ Blessed is ᵗʰᵉ_ₜₕₐₜ man that maketh the LORD his
   trust,
   And respecteth not the proud, nor such as
   ¹turn aside to lies.
⁵ Many, O LORD my God, are ᵗʰᵉ_ₜₕy wonderful
   works which thou hast done,
   And thy thoughts which are to us-ward:
   ²They cannot be ᵣₑcₖₒₙₑd ᵤₚ^set in order unto ᵗʰᵉᵉ:
   If I would declare and speak of them,
   They are more than can be numbered.
⁶ Sacrifice and ³offering thou ʰᵃˢᵗ ⁿᵒ ᵈᵉˡⁱᵍʰᵗ ⁱⁿ .
   ⁴Mine ears hast thou opened:
   Burnt offering and sin offering hast thou not
   required.
⁷ Then said I, Lo, I ᵃᵐ ᶜᵒᵐᵉ;
   In the ᵥₒₗᵤₘₑ^roll of the book it is ⁵written of ᵐᵉ:
⁸ I delight to do thy will, O my ᴳᵒᵈ;
   Yea, thy law is within my heart.
⁹ I have ⁶ᵖᵘᵇˡⁱˢʰᵉᵈ_ₚᵣₑₐcₕₑd righteousness in the great
   congregation;
   Lo, I ʰᵃᵛᵉ^will not ᵣₑfᵣₐiₙₑd^refrain my lips,
   O LORD, thou knowest.

R.V.   ¹ Or, *fall away treacherously*   ² Or, *There is none to
be compared unto thee*   ³ Or, *meal offering*   ⁴ Heb. *Ears
hast thou digged* (or, *pierced*) *for me.*   ⁵ Or, *prescribed to
*⁶ Or, *proclaimed glad tidings of*

¹⁰ I have not hid thy righteousness within my
heart;
I have declared thy faithfulness and thy salvation:
I have not concealed thy lovingkindness and
thy truth from the great congregation.

¹¹ Withhold not thou thy tender mercies from
me, O LORD:
Let thy lovingkindness and thy truth continually preserve me.

¹² For innumerable evils have compassed me
about,
Mine iniquities have taken hold upon me, so that I
am not able to look up;
They are more than the hairs of mine head:
and therefore my heart hath failed me.

¹³ Be pleased, O LORD, to deliver me:
O LORD, make haste to help me.

¹⁴ Let them be ashamed and confounded together
That seek after my soul to destroy it;
Let them be driven backward and put to
dishonour
That wish me evil.

¹⁵ Let them be ²desolate for a reward of their shame
That say unto me, Aha, aha.

¹⁶ Let all those that seek thee rejoice and be
glad in thee:

R.V. ¹ Heb. *forsaken.*   ² Or, *astonished*   ³ Or, *for a reward of*

69

Let such as love thy salvation say continually,
The LORD be magnified.
¹⁷ But I am poor and needy;
Yet the Lord thinketh upon me:
Thou art my help and my deliverer;
Make no tarrying, O my God.

41

For the Chief Musician. A Psalm of David.
~~To the Chief Musician,~~

¹ Blessed is he that considereth ¹the poor:
The LORD will deliver him in ^the day of evil._the time of trouble.
² ²The LORD will preserve him, and keep him ^alive,_alive; and he shall be blessed ³upon the ^earth:_earth:
And ^deliver not thou_thou wilt not deliver him unto the will of his enemies.
³ ⁴The LORD will ^support_strengthen him upon the ^couch_bed of languishing:
Thou ^makest_wilt make all his bed in his sickness.
⁴ I said, ^O LORD, have mercy upon_LORD, be merciful unto me:
Heal my soul; for I have sinned against thee.
⁵ Mine enemies speak evil ^against_of me, *saying,*
When shall he die, and his name perish?
⁶ And if he come to see *me*, he speaketh ^vanity:_vanity:
His heart gathereth iniquity to ^itself:_itself;
When he goeth abroad, he telleth it.
⁷ All that hate me whisper together against me:

R.V.   ¹ Or, *the weak*   ² Or, *The LORD preserve*   ³ Or,
in the land   ⁴ Or, *The LORD support*   ⁵ Heb. *turnest,*
or, *changest.*   ⁶ Or, *falsehood*

Against me do they devise my hurt.
⁸ ¹An evil disease, *say they*, ²cleaveth fast unto
   him :
   And now that he lieth he shall rise up no
   more.
⁹ Yea, mine own familiar friend, in whom I
   trusted, which did eat of my bread,
   Hath lifted up his heel against me.
¹⁰ But thou, O Lord, ᵇᵉ ᵐᵉʳᶜⁱᶠᵘˡ ᵘⁿᵗᵒ me, and raise
   me up,
   That I may requite them.
¹¹ By this I know that thou ᶠᵃᵛᵒᵘʳᵉˢᵗ ⁱⁿ me,
   Because mine enemy doth not triumph over
   me.
¹² And as for me, thou upholdest me in mine
   integrity,
   And settest me before thy face for ever.

¹³ Blessed be the Lord, the God of Israel,
   From everlasting, and to everlasting.
   Amen, and Amen.

R.V. ¹ Or, *Some wicked thing*   ² Or, *is poured out upon him*

BOOK II

42 For the Chief Musician; Maschil of
To the chief Musician, Maschil, for the sons of Korah

¹ As the hart panteth after the water
   brooks,
So panteth my soul after thee, O God.
² My soul thirsteth for God, for the living God:
   When shall I come and appear before God?
³ My tears have been my meat day and night,
   While they ¹continually say unto me, Where
   is thy God?
⁴ These things I remember, and
When I remember these *things*, I pour out my soul ²within me,
   in me:
How I went with the throng, and ³led
for I had gone with the multitude, I went with them to
   the house of God,
With the voice of joy and praise, with a multitude keeping holyday.
   that kept
⁵ Why art thou ⁴cast down, O my soul?
And *why* art thou disquieted within me?
   in
Hope thou in God: for I shall yet praise him
⁵*For* the ⁶health of his countenance.
   help

⁶ O my God, my soul is cast down within me:
Therefore do I remember thee from the land
   will
   of Jordan,
And of the Hermons, from ⁷the hill Mizar.
   of the Hermonites,

R.V. ¹ Heb. *all the day.*   ² Heb. *upon.*   ³ Or, *went in
procession with them*   ⁴ Heb. *bowed down.*   ⁵ According
to some ancient authorities, *Who is the health of my countenance, and
my God. My soul &c.*   ⁶ Or, *help*   ⁷ Or, *the little mountain*

7 Deep calleth unto deep at the noise of thy
   ¹waterspouts :
  All thy waves and thy billows are gone over
   me.
8 *Yet* the LORD will command his lovingkindness
   in the ^day-time,_daytime,
  And in the night his song shall be with me,
  ^Even a_and my prayer unto the God of my life.
9 I will say unto God my rock, Why hast thou
   forgotten me?
  Why go I mourning ²because of the oppression
   of the enemy?
10 As with ³a sword in my bones, mine ^adversaries_enemies
   reproach me ;
  While they ^continually say_say daily unto me, Where is thy
   God?
11 Why art thou cast down, O my soul?
  And why art thou disquieted within me?
  Hope thou in God : for I shall yet praise him,
  Who is the ⁴health of my countenance, and
   my God.

43 ¹ Judge me, O God, and plead my cause
       against an ungodly nation :
       O deliver me from the deceitful and un-
       just man.
2 For thou art the God of my ^strength_strength: why ^hast_dost thou
   cast me off?

---

*R.V.   ¹ Or, *cataracts*   ² Or, *while the enemy oppresseth*
³ Or, *crushing*   ⁴ Or, *help*

73   C 5

Why go I mourning [1]because of the oppression
of the enemy?

[3] O send out thy light and thy truth: let them
lead me:

Let them bring me unto thy holy hill,
And to thy tabernacles.

[4] Then will I go unto the altar of God,
Unto God [2]my exceeding joy:
And upon the harp will I praise thee, O God, my
God.

[5] Why art thou cast down, O my soul?
And why art thou disquieted within me?
Hope thou in God: for I shall yet praise
him,
Who is the [3]health of my countenance, and
my God.

44 For the Chief Musician; *a Psalm* of the sons of Korah.
To the chief Musician for the sons of Korah,
Maschil.

[1] We have heard with our ears, O God, our
fathers have told us,
What work thou didst in their days, in the
days of old.

[2] Thou didst drive out the nations with thy hand,
How thou heathen
and plantedst them in;
Thou didst afflict the peoples, and [4]didst spread them
how thou people, cast
abroad.
out.

R.V. [1] Or, *while the enemy oppresseth*   [2] Heb. *the gladness
of my joy*.   [3] Or, *help*   [4] Or, *cast them forth*

³ For they ᵍᵃᵗ_ᵍₒₜ not the land in possession by their
　　own sword,
　Neither did their own arm save them :
　But thy right hand, and thine arm, and the
　　light of thy countenance,
　Because thou hadst a favour unto them.
⁴ Thou art my King, O God :
　Command ¹ᵈᵉˡⁱᵛᵉʳᵃⁿᶜᵉ_ᵈᵉˡⁱᵛᵉʳᵃⁿᶜᵉˢ for Jacob.
⁵ Through thee will we push down our ᵃᵈᵛᵉʳˢᵃʳⁱᵉˢ_ᵉⁿᵉᵐⁱᵉˢ :
　Through thy name will we tread them under
　　that rise up against us.
⁶ For I will not trust in my bow,
　Neither shall my sword save me.
⁷ But thou hast saved us from our ᵃᵈᵛᵉʳˢᵃʳⁱᵉˢ,_ᵉⁿᵉᵐⁱᵉˢ,
　And hast put them to shame that ʰᵃᵗᵉ_ʰᵃᵗᵉᵈ us.
⁸ In God ʰᵃᵛᵉ we ᵐᵃᵈᵉ ᵒᵘʳ boast all the day long,
　And ʷᵉ ʷⁱˡˡ ᵍⁱᵛᵉ ᵗʰᵃⁿᵏˢ ᵘⁿᵗᵒ_ᵖʳᵃⁱˢᵉ thy name for ever.　ˢᵉˡᵃʰ_ˢᵉˡᵃʰ.

⁹ But ⁿᵒʷ thou hast cast ᵘˢ off, and ᵇʳᵒᵘᵍʰᵗ_ᵖᵘᵗ us to
　ᵈⁱˢʰᵒⁿᵒᵘʳ .
　ˢʰᵃᵐᵉ
　And goest not forth with our ʰᵒˢᵗˢ._ᵃʳᵐⁱᵉˢ.
¹⁰ Thou makest us to turn back from the ᵃᵈᵛᵉʳˢᵃʳʸ_ᵉⁿᵉᵐʸ :
　And they which hate us spoil for themselves.
¹¹ Thou hast given us like sheep *appointed* for
　　meat ;
　And hast scattered us among the ⁿᵃᵗⁱᵒⁿˢ._ʰᵉᵃᵗʰᵉⁿ.
¹² Thou sellest thy people for nought,
　And ʰᵃˢᵗ_ᵈᵒˢᵗ not ⁱⁿᶜʳᵉᵃˢᵉᵈ_ⁱⁿᶜʳᵉᵃˢᵉ *thy wealth* by their price.

¹³ Thou makest us a reproach to our neighbours,
   A scorn and a derision to them that are round
     about us.
¹⁴ Thou makest us a byword among the ^nations,^heathen,
   A shaking of the head among the ^peoples.^people.
¹⁵ ^All the day long is my dishonour^My confusion *is* continually before me,
   And the shame of my face hath covered me,
¹⁶ For the voice of him that reproacheth and
     blasphemeth;
   By reason of the enemy and ^the avenger.
¹⁷ All this is come upon us; yet have we not
     forgotten thee,
   Neither have we dealt falsely in thy covenant.
¹⁸ Our heart is not turned back,
   Neither have our steps declined from thy way;
¹⁹ ^1 That^Though thou hast sore broken us in the place of
     ^jackals,^dragons,
   And covered us with the shadow of death.
²⁰ If we have forgotten the name of our God,
   Or ^spread forth^stretched out our hands to a strange god;
²¹ Shall not God search this out?
   For he knoweth the secrets of the heart.
²² Yea, for thy sake are we killed all the day
     long;
   We are counted as sheep for the slaughter.
²³ Awake, why sleepest thou, O Lord?
   Arise, cast *us* not off for ever.
²⁴ Wherefore hidest thou thy face,

R.V.   ¹ Or, *Though*

And forgettest our affliction and our oppression?
²⁵ For our soul is bowed down to the dust :
Our belly cleaveth unto the earth.
²⁶ ^{Rise up}_{Arise} for our help,
And redeem us for thy ^{lovingkindness'}_{mercies'} sake.

45
For the Chief Musician; set to ¹Shoshannim; *a Psalm* of the sons
To the chief Musician upon Shoshannim, for
of Korah. Maschil. A Song of loves.
Korah, Maschil,

¹ My heart ^{overfloweth. with a goodly}_{is inditing a good} matter :
²I speak _{of} the things which I have made
touching the king :
My tongue is the pen of a ready writer.
² Thou art fairer than the children of ^{men:}_{men:}
Grace is poured ³into thy lips :
Therefore God hath blessed thee for ever.
³ Gird thy sword upon thy thigh, O ^{mighty one,}_{*most* mighty,}
_{with thy}^{Thy} glory and thy majesty.
⁴ And in thy majesty ride ^{on prosperously,}_{prosperously}
⁴Because of truth and meekness *and* ^{righteousness:}_{righteousness :}
And ⁵thy right hand shall teach thee terrible
things.
⁵ Thine arrows are ^{sharp:}_{sharp}
The peoples fall under thee;
in the heart of the king's enemies;   *L.A.V.*
They are in the heart of the king's enemies.
_{whereby} the people fall under thee.

R.V. ¹ That is, *Lilies.*   ² Or, *I speak; my work is for a*
king   ³ Or, *upon*   ⁴ Or, *In behalf of*   ⁵ Or, *let thy right*
hand teach

⁶ ¹Thy throne, O God, is for ever and ever:

_{the}^A sceptre of ^{equity is the sceptre of thy kingdom.}_{thy kingdom *is* a right sceptre.}

⁷ Thou ^{hast loved}_{lovest} righteousness, and ^{hated}_{hatest} wickedness:

Therefore God, thy God, hath anointed thee
With the oil of gladness above thy fellows.

⁸ All thy garments *smell of* myrrh, and aloes, *and* _{cassia;}_{cassia,}

Out of _{the} ivory ^{palaces stringed instruments}_{palaces, whereby they} have made thee glad.

⁹ Kings' daughters ^{are}_{were} among thy honourable women:

_{upon}^{At} thy right hand ^{doth}_{did} stand the queen in gold of Ophir.

¹⁰ Hearken, O daughter, and consider, and incline thine ear;

Forget also thine own people, and thy father's house;

¹¹ So shall the king _{greatly} desire thy beauty:

For he is thy Lord; and worship thou him.

¹² And the daughter of Tyre *shall be there* with a gift;

Even the rich among the people shall intreat thy favour.

¹³ The king's daughter ²^{within *the palace* is all glorious}_{*is* all glorious within}:

Her clothing is ^{inwrought with}_{of wrought} gold.

R.V.   ¹ Or, *Thy throne is* the throne of *God &c.*   ² Or, *in the inner part* of the palace

¹⁴ She shall be $_{brought}^{led}$ unto the king ¹in $_{work}^{broidered}$ $_{needlework}^{raiment of}$:
   The virgins her companions that follow her
   Shall be brought unto thee.
¹⁵ With gladness and rejoicing shall they be $_{brought}^{led}$:
   They shall enter into the king's palace.
¹⁶ Instead of thy fathers shall be thy children,
   Whom thou $_{mayest}^{shalt}$ make princes in all the earth.
¹⁷ I will make thy name to be remembered in all
     generations:
   Therefore shall the $_{people\ praise\ thee}^{peoples\ give\ thee\ thanks}$ for ever
   and ever.

46 For the Chief Musician; *a Psalm* of the sons of Korah; set to Alamoth. A Song.
To the chief Musician for the sons of Korah, A Song upon Alamoth.

¹ God is our refuge and strength,
   A very present help in trouble.
² Therefore will $_{not\ we}^{we\ not}$ fear, though the earth $_{be\ removed,}^{do\ change,}$
   And though the mountains be $_{carried\ into}^{moved\ in}$ the $_{midst}^{heart}$
   of the $_{sea}^{seas}$;
³ Though the waters thereof roar and be troubled,
   Though the mountains shake with the ²swell-
     ing thereof. Selah. [Selah

⁴ There is a river, the streams whereof $_{shall}$ make
   glad the city of God,

R.V. ¹ Or, *upon* ² Or, *pride*

The holy place of the tabernacles of the ^{Most}_{most} High.

5 God is in the midst of her; she shall not be moved:
God shall help her, [1]and that right early.

6 The ^{nations}_{heathen} raged, the kingdoms were moved:
He uttered his voice, the earth melted.

7 The LORD of hosts is with us;
The God of Jacob is our [2]refuge.   Selah.   [Selah

8 Come, behold the works of the LORD,
[3]What desolations he hath made in the earth.

9 He maketh wars to cease unto the end of the earth;
He breaketh the bow, and cutteth the spear in sunder;
He burneth the ^{chariots}_{chariot} in the fire.

10 [4]Be still, and know that I am God:
I will be exalted among the ^{nations,}_{heathen,}
I will be exalted in the earth.

11 The LORD of hosts is with us;
The God of Jacob is our [2]refuge.   Selah.   [Selah

47

For the Chief Musician; a ^{Psalm} ^{of} the sons of Korah.
To the chief Musician, A _{for}

1 O clap your hands, all ye ^{peoples}_{people};
Shout unto God with the voice of triumph.

R.V.   [1] Heb. *at the dawn of morning.*   [2] Or, *high tower*
[3] Or, *Who hath made desolations &c.*   [4] Or, *Let be*

2 For ¹the LORD ᴹᵒˢᵗ ᴴⁱᵍʰ is terrible ;
 He is a great King over all the earth.
3 He ²shall subdue the peoples under us,
 And the nations under our feet.
4 He ³shall choose our inheritance for us,
 The excellency of Jacob whom he ⁴loved.
            [Selah
 Selah.
5 God is gone up with a shout,
 The LORD with the sound of a trumpet.
6 Sing praises to God, sing praises :
 Sing praises unto our King, sing praises.
7 For God is the King of all the earth :
 Sing ye praises ⁵with understanding.
3 God reigneth over the nations :
 God sitteth upon the throne of his holiness.
9 The princes of the peoples are gathered together,
 ⁶To be even the people of the God of Abraham :
 For the shields of the earth belong unto God :
 He is greatly exalted.

48

  A Song; a Psalm of the sons of Korah.

1 Great is the LORD, and highly to be praised,
 In the city of our God, in his holy mountain.
2 Beautiful in elevation, the joy of the whole earth,
 Is mount Zion, *on* the sides of the north,
 The city of the great King.

R.V. ¹Or, *the LORD is most high* and *terrible* ²Or, *subdueth*
³Or, *chooseth* ⁴Or, *loveth* ⁵Or, *in a skilful psalm*
Heb. *Maschil.* ⁶Or, Unto *the people*

³ God ^{hath made himself}_{is} known in her palaces for a
   ¹refuge.
⁴ For, lo, the kings ^{assembled themselves.}_{were assembled,}
   They ²passed by together.
⁵ They saw it, ^{then were}_{and so} they ^{amazed}_{marvelled;}
   They were ^{dismayed, they}_{troubled, and} ³hasted away.
⁶ ^{Trembling}_{Fear} took hold _{upon} them ^{there;}_{there,}
   ^{Pain,}_{and pain,} as of a woman in travail.
⁷ ⁴With the east wind

   Thou breakest the ships of _{Tarshish} ^{Tarshish.}_{with an east wind.}
⁸ As we have heard, so have we seen
   In the city of the LORD of hosts, in the city of
     our God:
   God will establish it for ever. _{Selah.}   [Selah
⁹ We have thought ^{on}_{of} thy lovingkindness, O God,
   In the midst of thy temple.
¹⁰ ^{As is}_{According to} thy name, O God,
   So is thy praise unto the ends of the earth:
   Thy right hand is full of righteousness.
¹¹ Let mount Zion ^{be glad,}_{rejoice,}
   Let the daughters of Judah ^{rejoice,}_{be glad,}
   Because of thy ^{judgements.}_{judgments.}
¹² Walk about Zion, and go round about her:
   Tell the towers thereof.
¹³ Mark ye well her bulwarks,
   ⁵Consider her palaces;

R.V. ¹ Or, *high tower*   ² Or, *passed away*   ³ Or, *were
stricken with terror*   ⁴ Or, As *with the east wind that breaketh*
⁵ Or, *Traverse*

That ye may tell it to the generation following.
14 For this God is our God for ever and ever:
He will be our guide *even* ¹unto death.

49 For the Chief Musician; a Psalm of the sons of Korah.
To the chief Musician, A Psalm for the sons of Korah.

¹ Hear this, all ye peoples;
people;
Give ear, all ye inhabitants of the world:
² Both low and high,
Rich and poor, together.
poor,
³ My mouth shall speak of wisdom;
And the meditation of my heart shall be of understanding.
⁴ I will incline mine ear to a parable:
I will open my dark saying upon the harp.
⁵ Wherefore should I fear in the days of evil,
When the ²iniquity at my heels compasseth me
of shall compass
about?
⁶ They that trust in their wealth,
And boast themselves in the multitude of their riches;
⁷ None *of them* can by any means redeem his brother,
Nor give to God a ransom for him:
⁸ (For the redemption of their soul is costly,
precious,
And must be let alone for ever:)
it ceaseth
⁹ That he should still live alway,
for ever,

R.V. ¹ Or, according to some ancient authorities, *for evermore*
² Or, *the iniquity of them that would supplant me compasseth me
about, even of them that trust...riches?*

^{That he should and} not see ¹corruption.

¹⁰ ²For he seeth that wise men die,
^{The likewise the} fool and the brutish ^{together person} perish,
And leave their wealth to others.

¹¹ ³Their inward thought is, *that* their houses
shall continue for ever,
And their dwelling places to all generations;
They call their lands after their own names.

¹² ^{But Nevertheless} ⁴man ^{abideth not in honour *being* in honour abideth not} :
He is like the beasts that perish.

¹³ ⁵This their way is ⁶their folly :
Yet ^{after them men their posterity} approve their sayings.   Selah.   [Selah

¹⁴ They are appointed as a flock for Sheol .
Like sheep they are laid in the grave ;
Death shall ^{be their shepherd: feed on them;}
And the upright shall have dominion over
them in the morning;
And their ⁷beauty shall ^{be for Sheol to consume, that there consume in the grave from}
be no habitation for it.
their dwelling.

¹⁵ But God will redeem my soul from the ⁸power
of ^{Sheol the grave} :
For he shall receive me.   Selah.   [Selah

¹⁶ Be not thou afraid when one is made rich,
When the ⁹glory of his house is ^{increased: increased;}

¹⁷ For when he dieth he shall carry nothing ^{away: away:}
His glory shall not descend after him.

R.V. ¹ Or, *the pit*   ² Or, *Yea, he shall see it : wise men &c.*
³ Some ancient versions read, *Their graves are their houses for ever.*
⁴ Or, *man* being *in honour abideth not*   ⁵ Or, *This is the way of them that are foolish*   ⁶ Or, *their confidence: and after &c.*
⁷ Or, *form*   ⁸ Heb. *hand.*   ⁹ Or, *wealth*

¹⁸ Though while he lived he blessed his ^{soul:}_{soul.}
   And men _{will} praise thee, when thou doest well
     to ^{thyself.}_{thyself.}
¹⁹ ¹He shall go to the generation of his fathers ;
   ²They shall never see ^{the} light.
²⁰ Man that is in honour, and understandeth not,
   Is like the beasts that perish.

50   A Psalm of Asaph.

¹   ³God, *even* God,
    The mighty God, *even* the Lord, hath spoken,
   And called the earth from the rising of the sun
     unto the going down thereof.
² Out of Zion, the perfection of beauty,
   God hath ^{shined forth.}_{shined.}
³ Our God ⁴shall come, and shall not keep
   silence :
   A fire shall devour before him,
   And it shall be very tempestuous round about
    him.
⁴ He shall call to the heavens _{from} above,
   And to the earth, that he may judge his ^{people:}_{people.}
⁵ Gather my saints together unto me ;
   Those that have made a covenant with me by
    sacrifice.
⁶ And the heavens ⁵shall declare his ^{righteousness;}_{righteousness:}
   For God is judge himself.   _{Selah.}   [Selah

R.V. ¹ Heb. *Thou shalt go,* or, *It shall go.*   ² Or, *Which
never more see*   ³ Or, *The God of gods* Heb. *El Elohim.*
⁴ Or, *cometh...devoureth...is &c.*   ⁵ Or, *declare*

⁷ Hear, O my people, and I will speak;
O Israel, and I will testify ^{1 unto}_{against} thee:
I am God, *even* thy God.
⁸ I will not reprove thee for thy ^{sacrifices;}_{sacrifices}
^{2And}_{or} thy burnt _{offerings, *to have been*}offerings are continually before
me.
⁹ I will take no bullock out of thy house,
Nor ^{he-goats}_{he goats} out of thy folds.
¹⁰ For every beast of the forest is mine,
And the cattle ³upon a thousand hills.
¹¹ I know all the fowls of the mountains:
And the wild beasts of the field are ⁴mine.
¹² If I were hungry, I would not tell thee:
For the world is mine, and the fulness thereof.
¹³ Will I eat the flesh of bulls,
Or drink the blood of goats?
¹⁴ Offer unto God ^{the sacrifice of} thanksgiving;
And pay thy vows unto the ^{Most}_{most} High:
¹⁵ And call upon me in the day of ^{trouble:}_{trouble:}
I will deliver thee, and thou shalt glorify me.

¹⁶ But unto the wicked God saith,
What hast thou to do to declare my statutes,
^{And}_{or} that thou ^{hast taken}_{shouldest take} my covenant in thy
mouth?
¹⁷ Seeing thou hatest ⁵instruction,
And castest my words behind thee.

R.V. ¹ Or, *against*   ² Or, *Nor for thy burnt offerings, which
are &c.*   ³ Or, *upon the mountains where thousands are*
⁴ Or, *in my mind* Heb. *with me.*   ⁵ Or, *correction*

86

¹⁸ When thou sawest a thief, _{then} thou consentedst
     with him,
   And ¹hast been partaker with adulterers.
¹⁹ Thou givest thy mouth to evil,
   And thy tongue frameth deceit.
²⁰ Thou sittest and speakest against thy brother;
   Thou ²slanderest thine own mother's son.
²¹ These things hast thou done, and I kept
     silence;
   Thou thoughtest that I was altogether such
     an one as thyself:
   But I will reprove thee, and set *them* in order
     before thine eyes.

²² Now consider this, ye that forget God,
   Lest I tear you in pieces, and there be none
     to deliver:
²³ Whoso offereth the sacrifice of thanksgiving glorifieth me;
   ³And to him that ordereth his ⁴conversation
   aright
   Will I shew the salvation of God.

51 For the Chief Musician. A Psalm of David: when Nathan the prophet came unto him, after he had gone in to Bath-sheba.

¹ Have mercy upon me, O God, according to
   thy lovingkindness:

R.V. ¹ Heb. *thy portion was with adulterers.*   ² Or, *givest
a thrust against*   ³ Or, *And prepareth a way that I may shew
him*   ⁴ Heb. *way.*

According _{unto}^{to} the multitude of thy tender
　mercies blot out my transgressions.
2 Wash me throughly from mine iniquity,
　And cleanse me from my sin.
3 For I [1]acknowledge my transgressions:
　And my sin is ever before me.
4 Against thee, thee only, have I sinned,
　And done ^{that} _{this}which is evil in thy sight:
　That thou ^{mayest}_{mightest} be justified when thou
　　speakest,
　And be clear when thou judgest.
5 Behold, I was shapen in iniquity;
　And in sin did my mother conceive me.
6 Behold, thou desirest truth in the inward
　　parts:
　And in the hidden part thou shalt make me to
　　know wisdom.
7 Purge me with hyssop, and I shall be clean:
　Wash me, and I shall be whiter than snow.
8 Make me to hear joy and gladness;
　That the bones which thou hast broken may
　　rejoice.
9 Hide thy face from my sins,
　And blot out all mine iniquities.
10 Create [2]in me a clean heart, O God;
　And renew a [3]right spirit within me.
11 Cast me not away from thy presence;
　And take not thy holy spirit from me.

R.V. [1] Heb. *know.*　　　[2] Or, *for me*　　　[3] Or, *stedfast*

12 Restore unto me the joy of thy {salvation: / salvation;}
And uphold me {with a / *with thy*} [1]free spirit.
13 Then will I teach transgressors thy ways;
And sinners shall [2]be converted unto thee.
14 Deliver me from bloodguiltiness, O God, thou God of my {salvation; / salvation:}
And my tongue shall sing aloud of thy righteousness.
15 O Lord, open thou my lips;
And my mouth shall shew forth thy praise.
16 For thou {delightest not in / desirest not} sacrifice; [3]else would I give it:
Thou {hast no pleasure / delightest not} in burnt offering.
17 The sacrifices of God are a broken spirit:
A broken and a contrite heart, O God, thou wilt not despise.

18 Do good in thy good pleasure unto Zion:
Build thou the walls of Jerusalem.
19 Then shalt thou {delight in / be pleased with} the sacrifices of righteousness, {in / with} burnt offering and whole burnt offering:
Then shall they offer bullocks upon thine altar.

52

{For the Chief Musician. Maschil of David: / To the chief Musician, Maschil, *A Psalm* of David,} when Doeg the Edomite came and told Saul, and said unto him, David is come to the house of Ahimelech.

1 Why boastest thou thyself in mischief, O mighty man?

R.V. [1] Or, *willing* [2] Or, *return* [3] Or, *that I should give it*

The ^{mercy}_{goodness} of God *endureth* continually.

2 Thy tongue deviseth ^{very wickedness}_{mischiefs} ;
   Like a sharp ^{razor,}_{rasor,} working deceitfully.

3 Thou lovest evil more than good ;
   And lying rather than to speak righteous-
       ness. Selah.   [Selah

4 Thou lovest all devouring words,
   ¹O thou deceitful tongue.

5 God shall likewise ²destroy thee for ever,
   He shall take thee _{away,}^{up,} and pluck thee out of
       thy _{dwelling place,}^{tent,}
   And root thee out of the land of the living.
       Selah.   [Selah

6 The righteous also shall ^{see}_{see,} _{it,} and fear,
   And shall laugh at _{him :}^{him, *saying*,}

7 Lo, this is the man that made not God his
       ³strength ;
   But trusted in the abundance of his riches,
   And strengthened himself in his wickedness.

8 But ^{as for me,} I am like a green olive tree in the
       house of God :
   I trust in the mercy of God for ever and
       ever.

9 I will ^{give thee thanks}_{praise thee} for ever, because thou hast
       done it :
   And I will wait on thy ^{name,}_{name;} for it is ^{good, in the}_{good}
       ^{presence of}_{before} thy saints.

R.V.   ¹ Or, And *the deceitful tongue*   ² Or, *break thee down*
³ Or, *strong hold*

53 For the Chief Musician; set to Mahalath. Maschil
To the chief Musician upon Mahalath, Maschil, *A Psalm* of David.

¹ ¹The fool hath said in his heart, There is no
God.

Corrupt are they, and have done abominable
iniquity;
iniquity:

There is none that doeth good.

² God looked down from heaven upon the
children of men,

To see if there were any that did ²understand,

That did seek ᵃᶠᵗᵉʳ God.

³ Every one of them is gone ᵇᵃᶜᵏ; they are
back:

together become filthy;
altogether

There is none that doeth good, no, not one.

⁴ Have the workers of iniquity no knowledge?

Who eat up my people *as* they eat ᵇʳᵉᵃᵈ,
bread:

And call not
they have not called upon God.

⁵ There were they in great fear, where no fear was:

For God hath scattered the bones of him that
encampeth against ᵗʰᵉᵉ;
thee:

Thou hast put them to shame, because God
hath ʳᵉʲᵉᶜᵗᵉᵈ them.
despised

⁶ Oh that the salvation of Israel were come out
of Zion!

When God ³bringeth back the captivity of his
people,

Then shall Jacob
Jacob shall rejoice, *and* Israel shall be glad.

R.V.　¹ See Ps. 14.　　² Or, *deal wisely*　　³ Or, *returneth to*

54 For the Chief Musician; on stringed instruments. Maschil of David:
To the chief Musician on Neginoth, Maschil, *A Psalm* of David,
when the Ziphites/Ziphims came and said to Saul, Doth not David hide himself with us?

¹ Save me, O God, by thy name,
And judge me in/by thy might./strength.
² Hear my prayer, O God;
Give ear to the words of my mouth.
³ For ¹strangers are risen up against me,
And violent men have sought/and oppressors seek after my soul:
They have not set God before them.　Selah. [Selah
⁴ Behold, God is mine helper:
The Lord is ²of/with them that uphold my soul.
⁵ ³He shall requite the/reward evil unto ⁴mine enemies:
Destroy thou them/cut them off in thy truth.
⁶ With a freewill offering will I/I will freely sacrifice unto thee:
I will give thanks unto/praise thy name, O LORD,/LORD; for it is good.
⁷ For he hath delivered me out of all trouble;/trouble:
And mine eye hath seen my/his *desire* upon mine enemies.

55 For the Chief Musician; on stringed instruments. Maschil of David.
To the chief Musician on Neginoth, Maschil, *A Psalm* of David.

¹ Give ear to my prayer, O God;
And hide not thyself from my supplication.
² Attend unto me, and answer/hear me:
I am restless/mourn in my complaint, and moan/make a noise;

R.V. ¹ See Ps. 86. 14.　　² Or, *with*　　³ Another reading
is, *The evil shall return.*　⁴ Or, *them that lie in wait for me*

92

³ Because of the voice of the enemy,
  Because of the oppression of the ^(wicked;)_(wicked:)
  For they cast iniquity upon me,
  And in ^(anger)_(wrath) they ^(persecute)_(hate) me.
⁴ My heart is sore pained within me:
  And the terrors of death are fallen upon me.
⁵ Fearfulness and trembling are come upon me,
  And horror hath overwhelmed me.
⁶ And I said, Oh that I had wings like a dove!
  ^(Then)_(for then) would I fly away, and be at rest.
⁷ Lo, then would I wander far off,
  ^(I would lodge)_(and remain) in the wilderness. Selah. [Selah
⁸ I would ¹^(haste me to a shelter)_(hasten my escape)
  From the ^(stormy wind)_(windy storm) and tempest.
⁹ ²Destroy, O Lord, *and* divide their ^(tongue)_(tongues):
  For I have seen violence and strife in the city.
¹⁰ Day and night they go about it upon the walls
      thereof:
  ^(Iniquity)_(mischief) also and ^(mischief)_(sorrow) are in the midst of it.
¹¹ Wickedness is in the midst thereof:
  ³^(Oppression)_(deceit) and guile depart not from her streets.
¹² For it was not an enemy that reproached me;
  Then I could have borne it:
  Neither was it he that hated me that did
      magnify himself against me;
  Then I would have hid myself from him:
¹³ But it was thou, a man mine equal,
  My ^(companion,)_(guide,) and ^(my familiar friend.)_(mine acquaintance.)

R.V. ¹ Or, *hasten my escape* ² Heb. *Swallow up.* ³ Or, *Fraud*

¹⁴ We took sweet counsel together,
_{and} ^{We} walked _{unto} ⁱⁿ the house of God ^{with the throng.}_{in company.}

¹⁵ ¹Let death ^{come suddenly}_{seize} upon them,
_{and let} ^{Let} them go down ^{alive}_{quick} into ²the pit:_{hell}
For wickedness is in their ^{dwelling, in}_{dwellings, and} ³the midst of among them.

¹⁶ As for me, I will call upon God;
And the LORD shall save me.

¹⁷ Evening, and morning, and at ^{noonday,}_{noon,} will I
_{pray,} ^{complain,} and _{cry aloud} ^{moan}:
And he shall hear my voice.

¹⁸ He hath ^{redeemed}_{delivered} my soul in peace ⁴from the battle that was against me:
For _{there} ^{they} were many ^{that strove} with me.

¹⁹ God shall hear, and ⁵^{answer}_{afflict} them,
Even he that abideth of ^{old.}_{old.} Selah.   [Selah
^{The men} who_{Because they} have no changes,
^{And who}_{therefore they} fear not God.

²⁰ He hath put forth his hands against such as
^{were}_{be} at peace with him:
He hath ^{profaned}_{broken} his covenant.

²¹ ^{His}_{The words} of his mouth ^{was smooth as}_{were smoother than} butter,
But ^{his heart was war}_{war was in his heart}:
His words were softer than oil,
Yet were they drawn swords.

²² Cast ⁶thy burden upon the LORD, and he shall sustain thee:

R.V. ¹ Or, as otherwise read, *Desolations be upon them!*
² Heb. *Sheol.*   ³ Or, *their inward part*   ⁴ Or, *so that none came nigh me*   ⁵ Or, *afflict*   ⁶ Heb. *that he hath given thee.*

He shall never suffer the righteous to be moved.
23 But thou, O God, shalt bring them down into
the pit of destruction:
Bloodthirsty and deceitful men shall not live out
bloody
half their days;
But I will trust in thee.

56 For the Chief Musician; set to ¹Jonath elem rehokim. *A Psalm*
To the chief Musician upon Jonath-elem-rechokim, Michtam
of David: Michtam: when the Philistines took him in Gath.
of David,

¹ Be merciful unto me, O God: for man would
God
swallow me up:
up:
All the day long he fighting oppresseth me.
he fighting daily
² ²Mine enemies would daily swallow me up all the
day long:

For they be many that fight proudly against me.
against me, O thou most High.
³ What time I am afraid,
I will put my trust in thee.
⁴ In God I will praise his word:
word,
In God have I put my trust, I will not be afraid;
I have trust; fear
What can flesh do unto me?
flesh can me.
⁵ All the day long they wrest my words:
Every day
All their thoughts are against me for evil.
⁶ They gather themselves together, they hide
themselves,
They mark my steps,
³Even as they have waited for my soul.
when wait

R.V. ¹ That is, *The silent dove of them that are afar off* or,
as otherwise read, *The dove of the distant terebinths* ² Or,
They that lie in wait for me ³ Or, *Inasmuch as*

7 ¹Shall they escape by iniquity?
In ^{In} <i>thine</i> anger cast down the ^{peoples,}_{people,} O God.

8 Thou tellest my wanderings:
Put thou my tears into thy ^{bottle:}_{bottle:}
Are they not in thy ²book?

9 ^{Then} When I cry <i>unto thee,</i> then shall mine enemies turn
back in the day that I call_{back}.
This I ^{know,}_{know;} ^{3that}_{for} God is for me.

10 In God will I praise <i>his</i> word:
In the Lord will I praise <i>his</i> word.

11 In God have I put my ^{trust:}_{trust:} I will not be ^{afraid;}_{afraid}
What ^{can man}_{man can} do unto ^{me?}_{me.}

12 Thy vows are upon me, O God:
I will render ^{thank offerings}_{praises} unto thee.

13 For thou hast delivered my soul from death:
Hast thou_{wilt} not delivered_{thou deliver} my feet from ^{falling?}_{falling,}
That I may walk before God
In the light of ⁴the ^{living.}_{living?}

57 For the Chief Musician; <i>set to</i> Al-tashheth. <i>A Psalm</i> of David:
To the chief Musician, Al-taschith, Michtam of
Michtam: David, when he fled from ^{Saul,}_{Saul} in the cave.

1 Be merciful unto me, O God, be merciful
unto ^{me;}_{me:}
For my soul ^{taketh refuge}_{trusteth} in thee:
Yea, in the shadow of thy wings will I _{make my}^{take}
refuge,

R.V.　¹ Or, <i>They think to escape</i>　　² Or, <i>record</i>　　³ Or, <i>for</i>
⁴ Or, life

Until *these* [1]calamities be overpast.

2 I will cry unto God ^{Most High} ;
                  _{most high}
Unto God that performeth *all things* for me.

3 He shall send from heaven, and save ^{me,}_{me}
from the reproach of him that would swallow me
   ^{When he} _{up reproacheth;}
   up reproacheth; Selah.   [Selah
God shall send forth his mercy and his truth.

4 My soul is among ^{lions;}
               _{lions: *and*}
[2]I lie ^{among} them that are set on fire,
   _{*even among*}
Even the sons of men, whose teeth are spears
   and arrows,
And their tongue a sharp sword.

5 Be thou exalted, O God, above the heavens ;
Let thy glory *be* above all the earth.

6 They have prepared a net for my steps ;
My soul is bowed down:
^{They} have digged a pit before ^{me;}
_{they}   _{me,}
^{They are fallen into the midst thereof} themselves. Selah. [Selah
_{into the midst whereof they are fallen}

7 My heart is fixed, O God, my heart is fixed:
I will ^{sing, yea, I will sing praises.}
     _{sing and give praise.}

8 Awake up, my glory; awake, psaltery and
harp :
[3]I myself will awake ^{right} early.

9 I will ^{give thanks unto} thee, O Lord, among the
     _{praise}
^{peoples}.
_{people} :
I will sing ^{praises} unto thee among the nations.

10 For thy mercy is great unto the heavens,

R.V. [1] Or, *wickednesses*   [2] Or, *I must lie*   [3] Or, *I will*
awake the dawn

And thy truth unto the skies. / clouds.

11 Be thou exalted, O God, above the heavens; / heavens:
Let thy glory *be* above all the earth.

58 For the Chief Musician; *set to* Al-tashheth. *A Psalm* of David:
To the chief Musician, Al-taschith, Michtam of Michtam. David.

1 1Do ye indeed in silence speak righteousness / speak righteousness, O congregation ?
Do ye 0judge uprightly, O ye sons of men?

2 Yea, in heart ye work wickedness ;
Ye weigh out the violence of your hands in the earth.

3 The wicked are estranged from the womb :
They go astray as soon as they be born, speaking lies.

4 Their poison is like the poison of a serpent :
They are like the deaf adder that stoppeth her ear;

5 Which hearkeneth not / will not hearken to the voice of 4charmers,
Charming never so wisely.

6 Break their teeth, O God, in their mouth :
Break out the great teeth of the young lions, O Lord.

7 Let them melt away as water that runneth apace / waters *which* run continually :
When he bendeth *his bow to shoot* / aimeth his arrows, let them be as though they were cut off. / cut in pieces.

8 *Let them be* as / As a snail which melteth and passeth / melteth, let *every one of them* pass away :

R.V. 1 Or, *Is the righteousness ye should speak dumb ?*   2 Or,
as otherwise read, *O ye gods* or, *O ye mighty ones*   3 Or, *judge
uprightly the sons of men*   4 Or, *enchanters*

Like the untimely birth of a woman, ¹that _{hath not seen}_{they may not see} the sun.

⁹ Before your pots can feel the thorns,

²He shall take them away _{as} with a whirlwind, _{the green and the burning alike.}_{both living, and in *his* wrath.}

¹⁰ The righteous shall rejoice when he seeth the vengeance:

He shall wash his feet in the blood of the wicked.

¹¹ So that _{a men}_{a man} shall say, Verily there is ³a reward for the righteous:

Verily _{there}_{he} is a God that judgeth in the earth.

59 For the Chief Musician; *set to* Al-tashheth. *A Psalm* of David: To the chief Musician, Al-taschith, Michtam of Michtam: when Saul sent, and they watched the house to kill him. David;

¹ Deliver me from mine enemies, O my God:

_{Set me on high}_{defend me} from them that rise up against me.

² Deliver me from the workers of iniquity,

And save me from _{the bloodthirsty}_{bloody} men.

³ For, lo, they lie in wait for my _{soul:}_{soul:}

The mighty _{gather themselves together}_{are gathered} against _{me:}_{me;}

Not for my transgression, nor for my sin, O LORD.

⁴ They run and prepare themselves without *my* fault:

Awake _{thou} to ⁴help me, and behold.

R.V.   ¹ Or, like them *that have not seen the sun as raw flesh, even so, shall fury sweep them away fruit.*   ⁴ Heb. *meet.*   ² Or, *Even* ³ Heb.

5 Even thou, Thou therefore, O LORD God of hosts, the God of
  Israel,
  Arise awake to visit all the ¹heathen:
  Be not merciful to any wicked transgressors.
                                              [Selah

⁶ They return at evening; evening: they make a noise like a
  dog,
  And go round about the city.
⁷ Behold, they belch out with their mouth; mouth:
  Swords are in their lips:
  For who, *say they*, doth hear?
⁸ But thou, O LORD, shalt laugh at them;
  Thou shalt have all the ¹heathen in derision.
⁹ ²O my strength, I will Because of his strength will I wait upon thee:
  For God is my high tower. defence.
¹⁰ ³The God of my mercy shall prevent me:
  God shall let me see *my desire* upon ⁴mine
  enemies.
¹¹ Slay them not, lest my people forget:
  ⁵Scatter them by thy power; power; and bring them
  down,
  O Lord our shield.
¹² *For* the sin of their mouth, mouth *and* the words of
  their lips, lips
  Let them even be taken in their pride, pride:
  And for cursing and lying which they speak.

R.V. ¹ Or, *nations*   ² So some ancient authorities. The
Hebrew text has, *His strength.*   ³ According to some ancient
authorities, *My God with his mercy.*   ⁴ Or, *them that lie in
wait for me*   ⁵ Or, *Make them wander to and fro*

¹³ Consume them in wrath, consume them, that they _{may not *be*}^{be no more}:

And let them know that God ruleth in J^{acob,}_{acob}

Unto the ends of the earth.   _{Selah.}   [Selah

¹⁴ And at evening let them _{return; *and*}^{return,} let them make a noise like a dog,

And go round about the city.

¹⁵ ^{They shall}_{Let them} wander up and down for meat,

And ^{tarry all night}_{grudge} if they be not satisfied.

¹⁶ But I will sing of thy ^{strength}_{power};

Yea, I will sing aloud of thy mercy in the morning:

For thou hast been my ^{high tower,}_{defence}

And ^{a refuge}_{refuge} in the day of my ^{distress.}_{trouble.}

¹⁷ Unto thee, O my strength, will I sing ^{praises}:

For God is my ^{high tower,}_{defence, *and*} the God of my mercy.

60

For the Chief Musician; set to ¹Shushan Eduth: Michtam of David,
To the chief Musician upon Shushan-eduth, to ^{teach}_{teach}: when he strove with Aram-naharaim and with Aram-zobah, ^{and}_{when} Joab returned, and smote of Edom in the ^{Valley}_{valley} of Salt _{of salt} twelve thousand.

¹ O God, thou hast cast us off, thou hast _{broken us down;}_{scattered us,}

Thou hast been _{displeased}^{angry}; O _{turn thyself to}^{restore} us again.

² Thou hast made the _{earth}^{land} to tremble; thou hast _{broken}^{rent} it:

Heal the breaches thereof; for it shaketh.

R.V. ¹ That is, *The lily of testimony.*

³ Thou hast shewed thy people hard things:
Thou hast made us to drink the wine of
staggering.
astonishment.

⁴ Thou hast given a banner to them that fear thee,
¹That it may be displayed because of the
truth. Selah.   [Selah

⁵ That thy beloved may be delivered,
delivered;
Save with thy right hand, and answer ²us.
hear me.

⁶ God hath spoken in his holiness; I will exult:
rejoice,
I will divide Shechem, and mete out the valley
of Succoth.

⁷ Gilead is mine, and Manasseh is mine;
Ephraim also is the defence of mine head;
strength
Judah is my ³sceptre.
lawgiver;

⁸ Moab is my washpot;
⁴Upon Edom will I cast out my shoe:
over
Philistia, shout thou because of me.
triumph

⁹ Who will bring me into the strong city?
⁵Who hath led me unto Edom?
will lead into

¹⁰ ⁶Hast not thou, O God, which hadst cast us off?
Wilt
And thou, O God, which didst not go out with our hosts.
thou goest not forth, O God,   armies?

¹¹ Give us help against the adversary:
from trouble
For vain is the ⁷help of man.

¹² Through God we shall do valiantly:
For he it is that shall tread down our adversaries.
enemies.

R.V. ¹ Many ancient authorities render, *That they may flee from
before the bow.* ² Another reading is, *me.* ³ Or, *lawgiver*
⁴ Or, *unto* ⁵ Or, *Who will lead me &c.* ⁶ Or, *Wilt not
thou, O God, which hast cast us off, and goest...hosts?* ⁷ Heb.
salvation.

61 For the Chief Musician; on a stringed instrument.
To the chief Musician upon Neginah,
A Psalm of David.

[1] Hear my cry, O God;
Attend unto my prayer.
[2] From the end of the earth will I ^{call}_{cry} unto thee,
when my heart [1]is overwhelmed:
Lead me to [2]the rock that is higher than I.
[3] For thou hast been a ^{refuge}_{shelter} for me,
^A_{*and* a} strong tower from the enemy.
[4] I will ^{dwell}_{abide} in thy [3]tabernacle for ever:
I will ^{take refuge}_{trust} in the covert of thy wings. _{Selah.} [Selah
[5] For thou, O God, hast heard my vows:
Thou hast [4]given *me* the heritage of those that
fear thy name.
[6] Thou wilt prolong the king's life:
^{His}_{*and* his} years ^{shall be} as many generations.
[7] He shall abide before God for ever:
O prepare ^{lovingkindness}_{mercy} and truth, ^{that they}_{*which*} may
preserve him.
[8] So will I sing praise unto thy name for ever,
That I may daily perform my vows.

62 For the Chief Musician; after the manner of Jeduthun.
To the chief Musician, to Jeduthun,
A Psalm of David.

[1] ^{My}_{Truly my} soul [5]waiteth ^{only} upon God:
From him *cometh* my salvation.

R.V. [1] Or, *fainteth*   [2] Or, *a rock that is too high for me*
[3] Heb. *tent.*   [4] Or, *given an heritage unto those &c.*   [5] Heb.
is silent unto God.

103

² He only is my rock and my ^{salvation:}
He is my ^{high tower}_{defence}; I shall not be greatly moved.

³ How long will ye _{imagine mischief against a man?}^{set upon a man,}
^{¹That ye may slay *him,*}_{ye shall be slain} all of ^{you,}_{you:}
^{Like}_{as} a bowing _{wall *shall ye be, and as*}^{wall, like} a tottering ^{fence?}_{fence.}

⁴ They only consult to ^{thrust}_{cast} him down from his
^{excellency;}_{excellency:}
They delight in lies:
They bless with their mouth, but they curse
inwardly. _{Selah.}   [Selah

⁵ My soul, ²wait thou only upon God;
For my expectation is from him.

⁶ He only is my rock and my salvation:
He is my ^{high tower}_{defence}; I shall not be moved

⁷ ^{With}_{In} God is my salvation and my glory:
The rock of my strength, and my refuge, is in
God.

⁸ Trust in him at all ^{times,}_{times;} ye ^{people;}_{people,}
Pour out your heart before him:
God is a refuge for us. _{Selah.}   [Selah

⁹ Surely men of low degree are ³vanity, and men
of high degree are a lie:
In the balances they will go up;
_{to be laid in the balance,}
They are ^{together}_{altogether} lighter than ³vanity.

¹⁰ Trust not in oppression,
And become not vain in robbery:
If riches increase, set not your heart ^{thereon.}_{upon them.}

R.V. ¹ Or, as otherwise read, *Ye shall be slain &c.*   ² Heb.
be thou silent unto God.   ³ Heb. *a breath.*

¹¹ God hath spoken ^{once,} _{once;}
Twice have I heard this;
That power belongeth unto ^{God:} _{God.}
¹² Also unto thee, O Lord, belongeth mercy:
For thou renderest to every man according to
    his work.

63   A Psalm of David, when he was in the wilderness of Judah.

¹ O God, thou art my God; ¹early will I seek
    thee:
My soul thirsteth for thee, my flesh longeth
    for ^{thee,} _{thee}
In a dry and ^{weary} _{thirsty} land, where no water ^{is,} _{is;}
2 So have I looked upon thee in the sanctuary,

To see thy power and thy ^{glory;} _{glory,}

so *as* I have seen thee in the sanctuary.
3 ^{For} _{Because} thy lovingkindness is better than ^{life;} _{life,}
My lips shall praise thee.
⁴ ^{So} _{Thus} will I bless thee while I live:
I will lift up my hands in thy name.
⁵ My soul shall be satisfied as with ²marrow and
    fatness;
And my mouth shall praise thee with joyful ^{lips:} _{lips:}
⁶ When I remember thee upon my bed,
    ³*And* meditate on thee in the night watches.
7 ^{For} _{Because} thou hast been my help,
    ^{And} _{therefore} in the shadow of thy wings will I rejoice.

R.V. ¹ Or, *earnestly*   ² Heb. *fat.*   ³ Or, *I meditate*

⁸ My soul followeth hard after thee:
Thy right hand upholdeth me.

⁹ But those that seek my soul, ¹to destroy it,
Shall go into the lower parts of the earth.

¹⁰ They shall be ²given over to the power of the sword:
fall by
They shall be a portion for ³foxes.

¹¹ But the king shall rejoice in God:
God;
Every one that sweareth by him shall glory;
glory;
For the mouth of them that speak lies shall be
but
stopped.

64

For the Chief Musician.
To the chief Musician,   A Psalm of David.

¹ Hear my voice, O God, in my complaint:
prayer
Preserve my life from fear of the enemy.

² Hide me from the secret counsel of evil-doers;
the wicked
From the ⁴tumult of the workers of iniquity:
insurrection

³ Who have whet their tongue like a sword,
And bend their bows to shoot their arrows, even bitter
have aimed
words:

⁴ That they may shoot in secret places at the
perfect:
Suddenly do they shoot at him, and fear
not.

⁵ They encourage themselves in an evil purpose;
matter:
They commune of laying snares privily;
They say, Who shall see them?

R.V. ¹ Or, *shall be destroyed; they shall &c.*   ² Or, *poured*
out by   ³ Or, *jackals*   ⁴ Or, *throng*

⁶ They search out iniquities; ¹We have accomplished, *say they, they accomplish*
  a diligent search :
  And both the inward thought of every one, *of them,* and
  the heart, is deep.
⁷ But God shall shoot at them; them
  With an arrow, arrow; suddenly shall they be wounded.
⁸ ²So they shall be made to stumble, make their own tongue
  being against them to fall upon themselves :
  All that see them shall ³wag the head. flee away.
⁹ And all men shall fear; fear,
  And they shall declare the work of God; God;
  And for they shall wisely consider of his doing.
¹⁰ The righteous shall be glad in the LORD, and
  shall trust in him ;
  And all the upright in heart shall glory.

65

For the Chief Musician. A Psalm. A Song of David
To the chief Musician, A Psalm *and*

¹ ⁴Praise waiteth for thee, O God, in Zion: Sion:
  And unto thee shall the vow be performed.
² O thou that hearest prayer,
  Unto thee shall all flesh come.
³ ⁵Iniquities prevail against me :
  As for our transgressions, thou shalt purge
  them away.

R.V. ¹ Or, as otherwise read, *they have accomplished* or *have hidden* ² Or, *So shall they against whom their tongue was make them to stumble* ³ Or, *flee away* ⁴ Or, *There shall be silence before thee,* and *praise, O God &c.* ⁵ Heb. *Words* (or, *Matters*) *of iniquities.*

⁴ Blessed is the man whom thou choosest, and
    causest to approach *unto thee*,
That he may dwell in thy courts:
We shall be satisfied with the goodness of thy
    house,
The holy place of thy *even* of thy holy temple.
⁵ By terrible things thou wilt answer us in righteousness, in righteousness wilt thou answer us,
O God of our salvation;
Thou that art *who art* the confidence of all the ends of the
    earth,
    ¹And of them that are afar off upon the sea:
⁶ Which by his strength setteth fast the moun-
    tains;
Being girded about with might: power:
⁷ Which stilleth the roaring noise of the seas, the roaring noise of
    their waves,
And the tumult of the peoples. people.
⁸ They also that dwell in the uttermost parts are
    afraid at thy tokens:
Thou makest the outgoings of the morning
    and evening to rejoice.
⁹ Thou visitest the earth, and waterest it: it:
Thou greatly enrichest it: it
The with the river of God, God which is full of water:
Thou providest preparest them corn, ²when thou hast so
    prepared ³the earth. provided for it.
¹⁰ Thou waterest her furrows abundantly; the ridges thereof abundantly:

R.V. ¹ Or, *And of the sea, afar off*   ² Or, *for so preparest*
thou   ³ Heb. *her*.

108

Thou ¹settlest the ₍ᵣᵢᵈᵍₑₛ₎ thereof :
Thou makest it soft with ₍ₛₕₒwₑᵣₛ₎:
Thou blessest the springing thereof.
¹¹ Thou crownest ²the year with thy goodness ;
And thy paths drop fatness.
¹² ³They drop upon the pastures of the wilder-
ness :
And the ₗᵢₜₜₗₑ hills ₐᵣₑ ᵍᵢᵣᵈₑᵈ wᵢₜₕ ⱼₒy.
¹³ The pastures are clothed with flocks ;
The valleys also are covered over with corn ;
They shout for joy, they also sing.

66   For the Chief Musician. A Song, a ₚₛₐₗₘ.
To the chief Musician, A Song *or*

¹ Make a joyful noise unto God, all ₜₕₑ ₑₐᵣₜₕ :
² Sing forth the ₍ᵍₗₒᵣy₎ of his name :
Make his praise glorious.
³ Say unto God, How terrible ₐᵣₜ ₜₕₒᵤ ᵢₙ thy works !
Through the greatness of thy power shall thine
enemies ⁴submit themselves unto thee.
⁴ All the earth shall worship thee,
And shall sing unto thee ;
They shall sing to thy name.   Selah.   [Selah
⁵ ₍Cₒₘₑ₎ and see the works of ₍Gₒᵈ₎:
He is terrible in his doing toward the children
of men.
⁶ He turned the sea into dry land :

R.V. ¹ Heb. *lowerest.*   ² Heb. *the year of thy goodness.*
³ Or, *The pastures...do drop*   ⁴ Or, *yield feigned obedience*
Heb. *lie.*

They went through the ^{river}/_{flood} on foot:
There ¹did we rejoice in him.
⁷ He ruleth by his ^{might}/_{power} for ever;
His eyes ^{observe}/_{behold} the nations:
Let not the rebellious exalt themselves.   _{Selah.} [Selah
⁸ O bless our God, ye ^{peoples,}/_{people,}
And make the voice of his praise to be heard:
⁹ Which ²holdeth our soul in life,
And suffereth not our feet to be moved.
¹⁰ For thou, O God, hast proved us:
Thou hast tried us, as silver is tried.
¹¹ Thou broughtest us into the net;
Thou ^{layedst a sore burden}/_{laidst affliction} upon our loins.
¹² Thou hast caused men to ride over our
    heads;
We went through fire and through ^{water:}/_{water:}
But thou broughtest us out into ³a wealthy
    place.
¹³ I will ^{come}/_{go} into thy house with burnt ^{offerings,}/_{offerings:}
I will pay thee my vows,
¹⁴ Which my lips have uttered,
And my mouth hath spoken, when I was in
    ^{distress.}/_{trouble.}
¹⁵ I will offer unto thee burnt ^{offerings}/_{sacrifices} of fatlings,
With the incense of rams;
I will offer bullocks with goats.   _{Selah.}   [Selah
¹⁶ ^{Come,}/_{Come} and hear, all ye that fear God,

R.V. ¹ Or, *let us rejoice*   ² Heb. *putteth*.   ³ Heb. *abun-*
dance.

And I will declare what he hath done for my
　　soul.
¹⁷ I cried unto him with my mouth,
　　And ¹he was extolled with my tongue.
¹⁸ If I ²regard iniquity in my heart,
　　The Lord ³will not hear *me*:
¹⁹ But verily God hath heard *me*;
　　He hath attended to the voice of my prayer.
²⁰ Blessed be God,
　　Which hath not turned away my prayer, nor
　　　his mercy from me.

67 For the Chief Musician: on stringed instruments.
To the chief Musician on Neginoth,
A Psalm, a
A Psalm *or* Song.

¹ God be merciful unto us, and bless us; us;
　　And cause his face to shine ⁴upon us ; Selah. [Selah
² That thy way may be known upon earth,
　　Thy saving health among all nations.
³ Let the peoples ⁵praise thee, O God ;
　　people
　　Let all the peoples praise thee.
　　　　　people
⁴ O let the nations be glad and sing for joy :
　　For thou shalt judge the peoples with equity,
　　　　　　　　　　　people righteously,
　　And ⁶govern the nations upon earth. Selah. [Selah
⁵ Let the peoples praise thee, O God ;
　　　　　people
　　Let all the peoples praise thee.
　　　　　people

R.V. ¹ Or, as otherwise read, *high praise was under my tongue*
² Or, *had regarded* ³ Or, *would* ⁴ Heb. *with us.* ⁵ Or,
give thanks unto ⁶ Heb. *lead.*

111

6   The earth hath yielded *her* increase:
    Then shall the earth yield her increase; *and*
God, even our own God, shall bless us.
7 God shall bless us;
  And all the ends of the earth shall fear him.

68   For the Chief Musician.   A Psalm of David, a Song.
         To the chief Musician,   *or* Song of David.

1 Let God arise, let his enemies be scattered;
  Let them also that hate him flee before him.
2 As smoke is driven away, so drive them away:
  As wax melteth before the fire,
  So let the wicked perish at the presence of
      God.
3 But let the righteous be glad; let them exult rejoice
  before God:
  Yea, let them rejoice with gladness.
                 exceedingly rejoice.
4 Sing unto God, sing praises to his name:
  Cast up a high way for him that rideth through the deserts;
        extol   upon the heavens
  His name is JAH; and exult ye before him.
  by his name JAH,   rejoice
5 A father of the fatherless, and a judge of the
      widows,
  Is God in his holy habitation.
6 God [1]setteth the solitary in families:
  He bringeth out the prisoners into prosperity :
                 those which are bound with chains
  But the rebellious dwell in a parched land.
                            dry

7 O God, when thou wentest forth before thy
      people,

R.V.   [1] Heb. *maketh the solitary to dwell in a house.*

112

When thou didst march through the wilderness ;   Selah: [Selah

8 The earth trembled, shook,

The heavens also dropped at the presence of
God :

Even yon Sinai itself *trembled was moved* at the presence of
God, the God of Israel.

9 Thou, O God, didst send a plentiful rain,
whereby thou Thou didst confirm thine inheritance, when
it was weary.

10 Thy ¹congregation hath dwelt therein :
Thou, O God, didst prepare hast prepared of thy goodness for
the poor.

11 The Lord giveth gave the word :
The women that publish the tidings are a great host.
great *was* the company of those that published *it*.

12 Kings of armies flee, they flee ; did flee apace ·
And she that tarrieth tarried at home divideth divided the spoil.

13 ²Will ye lie have lien among the sheepfolds, pots,
As yet shall ye be as the wings of a dove covered with
silver,

And her pinions feathers with yellow gold? gold.

14 When the Almighty scattered kings therein, in it,
³*It was* *as when* it snoweth *white as snow* in Zalmon. Salmon.

15 A mountain The hill of God is the mountain *is as* the hill of Bashan ;
⁴An high mountain is hill *as* the mountain hill of Bashan.

16 Why look ye askance, leap ye, ye high mountains, hills?
At the mountain *this is* the hill which God hath desired for his abode? desireth to dwell in ;

R.V. ¹ Or, *troop*   ² Or, *When ye lie among the sheepfolds,*
it is as *the wings...gold.*   ³ Or, *It snowed*   ⁴ Heb. *A*
mountain of summits.

Yea, the LORD will dwell *in it* for ever.

¹⁷ The chariots of God are twenty thousand, even thousands ^{upon thousands}_{of angels} :

The Lord is among them, ¹*as in* Sinai, in the ^{sanctuary.} holy *place.*

¹⁸ Thou hast ascended on high, thou hast led *thy* captivity ^{captive;}_{captive:}

Thou hast received gifts ^{among men,}_{for men;}

Yea, ^{among}_{for} the rebellious also, that ²the LORD God might ³dwell ^{with}_{among} *them.*

¹⁹ ⁴Blessed be the Lord, who daily ^{beareth our} loadeth us *with* _{burden,} *benefits,*

Even the God ^{who is}_{of} our salvation.   Selah.   [Selah

²⁰   God is unto us a   God of ^{deliverances} _{*He that is* our God *is* the}   _{salvation} ;

And unto ^{JEHOVAH}_{GOD} the Lord belong the issues from death.

²¹ But God shall ^{smite through}_{wound} the head of his enemies,

^{The}_{*and* the} hairy scalp of such an one as goeth on still in his ^{guiltiness.}_{trespasses.}

²² The Lord said, I will bring again from Bashan,

I will bring ^{*them*}_{*my people*} again from the depths of the sea :

²³ That ^{thou mayest dip thy foot}_{thy foot may be dipped} in the blood ^{blood,} of *thine* enemies,

^{That}_{*and*} the tongue of thy dogs ^{may have its portion from}_{in the} *thine* enemies. _{same.}

R.V. ¹ Or, *Sinai* is *in the sanctuary*   ² Heb. *Jah.* See ver. 4.
³ Or, *dwell* there   ⁴ Or, *Blessed be the Lord day by day: if one oppresseth us, God is our salvation*

²⁴ They have seen thy goings, O _{God;}^{God,}
   Even the goings of my God, my King, ¹_{in}^{into} the
      sanctuary.
²⁵ The singers went before, the _{players on instruments}^{minstrels}
   followed _{after;}^{after,}
   _{among} ^{In the midst of} _{them were} the damsels playing with timbrels.
²⁶ Bless ye God in the congregations,
   Even the Lord, ^{ye} ^{that are} _{from} ^{of} the fountain of Israel.
²⁷ There is little Benjamin _{with} their ruler,
   The princes of Judah *and* their ²council,
   The princes of Zebulun, _{and} the princes of
      Naphtali.

²⁸ Thy God hath commanded thy strength :
   ³Strengthen, O God, that which thou ⁴hast
      wrought for us.
²⁹ Because of thy temple at Jerusalem
   _{shall kings}^{Kings shall} bring presents unto thee.
³⁰ Rebuke the _{company of spearmen,}^{wild beast of the reeds,}
   The multitude of the bulls, with the calves of
      the _{people,}^{peoples}
   ⁵Trampling under foot the _{till every one submit himself with} pieces of _{silver:}^{silver;}
   ⁶He hath scattered _{scatter thou} the _{people}^{peoples} that delight in war.
³¹ Princes shall come out of Egypt ;
   ⁷Ethiopia shall _{soon}^{haste to} stretch out her hands
      unto God.

R.V.   ¹ Or, *in the sanctuary*   Or, *in holiness*   ² Or, *company*
³ Or, *Be strong, O God, thou that hast &c.*   ⁴ Or, *hast wrought*
for us out of thy temple. Unto Jerusalem &c.   ⁵ Or, Every
one *submitting himself with pieces of silver*   ⁶ Or, as otherwise
read, *Scatter thou*   ⁷ Heb. *Cush.*

³² Sing unto God, ye kingdoms of the earth;
   O sing praises unto the Lord; _{Selah:}   [Selah

³³ To him that rideth upon the heavens of
   heavens, _{which are} _{which were} of old;
   Lo, he _{doth send out} _{uttereth} his voice, *and that* a mighty
   voice.

³⁴ Ascribe ye strength unto God:
   His excellency is over Israel,
   And his strength is in the _{skies.} _{clouds.}

³⁵ ¹O God, *thou art* terrible out of thy holy
   places:
   The God of _{Israel,} _{Israel} *is* he _{that} giveth strength and
   power unto *his* people.
   Blessed be God.

69

For the Chief Musician; set to ²Shoshannim.
To the chief Musician upon Shoshannim,   *A Psalm* of David.

¹ Save me, O God;
   For the waters are come in unto my soul.

² I sink in deep mire, where there is no standing:
   I am come into deep waters, where the floods
   overflow me.

³ I am weary _{with} _{of} my _{crying:} _{crying:} my throat is dried:
   Mine eyes fail while I wait for my God.

⁴ They that hate me without a cause are more
   than the hairs of mine head:
   They that would _{cut me off,} _{destroy me,} being mine enemies
   ³wrongfully, are mighty:

R.V.   ¹ Or, *Terrible is God*   ² That is, *Lilies.*   ³ Heb. *falsely.*

Then I ¹restored that which I took not away.

⁵ O God, thou knowest my foolishness;
And my ²sins are not hid from thee.

⁶ Let not them that wait on ^{thee be ashamed through me,} _{thee, O Lord GOD of hosts,}
^{O Lord GOD of hosts}
_{be ashamed for my sake} :
Let not those that seek thee be ^{brought to dishonour} _{confounded for}
^{through me,} _{my sake,} O God of Israel.

⁷ Because for thy sake I have borne reproach;
Shame hath covered my face.

⁸ I am become a stranger unto my brethren,
And an alien unto my mother's children.

⁹ For the zeal of thine house hath eaten me
up;
And the reproaches of them that _{reproached} ^{reproach} thee
are fallen upon me.

¹⁰ When I wept, *and chastened* my soul with
fasting,
That was to my reproach.

¹¹ ^{When} I made sackcloth _{also} my ^{clothing,} _{garment;}
_{and} I became a proverb ^{unto} _{to} them.

¹² They that sit in the gate _{speak against} ^{talk of} me;
And _I ^{I am} _{was} the song of the drunkards.

¹³ But as for me, my prayer is unto thee, O LORD,
in an acceptable time:
O God, in the multitude of thy ^{mercy,} _{mercy}
^{Answer me} _{hear me,} in the truth of thy salvation.

¹⁴ Deliver me out of the mire, and let me not
sink:

R.V.   ¹ Or, *had to restore*   ² Heb. *guiltinesses.*

Let me be delivered from them that hate me,
and out of the deep waters.

¹⁵ Let not the waterflood ^{overwhelm}_{overflow} me,
Neither let the deep swallow me ^{up;}_{up,}
And let not the pit shut her mouth upon me.

¹⁶ ^{Answer}_{Hear} me, O LORD; for thy lovingkindness is
good :
turn unto me according ^{According} to the multitude of thy tender
mercies _{turn thou unto me}.

¹⁷ And hide not thy face from thy servant ;
For I am in ^{distress; answer}_{trouble: hear} me speedily.

¹⁸ Draw nigh unto my soul, and redeem it :
^{Ransom}_{deliver} me because of mine enemies.

¹⁹ Thou ^{knowest}_{hast known} my reproach, and my shame,
and my dishonour :
Mine adversaries are all before thee.

²⁰ Reproach hath broken my heart; and I am
¹full of heaviness :
And I looked for some to take pity, but there
was none ;
And for comforters, but I found none.

²¹ They gave me also ²gall for my meat ;
And in my thirst they gave me vinegar to drink.

²² Let their table ^{before them become a snare;}_{become a snare before them:}
And *that which should have been* ^{when they are in peace,} for *their* welfare, *let it become*
a trap.

²³ Let their eyes be darkened, that they see not ;
And make their loins continually to shake.

R.V. ¹ Or, *sore sick*   ² See Deut. 29. 18.

²⁴ Pour out thine indignation upon them,
And let ^the fierceness of thine_thy wrathful anger ^overtake_take hold of them.
²⁵ Let their ¹habitation be desolate;
^Let_and let none dwell in their tents.
²⁶ For they persecute him whom thou hast smitten;
And they ^tell of_talk to the ²sorrow_grief of those whom thou hast wounded.
²⁷ Add iniquity unto their iniquity:
And let them not come into thy righteousness.
²⁸ Let them be blotted out of the book of ^³life,_the living,
And not be written with the righteous.
²⁹ But I am poor and ⁴sorrowful:
Let thy salvation, O God, set me up on high.
³⁰ I will praise the name of God with a song,
And will magnify him with thanksgiving.
³¹ ^And it_This also shall please the LORD better than an ^ox,_ox
Or ᵃ bullock that hath horns and hoofs.
³² The ^meek have seen it,_humble shall see this, and ^are_be glad:
Ye that seek after God, let your heart live.
and your heart shall live that seek God.
³³ For the LORD heareth the ^needy,_poor,
And despiseth not his prisoners.
³⁴ Let ₜₕₑ heaven and earth praise him,
The seas, and every thing that moveth therein.
³⁵ For God will save Zion, and ₜᵢₗₗ build the cities of ^Judah;_Judah:
^And they_that they ^shall abide_may dwell there, and have it in possession.

R.V.   ¹ Or, *encampment*   ² Or, *pain*   ³ Or, *the living*
⁴ Or, *in pain*

³⁶ The seed also of his servants shall inherit $^{it}_{it}$:
And they that love his name shall dwell therein.

70 For the Chief Musician. *A Psalm* of David;
To the chief Musician, David,
¹to bring to remembrance.

¹ ²*Make haste*, O God, to deliver me;
Make haste to help me, O Lord.
² Let them be ashamed and confounded
That seek after my soul:
Let them be turned $^{backward}_{backward}$, and $^{brought}_{put}$ to $^{dishonour}_{confusion}$,
That $^{delight\ in}_{desire}$ my hurt.
³ Let them be turned back $^{3by\ reason}_{for\ a\ reward}$ of their shame
That say, Aha, $^{Aha.}_{aha.}$
⁴ Let all those that seek thee rejoice and be
glad in $^{thee;}_{thee:}$
And let such as love thy salvation say con-
tinually,
Let God be magnified.
⁵ But I am poor and $^{needy;}_{needy:}$
Make haste unto me, O God:
Thou art my help and my deliverer;
O Lord, make no tarrying.

71 ¹ ⁴In thee, O Lord, do I put my trust:
Let me never be $^{ashamed.}_{put\ to\ confusion.}$
² Deliver me in thy righteousness, and
$^{rescue\ me}_{cause\ me\ to\ escape}$:

R.V. ¹ Or, *to make memorial*   ² See Ps. 40. 13–17.   ³ Or,
for a reward of   ⁴ See Ps. 31. 1–3.

^{Bow down}_{Incline} thine ear unto me, and save me.

³ Be thou ^{to me}_{my strong} ¹a rock of habitation, whereunto I
   may continually resort:

Thou hast given commandment to save me;

For thou art my rock and my fortress.

⁴ ^{Rescue}_{Deliver} me, O my God, out of the hand of the
   wicked,

Out of the hand of the unrighteous and cruel
   man.

⁵ For thou art my hope, O Lord GOD:

Thou art my trust from my youth.

⁶ By thee have I been holden up from the womb:

  ²Thou art he that took me out of my mother's
   bowels:

My praise shall be continually of thee.

⁷ I am as a wonder unto many;

But thou art my strong refuge.

⁸ ^{My mouth shall}_{Let my mouth} be filled with thy ^{praise,}_{praise}

And with thy honour all the day.

⁹ Cast me not off in the time of old age;

Forsake me not when my strength faileth.

¹⁰ For mine enemies speak ^{concerning}_{against} me;

And they that _{lay wait}^{watch} for my soul take counsel
   together,

¹¹ Saying, God hath forsaken him:

^{Pursue}_{persecute} and take him; for there is none to
    ^{deliver.}
    deliver *him.*

R.V. ¹ According to some ancient authorities, *a strong rock,*
whereunto &c.   ² Or, *Thou hast been my benefactor from &c.*

¹² O God, be not far from me:
O my God, make haste ^{to help me.}_{for my help.}

¹³ Let them be ^{ashamed}_{confounded} *and* consumed that are
adversaries to my soul;
Let them be covered with reproach and dishonour that seek my hurt.

¹⁴ But I will hope continually,
And will ^{praise thee yet}_{yet praise thee} more and more.

¹⁵ My mouth shall ^{tell of}_{shew forth} thy ^{righteousness,}_{righteousness}
And ^{of} thy salvation all the day;
For I know not the numbers *thereof.*

¹⁶ I will ^{come ¹with}_{go in} the ^{mighty acts}_{strength} of the Lord GOD:
I will make mention of thy righteousness, even
of thine only.

¹⁷ O God, thou hast taught me from my ^{youth:}_{youth:}
And hitherto have I declared thy wondrous
works.

¹⁸ ^{Yea, even ²}_{Now also}when I am old and grayheaded, O God,
forsake me not;
Until I have ^{declared}_{shewed} ³thy strength unto *the next*
this
generation,
^{Thy might}_{and thy power} to every one that is to come.

¹⁹ Thy righteousness also, O God, is very ^{high;}_{high,}
^{Thou} who hast done great ^{things,}_{things:}
O God, who is like unto ^{thee?}_{thee!}

²⁰ Thou, which has shewed ^{⁴us many}_{me great} and sore
troubles,

R.V. ¹ Or, *in the strength*
hairs.   ³ Heb. *thine arm.*   ² Heb. *unto old age and gray*   ⁴ Another reading is, *me.*

122

Shalt quicken ¹us/me again,
And shalt bring ¹us/me up again from the depths
    of the earth.
21 Increase thou/Thou shalt increase my greatness,
   And turn again and comfort me./comfort me on every side.
22 I will also praise thee with the psaltery,
   Even thy truth, O my God:
   Unto thee will I sing praises with the harp,
   O thou Holy One of Israel.
23 My lips shall greatly rejoice when I sing praises
       unto thee;
   And my soul, which thou hast redeemed.
24 My tongue also shall talk of thy righteousness
       all the day long:
   For they are ashamed,/confounded, for they are brought unto shame,/confounded,
       that seek my hurt.

72

A Psalm of/for Solomon.

1 Give the king thy judgements,/judgments, O God,
   And thy righteousness unto the king's son.
2 ²He shall judge thy people with righteousness,
   And thy poor with judgement./judgment.
3 The mountains shall bring peace to the people,
   And the little hills, in/by righteousness.
4 He shall judge the poor of the people,
   He shall save the children of the needy,

R.V. ¹ Another reading is, *me*.   ² Or, *Let him* and so throughout the Psalm.

123

And shall break in pieces the oppressor.

5 They shall fear thee _while_ _as long as_ the sun endureth,

And _¹so long as the moon endure,_ throughout all generations.

6 He shall come down like rain upon the mown grass:

As showers that water the earth.

7 In his days shall the righteous flourish;

And abundance of _peace, so_ _peace, till_ _long as_ the moon _be no more._ _endureth._

8 He shall have dominion also from sea to sea,

And from ²the _River_ _river_ unto the ends of the earth.

9 They that dwell in the wilderness shall bow before him;

And his enemies shall lick the dust.

10 The kings of Tarshish and of the isles shall ³bring presents:

The kings of Sheba and Seba shall offer gifts.

11 Yea, all kings shall fall down before him:

All nations shall serve him.

12 For he shall deliver the needy when he crieth;

And the poor, _the poor also, and him_ ⁴that hath no helper.

13 He shall _have pity on_ _spare_ the ⁵poor and needy,

And _shall save_ the souls of the needy _he shall save_

14 He shall redeem their soul from ⁶oppression _deceit_ and _violence:_ _violence:_

And precious shall their blood be in his _sight:_ _sight._

R.V.　¹ Heb. _before the moon._　² See Ex. 23. 31.　³ Or, _render_ _tribute_　⁴ Or, _and him that hath_　⁵ Or, _weak_　⁶ Or, _fraud_

124

¹⁵ And ^{1they}_{he} shall ^{live;}_{live,} and to him shall be given of
    the gold of Sheba:
    _{And men shall pray}
    _{prayer also shall be made} for him continually;
    ¹They shall bless him all the day long.
    _{and daily shall he be praised.}
¹⁶ There shall be ^{2abundance}_{an handful} of corn in the ³earth
    upon the top of the mountains;
    The fruit thereof shall shake like Lebanon:
    And they of the city shall flourish like grass of
    the earth.
¹⁷ His name shall endure for ^{ever;}_{ever:}
    His name shall ⁴be continued ⁵as long as the
    sun:
    And men shall ⁶be blessed in ^{him;}_{him:}
    All nations shall call him _{blessed.}^{happy;}

¹⁸ Blessed be the LORD God, the God of Israel,
    Who only doeth wondrous ^{things;}_{things.}
¹⁹ And blessed be his glorious name for ^{ever;}_{ever:}
    And let the whole earth be filled with his ^{glory.}_{glory;}
    Amen, and Amen.

²⁰ The prayers of David the son of Jesse are ended.

R.V. ¹ Or, *he*   ² Or, *an handful*   ³ Or, *land*   ⁴ Or,
have issue   ⁵ Heb. *before the sun.*   ⁶ Or, *bless themselves*

BOOK III

73

A Psalm of Asaph.

1 ¹Surely/Truly God is good to Israel,
Even to such as are ofpure ina clean heart.

2 But as for me, my feet were almost gone;
My steps had well nigh slipped.

3 For I was envious at the ²arrogant,foolish,
When I saw the prosperity of the wicked.

4 For there are no ³bands in their death:
But their strength is firm.

5 They are not ⁴in trouble as *other* men;
Neither are they plagued like *other* men.

6 Therefore pride is as a chaincompasseth them about their neck;as a chain;
Violence covereth them as a garment.

7 Their eyes stand out with fatness:
⁵They have more than heart could wish.

8 They scoff,are corrupt, and in wickedness utterspeak wickedly *concerning* oppression:
They speak ⁶loftily.

9 They have set their mouth ⁷inagainst the heavens,
And their tongue walketh through the earth.

10 Therefore ⁸his people return hither:
And waters of a full *cup* are ⁹wrung out byto them.

R.V.   ¹ Or, *Only good is God*   ² Or, *fools*   ³ Or, *pangs*
⁴ Heb. *in the trouble of men.*   ⁵ Or, *The imaginations of their
heart overflow*   ⁶ Or, *from on high*   ⁷ Or, *against*
⁸ Another reading is, *he will bring back his people.*   ⁹ Or,
drained

¹¹ And they say, How doth God know?
　　And is there knowledge in the ^{Most}_{most} High?
¹² Behold, these are the ^{wicked;}_{ungodly,}
　　^{And, being alway at ease,}_{who prosper in the world;} they increase in riches.
¹³ ^{Surely in vain have I}_{Verily I have} cleansed my ^{heart,}_{heart *in* vain,}
　　And washed my hands in ^{innocency;}_{innocency.}
¹⁴ For all the day long have I been plagued,
　　And ¹chastened every morning.
¹⁵ If I ^{had said,}_{say,} I will speak thus;
　　Behold, I ^{had dealt treacherously with}_{should offend *against*} the generation of
　　thy children.
¹⁶ When I thought ^{how I might}_{to} know this,
　　²It was too painful for me;
¹⁷ Until I went into the sanctuary of ^{God,}_{God;}
　　^{And considered}_{*then* understood I} their ^{latter} end.
¹⁸ Surely thou ^{settest}_{didst set} them in slippery places:
　　Thou ^{castest}_{castedst} them down ^{to}_{into} ³destruction.
¹⁹ How are they ^{become a desolation}_{*brought* into desolation,} as in a moment!
　　They are utterly consumed with terrors.
²⁰ As a dream when one awaketh;
　　So, O Lord, ⁴when thou awakest, thou shalt
　　despise their image.
²¹ ^{For}_{Thus} my heart ⁵was grieved,
　　And I was pricked in my ^{reins:}_{reins.}
²² So ^{brutish}_{foolish} ⁶was I, and ^{ignorant;}_{ignorant:}
　　I was *as* a beast ⁷before thee.

R.V. ¹ Heb. *my chastisement* was.　　　² Heb. *It was labour
in mine eyes.*　³ Heb. *ruins.*　　⁴ Or, *in the city*　　⁵ Heb.
was in a ferment.　⁶ Or, *am*　⁷ Heb. *with thee.*

²³ Nevertheless I am continually with thee:
  Thou hast holden *me* by my right hand.
²⁴ Thou shalt guide me with thy counsel,
  And afterward receive me ¹to glory.
²⁵ Whom have I in heaven *but thee*?
  And there is none upon earth that I desire
    ²beside thee.
²⁶ My flesh and my heart faileth:
  But God is the ³strength of my ᵇᵉᵃʳᵗ and my
    portion for ever.
²⁷ For, lo, they that are far from thee shall
    perish:
  Thou hast destroyed all them that go a whoring
    from thee.
²⁸ But it is good for me to draw near ᵘⁿᵗᵒ God:
  I have ᵐᵃᵈᵉ ᵗʰᵉ ᴸᵒʳᵈ ᴳᴼᴰ ᵐʸ ʳᵉᶠᵘᵍᵉ,
       ᵖᵘᵗ ᵐʸ ᵗʳᵘˢᵗ ⁱⁿ ᵗʰᵉ ᴸᵒʳᵈ ᴳᴼᴰ,
  That I may ᵗᵉˡˡ ᵒᶠ all thy works.

74   Maschil of Asaph.

¹ O God, why hast thou cast *us* off for ever?
  Why doth thine anger smoke against the sheep
    of thy pasture?
² Remember thy congregation, which thou hast
    purchased of ᵒˡᵈ;
  Which thou hast redeemed to be the tribe of thine inheritance;
    the rod of thine inheritance, *which* thou hast redeemed ;
  ᴬⁿᵈ mount Zion, wherein thou hast dwelt.
³ Lift up thy feet unto the perpetual ʳᵘⁱⁿˢ,
                                       ᵈᵉˢᵒˡᵃᵗⁱᵒⁿˢ;

R.V.   ¹ Or, *with*   ² Or, *with thee*   ³ Heb. *rock*.

¹All the evil *even* all that the enemy hath done wickedly in the sanctuary.

4 Thine adversaries have roared *enemies roar* in the midst of thine *thy* assembly. *congregations;*

They have set up their ensigns for signs.

5 They ²seemed as men that *A man* was famous according as he had lifted up Axes upon a thicket of *the thick* trees.

6 And now *But* they break down all *together* the carved work thereof *at once* They break down with hatchet *axes* and hammers.

7 They have set thy sanctuary on fire; *cast fire into thy sanctuary,* They have defiled *by casting down* *profaned* the dwelling place of thy name even to the ground.

8 They said in their heart, *hearts,* Let us make havoc of *destroy* them altogether. *together* They have burned up all the ³synagogues of God in the land.

9 We see not our signs: There is no more any prophet; *prophet:* Neither is there among us any that knoweth how long.

10 How long, O God, *O God, how long* shall the adversary reproach? Shall the enemy blaspheme thy name for ever?

11 Why drawest thou back *withdrawest thou* thy hand, even thy right hand? *Pluck it* out of thy bosom *and* consume *them.* *bosom.*

12 Yet *For* God is my King of old,

Working salvation in the midst of the earth.

¹³ Thou didst ¹divide the sea by thy strength:
Thou brakest the heads of the ²dragons in the waters.

¹⁴ Thou brakest the heads of leviathan in pieces,
Thou and gavest him to be meat to the people inhabiting the wilderness.

¹⁵ Thou didst cleave the fountain and the flood:
Thou driedst up ³mighty rivers.

¹⁶ The day is thine, the night also is thine:
Thou hast prepared the ⁴light and the sun.

¹⁷ Thou hast set all the borders of the earth:
Thou hast made summer and winter.

¹⁸ Remember this, that the enemy ⁵hath reproached, O Lord,
And that the a foolish people have blasphemed thy name.

¹⁹ O deliver not ⁶the soul of thy turtledove unto the multitude of the wicked wild beast:
Forget not the congregation ⁷life of thy poor for ever.

²⁰ Have respect unto the covenant:
For the dark places of the ⁸earth are full of the habitations of cruelty. violence.

²¹ O let not the oppressed return ashamed:
Let the poor and needy praise thy name.

²² Arise, O God, plead thine own cause:

R.V. ¹ Heb. *break up*.   ² Or, *sea-monsters*   ³ Or, *ever-flowing*   ⁴ Heb. *luminary*.   ⁵ Or, *hath reproached the Lord*   ⁶ Or, *thy turtledove unto the greedy multitude*   ⁷ Or, *multitude*   ⁸ Or, *land*

Remember how the foolish man reproacheth
   thee ^{all the day.}_{daily.}
23 Forget not the voice of thine ^{adversaries}_{enemies} :
The tumult of those that rise up against thee
   ^{1ascendeth}_{increaseth} continually.

75
For the Chief Musician; *set to* Al-tashheth. A Psalm
To the chief Musician, Al-taschith,
of Asaph, a Song.
or Song of Asaph.

1 We give thanks unto thee, O God;
Unto thee, O God, do we give thanks,
    We give thanks,
unto thee do we give thanks: ²for *that* thy name is ^{near:}_{near}
Men tell of thy wondrous ^{works declare.}_{works.}
2 When I shall ^{3find}_{receive} the ^{set time,}_{congregation}
  I will judge uprightly.
3 ⁴The earth and all the inhabitants thereof are
   dissolved :
I ^{have 5set}_{bear} up the pillars of it. Selah.   [Selah
4 I said unto the ^{6arrogant,}_{fools,} Deal not ^{arrogantly}_{foolishly} :
And to the wicked, Lift not up the horn :
5 Lift not up your horn on ^{high:}_{high:}
  ⁷Speak not with a stiff neck.
6 For _{promotion} *cometh* neither from the east, nor from
   the west,
Nor ^{yet} ⁸from the ^{9south,}_{south.} *cometh* lifting up.
7 But God is the judge :

R.V. ¹ Or, *which ascendeth*   ² Or, *for* that *thy name is near*
thy wondrous works declare   ³ Heb. *take.*   ⁴ Or, *When the*
earth...I set up   ⁵ Heb. *proportioned.*   ⁶ Or, *fools*   ⁷ Or,
Speak not insolently with a haughty *neck*   ⁸ Or, *from the*
wilderness of mountains, cometh judgement   ⁹ Heb. *wilderness.*

He putteth down one, and ^{lifteth}/_{sette'h} up another.
8 For in the hand of the LORD there is a cup,
    and the wine ^{1 foameth:}/_{is red} ;
    It is full of ^{mixture:}/_{mixture;} and he poureth out of the
    same :
    ^{Surely}/_{but} the dregs thereof, all the wicked of the
    earth shall ²wring them out, and drink them.
9 But I will declare for ^{ever,}/_{ever;}
    I will sing praises to the God of Jacob.
10 All the horns of the wicked also will I cut
    off ;
    But the horns of the righteous shall be ^{lifted up.}/_{exalted.}

76 For the Chief Musician; on stringed Instruments.
    To the chief Musician on Neginoth,
    A Psalm ^{of Asaph, a Song.}/_{or Song of Asaph.}

1 In Judah is God known :
    His name is great in Israel.
2 In Salem also is his ³tabernacle,
    And his ⁴dwelling place in Zion.
3 There ^{he brake}/_{brake he} the ⁵arrows of the ^{bow;}/_{bow,}
    The shield, and the sword, and the battle.
                                [Selah
4 ^{Selah.} Glorious art thou *and* excellent, ⁶from the mountains of
    Thou *art* more glorious *and* excellent than
    prey.
5 The stouthearted are spoiled, they have slept
    their ^{sleep;}/_{sleep;}

R.V. ¹ Or, *is red*   ² Or, *drain*   ³ Or, *covert*   ⁴ Or,
lair   ⁵ Or, *fiery shafts* Or, *lightnings*   ⁶ Or, *more than*

And none of the men of might have found
their hands.

⁶ At thy rebuke, O God of Jacob,
Both _{the} chariot and horse are cast into a dead
sleep.

⁷ Thou, even thou, art to be feared:
And who may stand in thy sight when once
thou art angry?

⁸ Thou didst cause _{judgment}^{sentence} to be heard from
heaven;
The earth feared, and was still,

⁹ When God arose to _{judgment,}^{judgement,}
To save all the meek of the earth.   Selah.   [Selah

¹⁰ Surely the wrath of man shall praise thee:
The _{remainder}^{residue} of wrath shalt thou ¹_{restrain.}^{gird upon thee.}

¹¹ Vow, and pay unto the LORD your God:
Let all that be round about him bring presents
unto him that ought to be feared.

¹² He shall cut off the spirit of princes:
He is terrible to the kings of the earth.

77 For the Chief Musician; after the manner of Jeduthun.
To the chief Musician, to Jeduthun,
A Psalm of Asaph.

¹ I _{cried}^{will cry} unto God with my _{voice,}^{voice;}
Even unto God with my _{voice;}^{voice,} and he _{gave}^{will give} ear
unto me.

² In the day of my trouble I sought the Lord:

R.V.   ¹ Or, *restrain*

My ^{hand was stretched out}_{sore ran} in the night, and ^{slacked not;}_{ceased not;}
My soul refused to be comforted.

3 I ^{remember}_{remembered} God, and ^{am disquieted}_{was troubled} :
I ^{complain,}_{complained,} and my spirit ^{¹is}_{was} overwhelmed.
[Selah

Selah.
4 Thou holdest mine eyes ^{watching}_{waking} :
I am so troubled that I cannot speak.

5 I have considered the days of old,
The years of ancient times.

6 I call to remembrance my song in the night :
I commune with mine own ^{heart:}_{heart:}
And my spirit made diligent search.

7 Will the Lord cast off for ever?
And will he be favourable no more?

8 Is his mercy clean gone for ever?
Doth his promise fail for evermore?

9 Hath God forgotten to be gracious?
Hath he in anger shut up his tender mercies?
[Selah

Selah.
10 And I said, This is my ^{infirmity;}_{infirmity:}
　²*But I will remember* the years of the right
　hand of the ^{Most}_{most} High.

11 I will ^{make mention of}_{remember} the ^{deeds}_{works} of ³the ^{LORD:}_{LORD:}
　^{For}_{surely} I will remember thy wonders of old.

12 I will meditate also ^{upon}_{of} all thy work,
And ^{muse on}_{talk of} thy doings.

13 Thy way, O God, is ⁴in the sanctuary :

R.V.　¹ Or, *fainteth*　　² Or, *That the right hand of the Most
High doth change*　　³ Heb. *Jah.*　　⁴ Or, *in holiness*

Who _{is so} ^{is a} great ^{god like unto}_{a God as our} God?

¹⁴ Thou art the God that doest wonders:
Thou hast ^{made known}_{declared} thy strength among the
_{peoples.}
_{people.}

¹⁵ Thou hast with thine arm redeemed thy people,
The sons of Jacob and Joseph.   Selah.   ^{(Selah}

¹⁶ The waters saw thee, O ^{God;}_{God,}
The waters saw ^{thee;}_{thee:} they ¹were afraid:
The depths also ^{trembled.}_{were troubled.}

¹⁷ The clouds poured out ^{water;}_{water:}
The skies sent out a sound:
Thine arrows also went abroad.

¹⁸ The voice of thy thunder was in the ^{whirlwind;}_{heaven:}
The lightnings lightened the world:
The earth trembled and shook.

¹⁹ Thy way ^{was}_{is} in the sea,
And thy ^{paths}_{path} in the great waters,
And thy footsteps ^{were}_{are} not known.

²⁰ Thou leddest thy people like a ^{flock,}_{flock.}
By the hand of Moses and Aaron.

78

Maschil of Asaph.

¹ Give ear, O my people, to my ²law:
Incline your ears to the words of my mouth.

² I will open my mouth in a ^{parable;}_{parable:}
I will utter dark sayings of old:

³ Which we have heard and known,

R.V.   ¹ Or, *were in pain*   ² Or, *teaching*

And our fathers have told us.
⁴ We will not hide them from their children,
　^{Telling}_{shewing} to the generation to come the praises of
　　the LORD
　And his strength, and his ^{wondrous}_{wonderful} works that he
　　hath done.
⁵ For he established a testimony in Jacob,
　And appointed a law in Israel,
　Which he commanded our fathers,
　That they should make them known to their
　　children :
⁶ That the generation to come might know *them*,
　even the children which should be born ;
　Who should arise and _{declare}^{tell} *them* to their
　　children :
⁷ That they might set their hope in God,
　And not forget the works of God,
　But keep his commandments :
⁸ And might not be as their fathers,
　A stubborn and rebellious generation ;
　A generation ¹that set not their heart aright,
　And whose spirit was not stedfast with God.
⁹ The children of Ephraim, being ^{armed}_{armed,} and carry-
　　ing bows,
　Turned back in the day of battle.
¹⁰ They kept not the covenant of God,
　And refused to walk in his law ;
¹¹ And ^{they} forgat his ^{doings,}_{works,}

R.V.　¹ Or, *that prepared not their heart*

And his ^{wondrous works}wonders that he had shewed them.

12 Marvellous things did he in the sight of their fathers,

In the land of Egypt, in the field of Zoan.

13 He clave divided the sea, and caused them to pass through;

And he made the waters to stand as an heap.

14 In the day-time daytime also he led them with a cloud,

And all the night with a light of fire.

15 He clave the rocks in the wilderness,

And gave them drink abundantly as out of the great depths.

16 He brought streams also out of the rock,

And caused waters to run down like rivers.

17 Yet went And they on still to sin sinned yet more against him, him

To rebel against by provoking the Most most High in ¹the desert. wilderness.

18 And they tempted God in their heart

By asking meat for their lust.

19 Yea, they spake against God;

They said, Can God prepare furnish a table in the wilderness?

20 Behold, he smote the rock, that the waters gushed out,

And the streams overflowed;

Can he give bread also?

Will can he provide flesh for his people?

21 Therefore the LORD heard, heard this, and was wroth:

And so a fire was kindled against Jacob,

And anger also ^went_came up against Israel;

22 Because they believed not in God,
And trusted not in his ^salvation._salvation:

23 ^Yet_Though he ^had commanded the ^skies_clouds from above,
And opened the doors of ^heaven;_heaven,

24 And ^he_had rained down manna upon them to eat,
And ^gave_had given them of the corn of heaven.

25 ¹Man did eat ^the bread of the mighty:_angels' food
He sent them meat to the full.

26 He ²caused ^the_an east wind to blow in the heaven:
And by his power he ^guided_brought in the south wind.

27 He rained flesh also upon them as ^the dust,
And ^winged fowl_feathered fowls like as the sand of the ^seas:_sea:

28 And he let it fall in the midst of their camp,
Round about their habitations.

29 So they did eat, and were well ^filled;_filled:
And ^for he gave them ^that they lusted after._their own desire;

30 They were not estranged from their ^lust._lust.
^Their_But while their meat was yet in their mouths,

31 ^When the anger_The wrath of God ^went up against_came upon them,
And slew ^of the fattest of them,
And smote down the ^young_chosen men of Israel.

32 For all this they sinned still,
And believed not ^in_for his wondrous works.

33 Therefore their days did he consume in vanity,
And their years in ^terror._trouble.

34 When he slew them, then they ^inquired after_sought him:

R.V. ¹ Or, *Every one*   ² Heb. *led forth the east wind.*

And they returned and _{inquired early after God.}^{sought God ¹early.}

35 And they remembered that God was their rock,
And the ^{Most High}_{high} God their redeemer.

36 _{Nevertheless}^{But} they ^{flattered}_{did flatter} him with their mouth,
And _{they} lied unto him with their ^{tongue.}_{tongues.}

37 For their heart was not ²right with him,
Neither were they _{stedfast}^{faithful} in his covenant.

38 But he, being full of compassion, forgave *their*
iniquity, and destroyed *them* not :
Yea, many a time turned he his anger away,
And did not stir up all his wrath.

39 ^{And}_{For} he remembered that they were but flesh ;
A wind that passeth away, and cometh not
again.

40 How oft did they ^{rebel against}_{provoke} him in the wilderness,
And grieve him in the desert !

41 ^{And}_{Yea,} they turned ^{again}_{back} and tempted God,
And ³^{provoked}_{limited} the Holy One of Israel.

42 They remembered not his hand,
Nor the day when he ^{redeemed}_{delivered} them from the
_{adversary.}
_{enemy.}

43 How he _{had wrought}^{set} his signs in Egypt,
And his wonders in the field of ^{Zoan:}_{Zoan:}

44 And _{had} turned their rivers into ^{blood,}_{blood;}
And their ^{streams,}_{floods,} that they could not drink.

45 He sent ^{among them swarms of flies,}_{divers sorts of flies among them,} which devoured
them ;

R.V.   ¹ Or, *earnestly*   ² Or, *stedfast*   ³ Or, *limited*

And frogs, which destroyed them.

⁴⁶ He gave also their increase unto the cater-
piller,

And their labour unto the locust.

⁴⁷ He ¹destroyed their vines with hail,

And their sycomore trees with ²frost.

⁴⁸ He gave ᵒᵛᵉʳᵤₚ their cattle also to the hail,

And their flocks to hot thunderbolts.

⁴⁹ He cast upon them the fierceness of his
anger,

Wrath, and indignation, and trouble,

³A band of by sending evil angels ᵒᶠ ᵉᵛⁱˡ. among them.

⁵⁰ He ⁴made a ᵖᵃᵗʰ ᶠᵒʳ ʷᵃʸ ᵗᵒ his anger;

He spared not their soul from death,

But gave ⁵their life over to the pestilence;

⁵¹ And smote all the firstborn in ᴱᵍʸᵖᵗ, ᴱᵍʸᵖᵗ;

The ⁶chief of their strength in the ᵗᵉⁿᵗˢ ᵗᵃᵇᵉʳⁿᵃᶜˡᵉˢ of
Ham:

⁵² But ʰᵉ ˡᵉᵈ ᶠᵒʳᵗʰ ᵐᵃᵈᵉ his own people ᵗᵒ ᵍᵒ ᶠᵒʳᵗʰ like sheep,

And guided them in the wilderness like a
flock.

⁵³ And he led them ₒₙ safely, so that they feared
not:

But the sea overwhelmed their enemies.

⁵⁴ And he brought them to ⁷the border of his
sanctuary,

R.V. ¹ Heb. *killed.*   ² Or, *great hailstones*   ³ Heb. *A
sending.*   ⁴ Heb. *levelled.*   ⁵ Or, *their beasts to the murrain*
⁶ Heb. *beginning.* See Deut 21. 17.   ⁷ Or, *his holy border*

^{even to} this ¹mountain, which his right hand had
purchased.

⁵⁵ He ^{drove}_{cast} out the ^{nations}_{heathen} also before them,
And ^{allotted}_{divided} them ^{for} an inheritance by line,
And made the tribes of Israel to dwell in their
tents.

⁵⁶ Yet they tempted and ^{rebelled against}_{provoked} the ^{Most High}_{most high}
God,
And kept not his ^{testimonies;}_{testimonies:}

⁵⁷ But turned back, and dealt ^{treacherously}_{unfaithfully} like their
fathers:
They were turned aside like a deceitful bow.

⁵⁸ For they provoked him to anger with their
high places,
And moved him to jealousy with their graven
images.

⁵⁹ When God heard *this*, he was wroth,
And greatly abhorred Israel:

⁶⁰ So that he forsook the tabernacle of Shiloh,
The tent which he placed among men;

⁶¹ And delivered his strength into captivity,
And his glory into the ^{adversary's}_{enemy's} hand.

⁶² He gave his people over also unto the sword;
And was wroth with his inheritance.

⁶³ ^{Fire devoured}_{The fire consumed} their young men;
And their maidens ^{had no marriage-song.}_{were not given to marriage.}

⁶⁴ Their priests fell by the sword;
And their widows made no lamentation.

R.V.   ¹ Or, *mountain land*

⁶⁵ Then the Lord awaked as one out of sleep,
  and ^{Like} like a mighty man that shouteth by reason
    of wine.
⁶⁶ And he smote his ^{adversaries backward}_{enemies in the hinder parts} :
  He put them to a perpetual reproach.
⁶⁷ Moreover he refused the ^{tent}_{tabernacle} of Joseph,
  And chose not the tribe of ^{Ephraim;}_{Ephraim:}
⁶⁸ But chose the tribe of Judah,
  The mount Zion which he loved.
⁶⁹ And he built his sanctuary like ^{the heights,}_{high *palaces,*}
  Like the earth which he hath established for
    ever.
⁷⁰ He chose David also his servant,
  And took him from the sheepfolds :
⁷¹ From following the ewes ^{that give suck}_{great with young} he brought
    _{him,}
    him
  To feed Jacob his people, and Israel his in-
    heritance.
⁷² So he fed them according to the integrity of
    his heart;
  And guided them by the skilfulness of his
    hands.

79
A Psalm of Asaph.

¹ O God, the ¹heathen are come into thine in-
    heritance ;
  Thy holy temple have they defiled ;

R.V.   ¹ Or, *nations*

They have laid Jerusalem on heaps.
² The dead bodies of thy servants have they
given to be meat unto the fowls of the
heaven,
The flesh of thy saints unto the beasts of the
earth.
³ Their blood have they shed like water round
about Jerusalem;
And there was none to bury them.
⁴ We are become a reproach to our neighbours,
A scorn and derision to them that are round
about us.
⁵ How long, O LORD, wilt thou be angry for ever?
Shall thy jealousy burn like fire?
⁶ Pour out thy wrath upon the heathen that
know thee not,
have not known thee,
And upon the kingdoms that have not called upon
and   call not
thy name.
⁷ For they have devoured Jacob,
And laid waste his dwelling place.
¹ habitation.
⁸ Remember not against us the iniquities of our forefathers:
O remember   former
Let thy tender mercies speedily prevent us:
For we are brought very low.
⁹ Help us, O God of our salvation, for the glory
of thy name:
And deliver us, and purge away our sins, for
thy name's sake.

R.V. ¹ Or, *pasture*
143

¹⁰ Wherefore should the heathen say, Where is
their God?
Let the revenging of the blood of thy servants which is shed
  him be known among the heathen in our sight
  Be known among the heathen in our sight,
  by the revenging of the blood of thy servants *which is* shed.

¹¹ Let the sighing of the prisoner come before
thee;
According to the greatness of ¹thy power preserve thou ²those that are appointed to $^{death}_{die}$;

¹² And render unto our neighbours sevenfold into
their bosom
Their reproach, wherewith they have reproached thee, O Lord.

¹³ So we thy people and sheep of thy pasture
Will give thee thanks for ever:
We will shew forth thy praise to all genera-
tions.

80 For the Chief Musician; set to ³Shoshannim Eduth
To the chief Musician upon Shoshannim-Eduth,
A Psalm of Asaph.

¹ Give ear, O Shepherd of Israel,
Thou that leadest Joseph like a flock;
Thou that $^{4sittest\ upon}_{dwellest\ between}$ the $^{cherubim,}_{cherubims,}$ shine forth.

² Before Ephraim and Benjamin and $^{Manasseh,}_{Manasseh}$ stir
up thy $^{might,}_{strength,}$
And come $^{to}_{and}$ save us.

³ ⁵'Turn us again, O $^{God;}_{God,}$

R.V. ¹ Heb. *thine arm.*   ² Heb. *the children of death.*
³ That is, *Lilies, a testimony.*   ⁴ Or, *dwellest between*   ⁵ Or,
Restore

144

And cause thy face to ^{shine,}_{shine}; and we shall be saved.

4 O Lord God of hosts,
How long ¹wilt thou be angry against the prayer of thy people?
5 Thou ^{hast fed}_{feedest} them with the bread of ^{tears,}_{tears};
And ^{given}_{givest} them tears to drink in ^{large}_{great} measure.
6 Thou makest us a strife unto our neighbours:
And our enemies laugh among themselves.
7 Turn us again, O God of ^{hosts}_{hosts};
And cause thy face to ^{shine,}_{shine}; and we shall be saved.

8 Thou ^{broughtest}_{hast brought} a vine out of Egypt:
Thou ^{didst drive}_{hast cast} out the ^{nations,}_{heathen}, and ^{plantedst}_{planted} it.
9 Thou preparedst *room* before it,
And _{didst cause it to take}^{it took} deep root, and _{it} filled the land.
10 The ^{mountains}_{hills} were covered with the shadow of it,
And ²the boughs thereof were *like* ^{³cedars of God.}_{the goodly cedars}
11 She sent out her ^{branches}_{boughs} unto the sea,
And her _{branches}^{shoots} unto the ^{River.}_{river}.
12 Why hast thou _{then} broken down her ^{fences,}_{hedges},
So that all they which pass by the way do pluck her?
13 The boar out of the wood doth ^{ravage}_{waste} it,
And the wild ^{beasts}_{beast} of the field _{doth devour}^{feed on} it.

R.V. ¹ Heb. *wilt thou smoke*. See Ps. 74. 1.   ² Or, *the cedars of God with the boughs thereof*   ³ Or, *goodly cedars*

¹⁴ ^{Turn again,}_{Return,} we beseech thee, O God of hosts:
　Look down from heaven, and behold, and visit
　　this ^{vine,}_{vine;}
¹⁵ And ¹the ^{stock}_{vineyard} which thy right hand hath
　　planted,
　And the ²branch that thou madest strong for
　　thyself.
¹⁶ It is burned with fire, it is cut down:
　They perish at the rebuke of thy countenance.
¹⁷ Let thy hand be upon the man of thy right
　　hand,
　Upon the son of man whom thou madest
　　strong for thyself.
¹⁸ So ^{shall we not}_{will not we} go back from thee:
　Quicken ^{thou} us, and we will call upon thy
　　name.
¹⁹ Turn us again, O Lord God of ^{hosts;}_{hosts,}
　Cause thy face to ^{shine,}_{shine;} and we shall be saved.

81

For the Chief Musician; set to the Gittith.
To the chief Musician upon Gittith,
A Psalm of Asaph.

¹ Sing aloud unto God our strength:
　Make a joyful noise unto the God of Jacob.
² Take ^{up the}_a psalm, and ³bring hither the timbrel,
　The pleasant harp with the psaltery.
³ Blow up the trumpet in the new moon,
　^{At the}_{in the} ^{full moon,}_{time appointed,} on our solemn feast day.

R.V.　¹ Or, *protect* (or *maintain*) *that which &c.*　² Heb.
son.　　³ Or, *strike the timbrel*

146

4 For _{this} _{*was*} ^{it is} a statute for Israel,
   ^{An ordinance} _{*and a law*} of the God of Jacob.
5 ^{He appointed it} _{This he ordained} in Joseph for a testimony,
   When he went out ^{1 over} _{through} the land of Egypt:
   Where I heard ²a language that I ^{knew} _{understood}
   not.
6 I removed his shoulder from the burden:
   His hands were _{delivered} ^{freed} from the ^{basket.} _{pots.}
7 Thou calledst in trouble, and I delivered thee;
   I answered thee in the secret place of ^{thunder:} _{thunder:}
   I proved thee at the waters of Meribah. _{Selah.} ^{[Selah}
8 Hear, O my people, and I will testify unto
   thee:
   O Israel, if thou ^{wouldest} _{wilt} hearken unto ^{me!} _{me;}
9 There shall no strange god be in thee;
   Neither shalt thou worship any strange god.
10 I am the LORD thy God,
   Which brought thee ^{up} out of the land of
      Egypt:
   Open thy mouth wide, and I will fill it.
11 But my people ^{hearkened not} _{would not hearken} to my voice;
   And Israel would none of me.
12 So I ^{let} _{gave} them ^{go after the stubbornness of their heart,} _{up unto their own hearts' lust:}
   ^{That} _{*and*} they ^{might walk} _{walked} in their own counsels.
13 Oh that my people ^{would hearken} _{had hearkened} unto me,
   ^{That} _{*and*} Israel ^{would walk} _{had walked} in my ways!
14 I should soon _{have} ^{subdue} _{subdued} their enemies,
   And _{turned} ^{turn} my hand against their adversaries.

R.V. ¹ Or, *against*   ² Or, *the speech of one that &c.*

¹⁵ The haters of the Lord should _{have submitted}^{¹submit} them-
    selves unto him :
    But their time should _{have endured}^{endure} for ever.
¹⁶ He should _{have fed}^{feed} them also with the ²finest of
    the wheat :
    And with honey out of the rock should I
    _{have satisfied}^{satisfy} thee.

82
A Psalm of Asaph.

¹ God standeth in the congregation of _{the mighty}^{God};
    He judgeth among the gods.
² How long will ye judge unjustly,
    And _{accept}^{respect} the persons of the wicked ?   _{Selah.}^{[Selah}
³ _{Defend}^{Judge} the ³poor and fatherless :
    Do justice to the afflicted and _{needy.}^{destitute.}
⁴ _{Deliver}^{Rescue} the ³poor and needy :
    _{rid}^{Deliver} them out of the hand of the wicked.
⁵ They know not, neither _{will}^{do} they understand ;
    They walk _{on}^{to and fro} in darkness :
    All the foundations of the earth are _{out of course}^{moved.}
⁶ I _{have} said, Ye are _{gods;}^{gods,}
    And all of you _{are} _{children}^{sons} of the _{most}^{Most} High.
⁷ _{But}^{Nevertheless} ye shall die like men,
    And fall like one of the princes.
⁸ Arise, O God, judge the earth :
    For thou shalt inherit all ^{the} nations.

R.V. ¹ Or, *yield feigned obedience* Heb. *lie.*   ² Heb. *fat of*
wheat.   ³ Or, *weak*

83

A Song, ^a Psalm of Asaph.
A Song *or*

¹ O God, keep not thou silence, O God :
   Keep   silence, O God

Hold not thy peace, and be not still, O God.

² For, lo, thine enemies make a tumult :
   And they that hate thee have lifted up the
   head.

³ They have taken crafty counsel against thy people,
         take
   And consult together against thy hidden ones.
       consulted

⁴ They have said, Come, and let us cut them off
   from being a nation ;
   That the name of Israel may be no more in
   remembrance.

⁵ For they have consulted together with one
   consent ;
   consent :
   Against thee do they make a covenant .
      they are confederate against thee   :

⁶ The tents of Edom, and the Ishmaelites ;
      tabernacles of Edom,
   of Moab, and the ¹Hagarenes ;

⁷ Gebal, and Ammon, and Amalek ;
   Philistia with the inhabitants of Tyre :
   the Philistines   Tyre ;

⁸ Assyria also is joined with them ;
   Assur   them :
   ²They have holpen the children of Lot.   [Selah
                                              Selah.

⁹ Do thou unto them as unto the Midian ;
                                  the Midianites ;
   As to Sisera, as to Jabin, at the river Kishon :
                                    brook of Kison :

¹⁰ Which perished at En-dor ;
                       En-dor :
   They became as dung for the earth.

¹¹ Make their nobles like Oreb, and like Zeeb ;
                            Oreb,   like Zeeb :

R.V. ¹ Or, *Hagrites* See 1 Chr. 5. 10.   ² Heb. *They have
been an arm to the children of Lot.*

Yea, all their princes ^{like Zebah}_{as Zebah,} and _{as} Zalmunna:

12 Who said, Let us take to ourselves ^{in possession}
The ^{1habitations of God.}_{houses of God in possession.}

13 O my God, make them like ^{the whirling dust}_{a wheel} ;
As _{the} stubble before the wind.

14 As the fire ^{that} burneth ^{the forest,}_{a wood,}
And as the flame ^{that} setteth the mountains on
fire ;

15 So ^{pursue}_{persecute} them with thy tempest,
And ^{terrify them}_{make them afraid} with thy storm.

16 Fill their faces with ^{confusion}_{shame} ;
That they may seek thy name, O LORD.

17 Let them be ^{ashamed}_{confounded} and ^{dismayed}_{troubled} for ever ;
Yea, let them be ^{confounded}_{put to shame,} and perish :

18 That ^{they}_{men} may know that ^{2thou alone,}_{thou,} whose name
_{alone} is JEHOVAH,
Art the ^{Most High}_{most high} over all the earth.

84 For the Chief Musician; set to the Gittith.
To the chief Musician upon Gittith,   A Psalm ^{of}_{for}
the sons of Korah.

1 How ³amiable are thy tabernacles,
O LORD of hosts !

2 My soul longeth, yea, even fainteth for the
courts of the ^{LORD;}_{LORD:}
^{My}_{my} heart and my flesh ^{4cry}_{crieth} out ^{unto}_{for} the living
God.

3 Yea, the sparrow hath found ^{her} an house,

R.V. ¹ Or, *pastures*   ² Or, *thou, whose name alone is*
JEHOVAH, art &c.   ³ Or, *lovely*   ⁴ Or, *sing for joy*

And the swallow a nest for herself, where she
  may lay her young,
Even thine altars, O LORD of hosts,
My King, and my God.

4 Blessed are they that dwell in thy house:
  They will be still praising thee.   Selah.   [Selah

5 Blessed is the man whose strength is in thee;
  In whose heart are the high ways to Zion.
  of them.

6 Passing
  Who passing through the valley of 1Weeping they make
  it a place of springs ;   Baca
  well
  Yea, the early rain covereth it with blessings.
  also filleth the pools.

7 They go from strength to strength,
  Every one of them in Zion appeareth before
  God in Zion.

8 O LORD God of hosts, hear my prayer:
  Give ear, O God of Jacob.   Selah.   [Selah

9 2Behold, O God our shield,
  And look upon the face of thine anointed.

10 For a day in thy courts is better than a
  thousand.
  I had rather 3be a doorkeeper in the house of
  my God,
  Than to dwell in the tents of wickedness.

11 For the LORD God is a sun and a shield :
  shield
  The LORD will give grace and glory:
  No good thing will he withhold from them that
  walk uprightly.

R.V   1 Or, *balsam trees* Heb. *Baca.* See 2 Sam. 5. 23.   2 Or,
Behold our shield, O God   3 Or, *stand at the threshold of &c.*

¹² O Lord of hosts,
  Blessed is the man that trusteth in thee.

85 For the Chief Musician. A Psalm of the sons of Korah.
       To the chief Musician,   for

¹ Lord, thou hast been favourable unto thy
    land :
  Thou hast ¹brought back the captivity of Jacob.
² Thou hast forgiven the iniquity of thy people,
  Thou hast covered all their sin.   Selah.   [Selah
³ Thou hast taken away all thy wrath :
  Thou hast turned *thyself* from the fierceness of
    thine anger.
⁴ ²Turn us, O God of our salvation,
  And cause thine indignation toward us to cease.
                           anger
⁵ Wilt thou be angry with us for ever?
  Wilt thou draw out thine anger to all genera-
    tions?
⁶ Wilt thou not quicken us again :
             revive
  That thy people may rejoice in thee?
⁷ Shew us thy mercy, O Lord,
  And grant us thy salvation.
⁸ I will hear what God the Lord will speak :
  For he will speak peace unto his people, and
    to his saints :
  But let them not turn again to folly.
⁹ Surely his salvation is nigh them that fear
    him ;

R.V.   ¹ Or, *returned to*   ² Or, *Turn to us*

That glory may dwell in our land.

¹⁰ Mercy and truth are met together;
Righteousness and peace have kissed each
other.

¹¹ Truth ^{springeth}_{shall spring} out of the earth;
And righteousness ^{hath looked}_{shall look} down from heaven.

¹² Yea, the LORD shall give that which is good;
And our land shall yield her increase.

¹³ Righteousness shall go before him;
And shall ¹make his footsteps a way to walk in.

86

A Prayer of David.

¹ Bow down thine ear, O LORD, and answer me; hear me:
For I am poor and needy.

² Preserve my soul; for I am godly:
O thou my God, save thy servant that trusteth
in thee.

³ Be merciful unto me, O Lord;
For unto thee do I cry all the day long.

⁴ Rejoice the soul of thy servant;
For unto thee, O Lord, do I lift up my soul.

⁵ For thou, Lord, art good, and ready to forgive;
And plenteous in mercy unto all them that call
upon thee.

⁶ Give ear, O LORD, unto my prayer;
And hearken unto the voice of my supplications.

⁷ In the day of my trouble I will call upon thee:

R.V.   ¹ Or, *set* us *in the way of his steps*

For thou wilt answer me.

8 There is none like unto thee among the gods, O Lord;
  Among the gods *there is* none like unto thee,
  Neither *are there any works* like unto thy works.

9 All nations whom thou hast made shall come and worship before thee, O Lord;
  And ^they shall glorify thy name.

10 For thou art great, and doest wondrous things:
  Thou art God alone.

11 Teach me thy way, O Lord; I will walk in thy truth:
  Unite my heart to fear thy name.

12 I will praise thee, O Lord my God, with my whole heart;
                                          all my heart:
  And I will glorify thy name for evermore.

13 For great is thy mercy toward me:
                                   me:
  And thou hast delivered my soul from ¹the lowest pit.
                                                  hell.

14 O God, the proud are risen ^up against me,
  And the congregation of violent men have sought
         assemblies
  after my soul,
           soul;
  And have not set thee before them.

15 But thou, O Lord, art a God full of compassion
                                         compassion,
  and gracious,
  Slow to anger, and plenteous in mercy and truth.
  longsuffering,

16 O turn unto me, and ²have mercy upon me;
  Give thy strength unto thy servant,

R.V. ¹ Or, *Sheol beneath*   ² Or, *be gracious unto*

And save the son of thine handmaid.

17 Shew me a token for good ;
That they which hate me may see it, and be ashamed,
Because thou, LORD, hast holpen me, and comforted me.

87 A Psalm _or_ Song for the sons of Korah ; a Song. Korah.

1 1 His foundation is in the holy mountains.
2 The LORD loveth the gates of Zion
More than all the dwellings of Jacob.
3 Glorious things are spoken of thee,
O city of God.   Selah.   [Selah
4 I will make mention of 2 Rahab and Babylon
as among them that know me :
to
Behold Philistia, and Tyre, with 3 Ethiopia ;
This one man was born there.
5 Yea, And of Zion it shall be said, This one and that
one man was born in her :
her :
And the Most High himself shall establish her.
highest
6 The LORD shall count, when he writeth up the
peoples,
people,
This one that this man was born there.   Selah.   [Selah
7 They that sing as well 4 they that dance
As well the singers as the players on instruments shall say, be there:
All my fountains springs are in thee.

R.V.   1 Or, _His foundation in the holy mountains the_ LORD
loveth, even the gates &c.   2 Or, _Egypt_   3 Heb. _Cush._
4 Or, _the players on instruments_ shall be there

88 A Song, a Psalm of the sons of Korah; for the Chief Musician;
A Song *or* for Korah, to the chief Musician
set to Mahalath ¹Leannoth. Maschil of Heman the Ezrahite.
upon Leannoth,

¹ O LORD, the God of my salvation,
   I have cried day and night before thee:
² Let my prayer enter into thy presence;
                   come before thee:
   Incline thine ear unto my cry:
                             cry;
³ For my soul is full of troubles,
                         troubles:
   And my life draweth nigh unto ²Sheol.
                               the grave.
⁴ I am counted with them that go down into
      the pit:
          pit:
   I am as a man that hath no help :
                                strength
⁵ ³Cast off among the dead,
   Free
   Like the slain that lie in the grave,
   Whom thou rememberest no more;
                             more:
   And they are cut off from thy hand.
⁶ Thou hast laid me in the lowest pit,
   In dark places, in the deeps.
      darkness,
⁷ Thy wrath lieth hard upon me,
   And thou hast afflicted me with all thy waves.
                                          [Selah
   Selah.
⁸ Thou hast put away mine acquaintance far from
      me ;
   Thou hast made me an abomination unto
      them :
   I am shut up, and I cannot come forth.
⁹ Mine eye wasteth away by reason of affliction :
            mourneth

R.V. ¹ Or, *for singing*   ² Or, *the grave*   ³ Or, *cast away*

LORD, I have called daily upon thee, O LORD.
I have spread forth / stretched out my hands unto thee.
¹⁰ Wilt thou shew wonders to the dead?
Shall ¹they that are deceased / the dead arise and praise thee?
[Selah
Selah.
¹¹ Shall thy lovingkindness be declared in the
grave?
Or thy faithfulness in ²Destruction / destruction?
¹² Shall thy wonders be known in the dark?
And thy righteousness in the land of forget-
fulness?
¹³ But unto thee, O LORD, have I cried, / thee have I cried, O LORD;
And in the morning shall my prayer come before / prevent
thee.
¹⁴ LORD, why castest thou off my soul?
Why hidest thou thy face from me?
¹⁵ I am afflicted and ready to die from my youth
up:
While I suffer thy terrors I am distracted.
¹⁶ Thy fierce wrath is gone / goeth over me;
Thy terrors have cut me off.
¹⁷ They came round about me daily / all the day long like water;
They compassed me about together.
¹⁸ Lover and friend hast thou put far from
me,
And mine acquaintance ³into darkness.

R.V. ¹ Or, *the shades* Heb. *Rephaim.*   ² Heb. *Abaddon.*
See Job 26. 6.   ³ Or, *are darkness*

157

89

Maschil of Ethan the Ezrahite.

¹ I will sing of the mercies of the Lord for
　　ever :
　With my mouth will I make known thy faith-
　　fulness to all generations.
² For I have said, Mercy shall be built up for
　　ever; _{ever:}
　Thy faithfulness shalt thou establish in the
　　very heavens.

³ I have made a covenant with my chosen,
　I have sworn unto David my servant; _{servant,}
⁴ Thy seed will I establish for ever,
　And build up thy throne to all generations.
　Selah. 　　　　　　　　　　　　　　　　[Selah
⁵ And the heavens shall praise thy wonders,
　O Lord; _{Lord:}
　Thy faithfulness also in the assembly _{congregation} of the
　　holy ones. _{saints.}
⁶ For who in the skies _{heaven} can be compared unto the
　　Lord?
　Who among the ¹ sons of the ² mighty can be likened _{is like}
　　unto the Lord, _{Lord?}
⁷ 　A God very terrible _{God is greatly to be feared} in the council _{assembly} of the holy ones, _{saints,}
　And to be feared above _{had in reverence of} all them that are round
　　about him? _{him.}
⁸ O Lord God of hosts,

R.V. 　¹ Or, *sons of God* 　　² Or, *gods* 　See Ps. **29. 1.**

158

Who is a *mighty one,* like unto *thee, O* JAH ?
strong LORD *thee*

And thy faithfulness *is* round about *thee.*
or to *thee?*

9 Thou rulest the *pride* of the sea :
raging

When the waves thereof arise, thou stillest
them.

10 Thou hast broken [1]Rahab in pieces, as one
that is slain ;

Thou hast scattered thine enemies with *the arm*
thy
of thy strength.
strong arm.

11 The heavens are thine, the earth also is thine :

The
as for the world and the fulness thereof, thou hast
founded them.

12 The north and the *south,* thou hast created them :
south

Tabor and Hermon *shall* rejoice in thy name.

13 Thou hast [2]a mighty arm :

Strong is thy hand, and high is thy right hand.

14 *Righteousness* and *judgement* are the *foundation* of thy
Justice *judgment* *habitation*
throne :

Mercy and truth *shall* go before thy face.

15 Blessed is the people that know the [3]joyful
sound :

They *shall* walk, O LORD, in the light of thy
countenance.

16 In thy name *do* they rejoice all the day :
shall

And in thy righteousness *are* they *be* exalted.
shall

17 For thou art the glory of their strength :

And in thy favour [4]our horn shall be exalted.

R.V. [1] Or, *Egypt*   [2] Heb. *an arm with might.*   [3] Or,
trumpet sound   [4] Another reading is, *thou shalt exalt our horn.*

¹⁸ For ^{our shield} belongeth unto the LORD ;
    _{the LORD} *is* our defence   ;
¹And ^{our king} ^{to} the Holy One of _{Israel} _{*is* our king.}^{Israel.}

¹⁹ Then thou spakest in vision to thy ^{2 saints,}_{holy one,}
    And saidst, I have laid help upon one that is
        mighty ;
    I have exalted one chosen out of the people.
²⁰ I have found David my servant ;
    With my holy oil have I anointed him :
²¹ With whom my hand shall be ^{established ;}_{established :}
    Mine arm also shall strengthen him.
²² The enemy shall not ³exact upon him ;
    Nor the son of wickedness afflict him.
²³ And I will beat down his ^{adversaries}_{foes} before _{his face,}^{him,}
    And ^{smite}_{plague} them that hate him.
²⁴ But my faithfulness and my mercy shall be
        with ^{him ;}_{him :}
    And in my name shall his horn be exalted.
²⁵ I will set his hand also ^{on}_{in} the sea,
    And his right hand ^{on}_{in} the rivers.
²⁶ He shall cry unto me, Thou art my father,
    My God, and the rock of my salvation.
²⁷ ^{I also}_{Also I} will make him *my* firstborn,
    ^{The highest of}_{higher than} the kings of the earth.
²⁸ My mercy will I keep for him for evermore,
    And my covenant shall ⁴stand fast with him.
²⁹ His seed also will I make to endure for ever,

R.V. ¹ Or, *Even to the Holy One of Israel our King*   ² Many
MSS. and ancient versions read the plural. Other authorities have
the singular.   ³ Or, *do him violence*   ⁴ Or, *be faithful*

And his throne as the days of heaven.
30 If his children forsake my law,
   And walk not in my judgements ;
31 If they [1]break my statutes,
   And keep not my commandments ;
32 Then will I visit their transgression with the
   rod,
   And their iniquity with stripes.
33 But Nevertheless my mercy lovingkindness will I not utterly take
   from him,
   Nor suffer my faithfulness to fail.
34 My covenant will I not [1]break,
   Nor alter the thing that is gone out of my
   lips.
35 [2]Once have I sworn by my holiness:
   that I will not lie unto David.
36 His seed shall endure for ever,
   And his throne as the sun before me.
37 [3]It shall be established for ever as the moon,
   [4]And as the faithful witness in the sky.   Selah.   [Selah

38 But thou hast cast off and rejected, abhorred,
   Thou hast been wroth with thine anointed.
39 Thou hast abhorred made void the covenant of thy servant :
   Thou hast profaned his crown by even casting it to the
   ground.

R.V.   [1] Heb. *profane.*   [2] Or, *One thing*   [3] Or, *As the
moon which is established for ever, and* as *the faithful witness &c.*
or, *and is a faithful witness &c.*   [4] Or, *And the witness in
the sky is faithful*

⁴⁰ Thou hast broken down all his hedges;
Thou hast brought his strong holds to ruin.
⁴¹ All that pass by the way spoil him:
He is ᵇᵉᶜᵒᵐᵉ a reproach to his neighbours.
⁴² Thou hast ᵉˣᵃˡᵗᵉᵈ_{set up} the right hand of his adversaries;
Thou hast made all his enemies to rejoice.
⁴³ ᵞᵉᵃ, ᵗʰᵒᵘ ᵗᵘʳⁿᵉˢᵗ ᵇᵃᶜᵏ_{Thou hast also turned} the edge of his sword,
And hast not made him to stand in the
battle.
⁴⁴ Thou hast made his ᵇʳⁱᵍʰᵗⁿᵉˢˢ_{glory} to cease,
And cast his throne down to the ground.
⁴⁵ The days of his youth hast thou shortened:
Thou hast covered him with shame. Selah. [Selah
⁴⁶ How long, ᴼ ᴸᴼᴿᴰ,_{O LORD?} wilt thou hide thyself for
ever?
How long shall thy wrath burn like fire?
⁴⁷ ᴼ ʳᵉᵐᵉᵐᵇᵉʳ_{Remember} how short my time is:
ᶠᵒʳ ʷʰᵃᵗ ᵛᵃⁿⁱᵗʸ_{wherefore} hast thou ᶜʳᵉᵃᵗᵉᵈ_{made} all ᵗʰᵉ ᶜʰⁱˡᵈʳᵉⁿ ᵒᶠ ᵐᵉⁿ!_{men in vain?}
⁴⁸ What man is he that ˢʰᵃˡˡ ˡⁱᵛᵉ ᵃⁿᵈ_{liveth, and shall} not see ᵈᵉᵃᵗʰ,_{death?}
ᵀʰᵃᵗ ˢʰᵃˡˡ_{shall he} deliver his soul from the ¹ᵖᵒʷᵉʳ ᵒᶠ ²ˢʰᵉᵒˡ_{hand of the grave}?
[Selah
Selah.
⁴⁹ Lord, where are thy former ᵐᵉʳᶜⁱᵉˢ,_{lovingkindnesses,}
Which thou swarest unto David in thy ᶠᵃⁱᵗʰᶠᵘˡⁿᵉˢˢ_{truth}?
⁵⁰ Remember, Lord, the reproach of thy servants;
How I do bear in my bosom *the reproach of*
all the ³mighty ᵖᵉᵒᵖˡᵉˢ_{people};

R.V.   ¹ Heb. *hand.*   ² Or, *the grave*   ³ Or, *many*

51 Wherewith thine enemies have reproached,
        O Lord,
          Lord;
    Wherewith they have reproached the footsteps
      of thine anointed.

52 Blessed be the Lord for evermore.
    Amen, and Amen.

BOOK IV

90   A Prayer of Moses the man of God.

1 Lord, thou hast been our dwelling place
    In all generations.
2 Before the mountains were brought forth,
    Or ever thou ¹hadst formed the earth and the
      world,
    Even from everlasting to everlasting, thou art
      God.
3 Thou turnest man to ²destruction;
    And sayest, Return, ye children of men.
4 For a thousand years in thy sight
    Are but as yesterday ³when it is past,
    And as a watch in the night.

R.V. ¹ Heb. *gavest birth to.*   ² Or, *dust* Heb. *crushing.*
³ Or, *when it passeth*

⁵ Thou carriest them away as with a flood ; they
    are as a sleep :
  In the morning they are like grass which
    groweth up.
⁶ In the morning it flourisheth, and groweth up ;
  In the evening it is cut down, and withereth.
⁷ For we are consumed $_{by}^{in}$ thine anger,
  And $_{by}^{in}$ thy wrath are we troubled.
⁸ Thou hast set our iniquities before thee,
  Our secret sins in the light of thy countenance.
⁹ For all our days are passed away in thy wrath :
  We $_{spend}^{bring}$ our years ᵗᵒ ᵃⁿ ᵉⁿᵈ as ¹a tale *that is told*.
¹⁰ The days of our years are threescore years
    and $_{ten;}^{ten,}$
  $_{and\ if}^{Or\ even}$ by reason of strength *they be* fourscore $_{years,}^{years;}$
  Yet is their $_{strength}^{pride\ but}$ labour and sorrow ;
  For it is soon $_{cut\ off,}^{gone,}$ and we fly away.
¹¹ Who knoweth the power of thine $_{anger?}^{anger,}$
  $_{even}^{And\ thy\ wrath}$ according to $_{thy\ fear,\ so\ is\ thy\ wrath.}^{the\ fear\ that\ is\ due\ unto\ thee?}$
¹² So teach us to number our days,
  That we may $_{apply\ our\ hearts\ unto}^{get\ us\ an\ heart\ of}$ wisdom.
¹³ Return, O $_{LORD,}^{LORD;}$ how long ?
  And let it repent thee concerning thy servants.
¹⁴ O satisfy us $_{early}^{in\ the\ morning}$ with thy mercy ;
  That we may rejoice and be glad all our days.
¹⁵ Make us glad according to the days wherein
    thou hast afflicted us,
  And the years wherein we have seen evil.

R.V.   ¹ Or, *a sound* or *sigh*

¹⁶ Let thy work appear unto thy servants,
And thy glory _{unto}^{upon} their children.
¹⁷ And let the ¹beauty of the LORD our God be
upon us :
And establish thou the work of our hands upon
us ;
Yea, the work of our hands establish thou it.

91 ¹ He that dwelleth in the secret place of
the _{most}^{Most} High
²Shall abide under the shadow of the
Almighty.
² I will say of the LORD, He is my refuge and
my _{fortress:}^{fortress:}
My _{God;}^{God,} in _{him will}^{whom} I trust.
³ _{Surely}^{For} he shall deliver thee from the snare of the
fowler,
And from the noisome pestilence.
⁴ He shall cover thee with his _{feathers,}^{pinions,}
And under his wings shalt thou _{trust}^{take refuge} :
His truth _{shall be thy}^{is a} shield and _{buckler.}^{a buckler.}
⁵ Thou shalt not be afraid for the terror by _{night;}^{night,}
Nor for the arrow that flieth by day ;
⁶ _{Nor for}^{For} the pestilence that walketh in _{darkness;}^{darkness,}
Nor for the destruction that wasteth at noonday.
⁷ A thousand shall fall at thy side,
And ten thousand at thy right hand ;
But it shall not come nigh thee.

R.V.   ¹ See Ps. 27. 4.   ² Or, *That abideth...Almighty ; even I &c.*

⁸ Only with thine eyes shalt thou _{behold,}^{behold,}
And see the reward of the wicked.

⁹ ¹For thou, O
Because thou hast made the LORD, *which is* ^{art} my ^{refuge!}_{refuge.}
Thou hast made _{*even*} the ^{Most High}_{most High,} thy habitation ;

¹⁰ There shall no evil befall thee,
Neither shall any plague come nigh thy ^{tent.}_{dwelling.}

¹¹ For he shall give his angels charge over thee,
To keep thee in all thy ways.

¹² They shall bear thee up in their hands,
Lest thou dash thy foot against a stone.

¹³ Thou shalt tread upon the lion and adder :
The young lion and the ^{serpent}_{dragon} shalt thou
trample under feet.

¹⁴ Because he hath set his love upon me, there-
fore will I deliver him :
I will set him on high, because he hath known
my name.

¹⁵ He shall call upon me, and I will answer ^{him;}_{him:}
I will be with him in ^{trouble:}_{trouble;}
I will deliver him, and honour him.

¹⁶ With long life will I satisfy him,
And shew him my salvation.

92

A Psalm, a
A Psalm *or* Song for the sabbath day.

¹ It is a good thing to give thanks unto the
LORD,
And to sing praises unto thy name, O ^{Most}_{most} High :

R.V. ¹ Or, *Because thou* hast said, *The* LORD *is my refuge;*

2 To shew forth thy lovingkindness in the
    morning,
  And thy faithfulness every night,
3 With/Upon an instrument of ten strings, and with/upon the
    psaltery;
  With a solemn sound upon the harp.
  upon the harp with a solemn sound.
4 For thou, LORD, hast made me glad through
    thy work:
  I will triumph in the works of thy hands.
5 How/O LORD, how great are thy works, O LORD/works !
  and Thy/thy thoughts are very deep.
6 A brutish man knoweth not;
  Neither doth a fool understand this:/this.
7 When the wicked spring as the grass,
  And when all the workers of iniquity do
    flourish;
  It is that they shall be destroyed for ever:
8 But thou, O LORD, art on/LORD, art most high for evermore.
9 For, lo, thine enemies, O LORD,
  For, lo, thine enemies shall perish;
  All the workers of iniquity shall be scattered.
10 But my horn hast/shalt thou exalted/exalt like *the horn of*
    the wild-ox.
    an unicorn ·
  I am/shall be anointed with fresh oil.
11 Mine eye also hath seen/shall see *my desire* on ¹mine
    enemies,
  Mine/and mine ears have heard/shall hear *my desire* of the evil-doers/wicked that
    rise up against me.

R.V.   ¹ Or, *them that lie in wait for me*

¹² The righteous shall flourish like the palm
  tree:
  He shall grow like a cedar in Lebanon.
¹³ ^They_Those that ^are_be planted in the house of the LORD
  Shall flourish in the courts of our God.
¹⁴ They shall still bring forth fruit in old age;
  They shall be ^full of sap_fat and ^green:_flourishing;
¹⁵ To shew that the LORD is ^upright;_upright:
  He is my rock, and there is no unrighteousness
  in him.

93 ¹ The LORD ^reigneth;_reigneth, he is ^apparelled_clothed with
         majesty;
       The LORD is ^apparelled,_clothed with strength, *wherewith* he
         hath girded himself ^with strength:
  The world also is stablished, that it cannot be
  moved.
² Thy throne is established of old:
  Thou art from everlasting.
³ The floods have lifted up, O LORD,
  The floods have lifted up their voice;
  The floods lift up their ¹waves.
⁴ ^Above the voices
  The LORD on high *is* mightier than the noise of many waters,
  ^The
  yea, than the mighty ^breakers_waves of the ^sea,_sea.
  The LORD on high is mighty.

⁵ Thy testimonies are very sure:
  Holiness becometh thine house,
  O LORD, for ^evermore._ever.

R.V.   ¹ Or, *roaring*
168

94

¹ O L<small>ORD</small>, thou God *LORD God,* to whom vengeance *belongeth,* *belongeth;*
Thou God *O God,* to whom vengeance belongeth,
shine forth.
shew thyself.

² Lift up thyself, thou judge of the earth:
Render <small>a reward</small> to the proud *their* desert.

³ L<small>ORD</small>, how long shall the wicked,
How long shall the wicked triumph?

⁴ *They prate.* *How long shall* they <small>utter and</small> speak *arrogantly:* *hard things?*
<small>and</small> All the workers of iniquity boast *themselves.* *themselves?*

⁵ They break in pieces thy people, O L<small>ORD</small>,
And afflict thine heritage.

⁶ They slay the widow and the stranger,
And murder the fatherless.

⁷ *And* *Yet* they say, ¹The L<small>ORD</small> shall not see,
Neither shall the God of Jacob *consider.* *regard it.*

⁸ *Consider,* *Understand,* ye brutish among the people:
And ye fools, when will ye be wise?

⁹ He that planted the ear, shall he not hear?
He that formed the eye, shall he not see?

¹⁰ He that ²chastiseth the *nations,* *heathen,* shall not he
correct, *correct?*
Even he that teacheth man <small>knowledge</small> *knowledge* *shall not he know* ?

¹¹ The L<small>ORD</small> knoweth the thoughts of man,
³That they are ⁴vanity.

¹² Blessed is the man whom thou chastenest,
¹O L<small>ORD</small>,
And teachest <small>him</small> out of thy law;

---

¹³ That thou mayest give him rest from the days
of adversity,
Until the pit be digged for the wicked.
¹⁴ For the LORD will not cast off his people,
Neither will he forsake his inheritance.
¹⁵ For judgement ᴮᵘᵗ ʲᵘᵈᵍᵐᵉⁿᵗ shall return unto righteousness:
And all the upright in heart shall follow it.
¹⁶ Who will rise up for me against the ᵉᵛⁱˡ-ᵈᵒᵉʳˢ?
ᵒʳ ʷʰᵒ will stand up for me against the workers
of iniquity?
¹⁷ Unless the LORD had been my help,
My soul had ˢᵒᵒⁿₐₗₘₒₛₜ dwelt in silence.
¹⁸ When I said, My foot slippeth;
Thy mercy, O LORD, held me up.
¹⁹ In the multitude of my ¹thoughts within me
Thy comforts delight my soul.
²⁰ Shall the ²throne of ʷⁱᶜᵏᵉᵈⁿᵉˢˢᵢₙᵢqᵤᵢₜy have fellowship
with thee,
Which frameth mischief by ˢᵗᵃᵗᵘᵗᵉₐ ₗₐw?
²¹ They gather themselves together against the
soul of the righteous,
And condemn the innocent blood.
²² But the LORD ʰᵃᵗʰ ᵇᵉᵉⁿᵢₛ my ʰⁱᵍʰ ᵗᵒʷᵉʳᵈₑfₑₙcₑ;
And my God ᵢₛ the rock of my refuge.
²³ And he ʰᵃᵗʰ ᵇʳᵒᵘᵍʰᵗₛₕₐₗₗ ᵦᵣᵢₙg upon them their own iniquity,
And shall cut them off in their own ʷⁱᶜᵏᵉᵈⁿᵉˢˢᵉᵛⁱˡ;
ₜₕₑyₑₐ, ₜₕₑ LORD our God shall cut them off.

R.V.   ¹ Or, *doubts*   ² Or, *seat*

95 ¹ O come, let us sing unto the Lord :
Let us make a joyful noise to the rock of
our salvation.

² Let us come before his presence with thanksgiving,
Let us _{and} make a joyful noise unto him with psalms.

³ For the Lord is a great God,
And a great King above all gods.

⁴ In his hand are the deep places of the ^{earth:}_{earth:}
The ¹_{strength}^{heights} of the ^{mountains are}_{hills is} his also.

⁵ The sea is his, and he made _{it:}^{it:}
And his hands formed the dry land.

⁶ O come, let us worship and bow ^{down:}_{down:}
Let us kneel before the Lord our ^{Maker:}_{maker.}

⁷ For he is our ^{God,}_{God;}
And we are the people of his pasture, and the
sheep of his hand.
²^{To-day, Oh that}_{To day if} ye ^{would}_{will} hear his ^{voice!}_{voice,}

⁸ Harden not your heart, as _{in the provocation,}^{at ³Meribah,}
_{and} ^{As} as in the day of _{temptation}^{⁴Massah} in the wilderness :

⁹ When your fathers tempted me,
Proved me, and saw my work.

¹⁰ Forty years long was I grieved with ^{that}_{this} generation,
And said, It is a people that do err in their
heart,
And they have not known my ways :

R.V. ¹ Or, *strength*   ² Or, *To-day, if ye will hear his voice,*
harden &c.   ³ That is, *strife.*   ⁴ That is, *temptation.*

¹¹ Wherefore <small>Unto whom</small> I sware in my <small>wrath,</small> wrath <small>.</small>
That they should not enter into my rest.

96 ¹ O sing unto the LORD a new song:
Sing unto the LORD, all the earth.
² Sing unto the LORD, bless his name;
Shew forth his salvation from day to day.
³ Declare his glory among the <small>nations,</small> heathen,
His <small>marvellous works</small> wonders among all <small>the peoples.</small> people.
⁴ For <small>great is the LORD,</small> the LORD *is* great, and <small>highly</small> greatly to be praised:
He is to be feared above all gods.
⁵ For all the gods of the <small>peoples</small> nations are ¹idols:
But the LORD made the heavens.
⁶ Honour and majesty are before him:
Strength and beauty are in his sanctuary.
⁷ Give unto the LORD, <small>O ye</small> ye kindreds of the <small>peoples,</small> people,
Give unto the LORD glory and strength.
⁸ Give unto the LORD the glory due unto his name:
Bring an offering, and come into his courts.
⁹ O worship the LORD ²in the beauty of holiness:
<small>Tremble</small> fear before him, all the earth.
¹⁰ Say among the <small>nations, The</small> heathen *that* the LORD reigneth:
The world also <small>is stablished</small> shall be established that it <small>cannot</small> shall not be moved:
He shall judge the <small>peoples with equity.</small> people righteously.
¹¹ Let the heavens <small>be glad,</small> rejoice, and let the earth <small>rejoice;</small> be glad;
Let the sea roar, and the fulness <small>thereof;</small> thereof.

R.V.   ¹ Or, *things of nought*   ² Or, *in holy array*

¹² Let the field _{be joyful,}^{exult,} and all that is ^{therein:}_{therein:}
Then shall all the trees of the wood ^{sing for joy:}_{rejoice}
¹³ Before the ^{LORD:}_{LORD:} for he ^{cometh:}_{cometh,}
For he cometh to judge the earth :
He shall judge the world with righteousness,
And the ^{peoples}_{people} ¹with his truth.

97 ¹ The LORD reigneth ; let the earth rejoice;
Let the multitude of isles be _{glad} ^{glad.} *thereof.*
² Clouds and darkness are round about him :
Righteousness and ^{judgement}_{judgment} are the ^{foundation}_{habitation} of his
throne.
³ A fire goeth before him,
And burneth up his ^{adversaries}_{enemies} round about.
⁴ His lightnings ^{lightened}_{enlightened} the world :
The earth saw, and trembled.
⁵ The hills melted like wax at the presence of
the LORD,
At the presence of the Lord of the whole
earth.
⁶ The heavens declare his righteousness,
And all the ^{peoples have seen}_{people see} his glory.
⁷ _{Confounded}^{Ashamed} be all they that serve graven images,
That boast themselves of idols :
Worship him, all ye gods.
⁸ Zion ^{heard}_{heard,} and was ^{glad.}_{glad;}
And the daughters of Judah ^{rejoiced:}_{rejoiced}
Because of thy ^{judgements,}_{judgments,} O LORD.

R.V.   ¹ Or, *in his faithfulness*

⁹ For thou, Lord, art ᵐᵒˢᵗ high above all the
   earth :
   Thou art exalted far above all gods.
¹⁰ O ye that love the Lord, hate evil :
   He preserveth the souls of his saints ;
   He delivereth them out of the hand of the
   wicked.
¹¹ Light is sown for the righteous,
   And gladness for the upright in heart.
¹² Be glad / Rejoice in the Lord, ye righteous ;
   And give thanks at the remembrance of his holiness. / to his holy ¹ name.

98
A Psalm.

¹ O sing unto the Lord a new song ;
   For he hath done marvellous things :
   His right hand, and his holy arm, hath wrought / gotten
   salvation for him. / him the victory.
² The Lord hath made known his salvation :
   His righteousness hath he openly shewed in
   the sight of the nations. / heathen.
³ He hath remembered his mercy and his faithfulness / truth
   toward the house of Israel :
   All the ends of the earth have seen the salvation
   of our God.
⁴ Make a joyful noise unto the Lord, all the
   earth :
   Break forth / make a loud noise, and sing for joy, yea, / rejoice, and sing praises. / praise.

R.V.   ¹ Heb. *memorial*.

⁵ Sing ᵖʳᵃⁱˢᵉˢ unto the LORD with the harp ;
With the ʰᵃʳᵖ harp, and the voice of ᵐᵉˡᵒᵈʸ· a psalm.

⁶ With trumpets and sound of cornet
Make a joyful noise before the ᴷⁱⁿᵍ, ᵗʰᵉ ᴸᴼᴿᴰ· LORD, the King.

⁷ Let the sea roar, and the fulness thereof ;
The world, and they that dwell ᵗʰᵉʳᵉⁱⁿ; therein.

⁸ Let the floods clap their ʰᵃⁿᵈˢ; hands:
Let the hills ˢⁱⁿᵍ ᶠᵒʳ ʲᵒʸ ᵗᵒᵍᵉᵗʰᵉʳ; be joyful together

⁹ Before the ᴸᴼᴿᴰ· LORD: for he cometh to judge the earth:
He shall judge the world with righteousness,
with righteousness shall he judge the world,
And the ᵖᵉᵒᵖˡᵉˢ people with equity.

99 ¹ The LORD reigneth ; let the ᵖᵉᵒᵖˡᵉˢ people tremble:
He ¹sitteth ᵘᵖᵒⁿ between the ᶜʰᵉʳᵘᵇⁱᵐ cherubims ; let the earth
be moved.

² The LORD is great in Zion ;
And he is high above all the ᵖᵉᵒᵖˡᵉˢ· people.

³ Let them praise thy great and terrible ⁿᵃᵐᵉ; name;
Holy is he.
for it *is* holy.

⁴ The king's strength also loveth ʲᵘᵈᵍᵉᵐᵉⁿᵗ; judgment ;
Thou dost establish equity,
Thou executest ʲᵘᵈᵍᵉᵐᵉⁿᵗ judgment and righteousness in
Jacob.

⁵ Exalt ye the LORD our God,
And worship at his ᶠᵒᵒᵗˢᵗᵒᵒˡ; footstool;
Holy is he.
for he *is* holy.

⁶ Moses and Aaron among his priests,

R.V. ¹ Or, *dwelleth between*

And Samuel among them that call upon his
   name ;
They called upon the Lord, and he answered
   them.

[7] He spake unto them in the ^{pillar of cloud}_{cloudy pillar} :
They kept his testimonies, and the _{ordinance}^{statute} that
   he gave them.

[8] Thou answeredst them, O Lord our God :
Thou wast a God that forgavest them,
Though thou tookest vengeance of their
   ^{doings.}_{inventions.}

[9] Exalt ^{ye} the Lord our God,
And worship at his holy hill ;
For the Lord our God is holy.

100

A Psalm [1]of ^{thanksgiving.}_{praise.}

[1] Make a joyful noise unto the Lord, [2]all ye
   lands.

[2] Serve the Lord with gladness :
Come before his presence with singing.

[3] Know ye that the Lord he is God :
It is he that hath made us, [3]and not ^{we are his}_{we ourselves} ;
We are his people, and the sheep of his
   pasture.

[4] Enter into his gates with [4]thanksgiving,
And into his courts with praise :

R.V. [1] Or, *for the thank offering*   [2] Heb. *all the earth.*
[3] Another reading is, *and not we ourselves.*   [4] Or, *a thank offering*

^{Give thanks}_{be thankful} unto him, and bless his name.

5 For the LORD is good; his mercy ^{endureth} for ever; _{is everlasting}
And his ^{faithfulness unto}_{truth endureth to} all generations.

101

A Psalm of David.

1 I will sing of mercy and ^{judgement}: _{judgment}
Unto thee, O LORD, will I sing ^{praises}.

2 I will ¹behave myself wisely in a perfect ^{way}: _{way}.
^{Oh}_O when wilt thou come unto me?
I will walk within my house ²with a perfect heart.

3 I will set no ^{base}_{wicked} thing before mine eyes:
I hate ³the work of them that turn aside;
It shall not cleave ^{unto}_{to} me.

4 A froward heart shall depart from me:
I will _{not} know ^{no}_{a wicked *person*.} ⁴evil thing.

5 Whoso privily slandereth his neighbour, him
will I ^{destroy}_{cut off}:
Him that hath an high look and a proud heart
will ^{I not}_{not I} suffer.

6 Mine eyes shall be upon the faithful of the
land, that they may dwell with me:
He that walketh in a perfect way, he shall
^{minister unto}_{serve} me.

7 He that worketh deceit shall not dwell within
my house:

R.V. ¹ Or, *give heed unto the perfect way* ² Or, *in the integrity of my heart* ³ Or, *the doing of unfaithfulness* ⁴ Or, *evil person.*

He that $^{\text{speaketh falsehood}}_{\text{telleth lies}}$ shall not $^{\text{be established before}}_{\text{tarry in my}}$ mine eyes. $_{\text{sight.}}$

8 Morning by morning will $^{\text{I}}_{\text{I will early}}$ destroy all the wicked of the land;

$_{\text{that I may}}^{\text{To}}$ cut off all $^{\text{the workers of iniquity}}_{\text{wicked doers}}$ from the city of the LORD.

102

A Prayer of the afflicted, when he [1]is overwhelmed, and poureth out his complaint before the LORD.

1 Hear my prayer, O LORD,
And let my cry come unto thee.

2 Hide not thy face from me in the day $^{\text{of my}}_{when\text{ I am}}$ $_{\text{distress:}}^{}$ $_{\text{in trouble;}}$
Incline thine ear unto $^{\text{me:}}_{\text{me:}}$
In the day when I call answer me speedily.

3 For my days $^{\text{consume away}}_{\text{are consumed}}$ [2]like smoke,
And my bones are burned [3]as $^{\text{a firebrand.}}_{\text{an hearth.}}$

4 My heart is $^{\text{smitten like grass, and withered}}_{\text{smitten, and withered like grass}}$;
$_{\text{so that}}^{\text{For}}$ I forget to eat my bread.

5 By reason of the voice of my groaning
My bones cleave to my $^{\text{flesh.}}_{\text{skin.}}$

6 I am like a pelican of the $^{\text{wilderness:}}_{\text{wilderness:}}$
I am $^{\text{become as}}_{\text{like}}$ an owl of the $^{\text{waste places.}}_{\text{desert.}}$

7 I watch, and am ^{become}
$^{\text{Like}}_{\text{as}}$ a sparrow $^{\text{that is}}$ alone upon the $^{\text{housetop.}}_{\text{house top.}}$

8 Mine enemies reproach me all the day;
$_{and\text{ they}}^{\text{They}}$ that are mad against me $^{\text{do curse by}}_{\text{are sworn against}}$ me.

9 For I have eaten ashes like bread,

R.V. [1] Or, fainteth   [2] Or, in smoke   [3] Or, as an hearth

And mingled my drink with weeping. weeping,
10 Because of thine indignation and thy wrath :
  For thou hast taken lifted me up, and cast me away. down.
11 My days are like a shadow that ¹declineth ;
  And I am withered like grass.

12 But thou, O Lord, ²shalt abide endure for ever ;
  And thy memorial remembrance unto all generations.
13 Thou shalt arise, and have mercy upon Zion :
  For it is the time to have pity upon favour her, yea, the set time time, is come.
14 For thy servants take pleasure in her stones,
  And have pity upon her dust. favour the dust thereof.
15 So the nations heathen shall fear the name of the Lord,
  And all the kings of the earth thy glory: glory.
16 For When the Lord hath built shall build up Zion,
  He hath appeared shall appear in his glory; glory.
17 He hath regarded will regard the prayer of the destitute,
  And hath not despised not despise their prayer.
18 This shall be written for the generation to come :
  And the a people which shall be created shall praise ³the Lord.
19 For he hath looked down from the height of his sanctuary ;
  From heaven did the Lord behold the earth ;
20 To hear the sighing groaning of the prisoner ;
  To loose ⁴those that are appointed to death ;

R.V. ¹ Or, *is stretched out*   ² Or, *sittest* as king   ³ Heb. *Jah.*   ⁴ Heb. *the children of death.*

²¹ That ^{men may}_{To} declare the name of the Lord in
Zion,
And his praise in Jerusalem ;
²² When the ^{peoples}_{people} are gathered together,
And the kingdoms, to serve the Lord.

²³ [1]He weakened my strength in the way ;
He shortened my days.
²⁴ I said, O my God, take me not away in the
midst of my days :
Thy years are throughout all generations.
²⁵ Of old hast thou laid the foundation of the
^{earth;}_{earth:}
And the heavens are the work of thy hands.
²⁶ They shall perish, but thou shalt endure :
Yea, all of them shall wax old like a garment ;
As a vesture shalt thou change them, and they
shall be changed :
²⁷ But thou art the same,
And thy years shall have no end.
²⁸ The children of thy servants shall continue,
And their seed shall be established before thee.

103   *A Psalm* of David.

¹ Bless the Lord, O my ^{soul:}_{soul:}
And all that is within me, *bless* his holy name.
² Bless the Lord, O my soul,

R.V.   [1] Another reading is, *He afflicted* me with *his strength.*

And forget not all his benefits :
³ Who forgiveth all thine iniquities ;
   Who healeth all thy diseases ;
⁴ Who redeemeth thy life from ¹destruction ;
   Who crowneth thee with lovingkindness and
      tender mercies:
⁵ Who satisfieth ²thy mouth with good things ;
   So that thy youth is renewed like the eagle's.
⁶ The LORD executeth righteous acts,
   And judgements for all that are oppressed.
⁷ He made known his ways unto Moses,
   His doings unto the children of Israel.
⁸ The LORD is full of compassion and gracious,
   Slow to anger, and plenteous in mercy.
⁹ He will not always chide:
   Neither will he keep *his anger* for ever.
¹⁰ He hath not dealt with us after our sins;
   Nor rewarded us according to our iniquities.
¹¹ For as the heaven is high above the earth,
   So great is his mercy toward them that fear
      him.
¹² As far as the east is from the west,
   So far hath he removed our transgressions
      from us.
¹³ Like as a father pitieth his children,
   So the LORD pitieth them that fear him.
¹⁴ For he knoweth our frame ;

R.V. ¹ Or, *the pit*   ² Or, *thy years* Or, *thy prime* Heb.
thine ornament.

He remembereth that we are dust.

15 As for man, his days are as grass;
   As a flower of the field, so he flourisheth.

16 For the wind passeth over it, and it is gone;
   And the place thereof shall know it no
   more.

17 But the mercy of the LORD is from everlasting
   to everlasting upon them that fear him,
   And his righteousness unto children's children;

18 To such as keep his covenant,
   And to those that remember his precepts to
   do them.

19 The LORD hath established his throne in the
   heavens;
   And his kingdom ruleth over all.

20 Bless the LORD, ye angels of his:
   Ye mighty that excel in strength, that fulfil his word,
   Hearkening unto the voice of his word.

21 Bless ye the LORD, all ye his hosts;
   Ye ministers of his, that do his pleasure.

22 Bless the LORD, all ye his works,
   In all places of his dominion:
   Bless the LORD, O my soul.

104
1 Bless the LORD, O my soul.
   O LORD my God, thou art very great;
   Thou art clothed with honour and
   majesty.

2 Who coverest thyself with light as with a
   garment:

Who stretchest out the heavens like a curtain :
3 Who layeth the beams of his chambers in the waters;
   waters:
  Who maketh the clouds his chariot:
   chariot:
  Who walketh upon the wings of the wind :
4 Who maketh ¹winds his messengers ;
            his angels spirits ;
  His ministers a flaming fire :
5 ²Who laid the foundations of the earth,
  That it should not be moved for ever.
                      removed
6 Thou coveredst it with the deep as with a vesture;
   garment:
  The waters stood above the mountains.
7 At thy rebuke they fled ;
  At the voice of thy thunder they hasted away;
                                          away.
8 ³They went up by the mountains; they went down by
       go   mountains;   go
  the valleys,
      valleys
  Unto the place which thou hadst founded for
                                  hast
  them.
9 Thou hast set a bound that they may not pass
  over ;
  That they turn not again to cover the earth.
10 He sendeth forth springs into the valleys;
               the   valleys,
   They run among the mountains:
   which   hills.
11 They give drink to every beast of the field:
                                       field:
   The wild asses quench their thirst.
12 By them shall the fowl of the heaven have their
            shall   fowls
   habitation,

R.V. ¹ Or, *his angels winds*   ² Heb. *He founded the earth
upon her bases.*   ³ Or, (*The mountains rose, the valleys sank
down;*)

^{They}_{which} ¹sing among the branches.

¹³ He watereth the ^{mountains}_{hills} from his chambers :

The earth is satisfied with the fruit of thy works.

¹⁴ He causeth the grass to grow for the cattle,

And herb for the ²service of ^{man}_{man} :

That he may bring forth ³food out of the ^{earth}_{earth} :

¹⁵ And wine that maketh glad the heart of man,

⁴*And* oil to make his face to shine,

And bread ^{that}_{which} strengtheneth man's heart.

¹⁶ The trees of the LORD are ⁵_{full} satisfied _{of sap} ;

The cedars of Lebanon, which he hath planted;

¹⁷ Where the birds make their nests :

As for the stork, the fir trees are her house.

¹⁸ The high ^{mountains are}_{hills *are* a refuge} for the wild goats ;

^{The}_{and the} rocks ^{are a refuge} for the ⁶conies.

¹⁹ He appointed the moon for seasons :

The sun knoweth his going down.

²⁰ Thou makest darkness, and it is ^{night}_{night} :

Wherein all the beasts of the forest do creep forth.

²¹ The young lions roar after their prey,

And seek their meat from God.

²² The sun ariseth, they _{gather} ^{get them away.}_{themselves together,}

And lay them down in their dens.

²³ Man goeth forth unto his work

R.V.   ¹ Heb. *utter their voice*.   ² Or, *labour*   ³ Heb. *bread*.
⁴ Heb. *To make his face to shine with oil*.   ⁵ See ver. 13.
⁶ See Lev. 11. 5.

And to his labour until the evening.
24 O Lord, how manifold are thy works!
In wisdom hast thou made them all:
The earth is full of thy ¹riches.
25 Yonder is the sea, great and wide,
   So is this   wide sea,
Wherein are things creeping innumerable,
Both small and great beasts.
26 There go the ships;
                 ships:
There is that leviathan, whom thou hast formed to
                                          made
   ²take his pastime therein.
    play
27 These wait all upon thee;
                     thee:
That thou mayest give them their meat in due
   season.
28 That thou givest unto them they gather;
                                   gather:
Thou openest thine hand, they are satisfied with
                                   filled
   good.
29 Thou hidest thy face, they are troubled;
                                 troubled:
Thou ³takest away their breath, they die,
And return to their dust.
30 Thou sendest forth thy spirit, they are created;
                                          created:
And thou renewest the face of the ground.
                                    earth.
31 Let the glory of the Lord shall endure for ever;
   The   ever:
Let the Lord rejoice in his works:
the Lord shall   works.
32 Who looketh on the earth, and it trembleth;
   He   trembleth:
He toucheth the mountains, and they smoke.
                 hills,
33 I will sing unto the Lord as long as I
   live:

R.V.   ¹ Or, *creatures*   ² Or, *play with him* See Job 41. 5.
³ Or, *gatherest in*

185

I will sing praise to my God while I have ^{any}_{my} being.

34 Let ^{my}_{My} meditation ^{be sweet unto him}_{of him shall be sweet} :
I will ^{rejoice}_{be glad} in the LORD.

35 Let _{the} sinners be consumed out of the earth,
And let the wicked be no more.
Bless _{thou} the LORD, O my soul.
¹Praise ye the LORD.

105 ¹ O give thanks unto the ^{LORD,}_{LORD;} call upon
his ^{name;}_{name:}

Make known his ^{doings}_{deeds} among the ^{peoples.}_{people.}
2 Sing unto him, sing ^{praises}_{psalms} unto ^{him:}_{him:}
²Talk ye of all his ^{marvellous}_{wondrous} works.
3 Glory ye in his holy name :
Let the heart of them rejoice that seek the LORD.
4 Seek ^{ye the LORD}_{the LORD,} and his ^{strength;}_{strength:}
Seek his face evermore.
5 Remember his marvellous works that he hath
done ;
His wonders, and the ^{judgements}_{judgments} of his mouth ;
6 O ye seed of Abraham his servant,
Ye children of ^{Jacob,}_{Jacob} his chosen ^{ones}.
7 He is the LORD our God :
His ^{Judgements}_{judgments} are in all the earth.
8 He hath remembered his covenant for ever,
The word which he commanded to a thousand
^{generations;}_{generations.}

R.V.   ¹ Heb. *Hallelujah.*   ² Or, *Meditate*

⁹ *The* Which *covenant* which he made with Abraham,
And his oath unto Isaac;

¹⁰ And confirmed the same unto Jacob for a statute, law,
To and to Israel for an everlasting covenant:

¹¹ Saying, Unto thee will I give the land of Canaan,
The ¹lot of your inheritance:

¹² When they were but a few men in number;
Yea, very few, and sojourners strangers in it; it.

¹³ And When they went about from from one nation to nation, another,
From one kingdom to another people. people;

¹⁴ He suffered no man to do them wrong: wrong:
Yea, he reproved kings for their sakes;

¹⁵ *Saying*, Touch not mine anointed ones,
And do my prophets no harm.

¹⁶ And Moreover he called for a famine upon the land; land:
He brake the whole staff of bread.

¹⁷ He sent a man before them; them,
even Joseph Joseph, *who* was sold for a servant:

¹⁸ His Whose feet they hurt with fetters; fetters:
²He was laid in *chains of* iron:

¹⁹ Until the time that his word came to pass; came:
The word of the LORD tried him.

²⁰ The king sent and loosed him;
Even the ruler of peoples, the people, and let him go free.

²¹ He made him lord of his house,
And ruler of all his substance:

²² To bind his princes at his pleasure; pleasure:

R.V.   ¹ Heb. *cord*, or, *line*.   ² Heb. *His soul entered into the iron.*

And teach his [1]senators wisdom.
23 Israel also came into Egypt;
And Jacob sojourned in the land of Ham.
24 And he increased his people greatly,
And made them stronger than their adversaries.
25 He turned their heart to hate his people,
To deal subtilly with his servants.
26 He sent Moses his servant;
And Aaron whom he had chosen.
27 [2]They set among them [3]his signs,
And wonders in the land of Ham.
28 He sent darkness, and made it dark;
And they rebelled not against his words.
29 He turned their waters into blood,
And slew their fish.
30 Their land swarmed with frogs,
In the chambers of their kings.
31 He spake, and there came swarms of flies,
And [4]lice in all their borders.
32 He gave them hail for rain,
And flaming fire in their land.
33 He smote their vines also and their fig trees;
And brake the trees of their borders.
34 He spake, and the locust came,
And the cankerworm, and that without number,
35 And did eat up every herb in their land,
And did eat up the fruit of their ground.

R.V. [1] Heb. *elders.*　　[2] Some ancient versions have, *He.*
[3] Heb. *the words of his signs.*　　[4] See Ex. 8. 16.

36 He smote also all the firstborn in their land,
   The ¹chief of all their strength.
37 ᴬⁿᵈ ʰᵉ/He brought them forth ₐₗₛₒ with silver and gold:
   And there was ²not one feeble person among
   ₜₕₑᵢᵣ/his tribes.
38 Egypt was glad when they departed:/departed:
   For the fear of them ʰᵃᵈ ᶠᵃˡˡᵉⁿ/fell upon them.
39 He spread a cloud for a covering;
   And fire to give light in the night.
40 ₜₕₑ ₚₑₒₚₗₑ/They asked, and he brought quails,
   And satisfied them with the bread of heaven.
41 He opened the rock, and ₜₕₑ waters gushed out;
   They ran in the dry places *like* a river.
42 For he remembered his holy ᵖʳᵒᵐⁱˢᵉ,/word,
   And Abraham his servant.
43 And he brought forth his people with joy,
   And his chosen with ᵍˡᵃᵈⁿᵉˢˢ:/singing.
44 And ʰᵉ gave them the lands of the ʰᵉᵃᵗʰᵉⁿ:/nations:
   And they ᵢₙₕₑᵣᵢₜₑд/took the labour of the ᵖᵉᵒᵖˡᵉˢ ⁱⁿ ᵖᵒˢˢᵉˢˢⁱᵒⁿ:/people;
45 That they might ₒᵦₛₑᵣᵥₑ/keep his statutes,
   And ᵏᵉᵉᵖ/observe his laws.
   ³Praise ye the LORD.

      ¹ ³Praise ye the LORD.
106 O give thanks unto the LORD; for he
         is good:
   For his mercy *endureth* for ever.

R.V. ¹ Heb. *beginning.* See Deut. 21. 17.   ² Or, *none that*
stumbled   ³ Heb. *Hallelujah.*

² Who can utter the mighty acts of the _{LORD:}^{LORD?}
 _{_who_ can}^{Or} shew forth all his praise?

³ Blessed are they that keep ^{judgement,}_{judgment,}
And he that doeth righteousness at all times.

⁴ Remember me, O LORD, with the favour that
 thou bearest unto thy ^{people:}_{people:}
O visit me with thy ^{salvation:}_{salvation:}

⁵ That I may see the ^{prosperity}_{good} of thy chosen,
That I may rejoice in the gladness of thy
 nation,
That I may glory with thine inheritance.

⁶ We have sinned with our fathers,
We have committed iniquity, we have done
 wickedly.

⁷ Our fathers understood not thy wonders in
 Egypt;
They remembered not the multitude of thy
 mercies;
But ^{were rebellious}_{provoked _him_} at the sea, even at the Red ^{Sea.}_{sea.}

⁸ Nevertheless he saved them for his name's
 sake,
That he might make his mighty power to be
 known.

⁹ He rebuked the Red ^{Sea}_{sea} also, and it was
 dried up:
So he led them through the depths, as through
 ^a_{the} ¹ wilderness.

R.V.   ¹ Or, _pasture land_

¹⁰ And he saved them from the hand of him that
hated them,
And redeemed them from the hand of the
enemy.
¹¹ And the waters covered their ^{adversaries}_{enemies}:
There was not one of them left.
¹² Then believed they his words;
They sang his praise.
¹³ They soon forgat his works;
They waited not for his counsel:
¹⁴ But lusted exceedingly in the wilderness,
And tempted God in the desert.
¹⁵ And he gave them their request;
But sent leanness into their soul.
¹⁶ They envied Moses also in the camp,
And Aaron the ¹saint of the LORD.
¹⁷ The earth opened and swallowed up Dathan,
And covered the company of Abiram.
¹⁸ And a fire was kindled in their company;
The flame burned up the wicked.
¹⁹ They made a calf in Horeb,
And worshipped ^a_{the} molten image.
²⁰ Thus they changed their glory
^{For}_{into} the ^{likeness}_{similitude} of an ox that eateth grass.
²¹ They forgat God their saviour,
Which had done great things in Egypt;
²² Wondrous works in the land of Ham,
And terrible things by the Red ^{Sea.}_{sea.}

R.V.   ¹ Or, *holy one*

²³ Therefore he said that he would destroy them,
    Had not Moses his chosen stood before him
      in the breach,
    To turn away his wrath, lest he should destroy
      them.
²⁴ Yea, they despised the pleasant land,
    They believed not his word:
²⁵ But murmured in their tents,
    And hearkened not unto the voice of the
      Lord.
²⁶ Therefore he lifted up his hand against them,
    That he would ¹overthrow them in the wilderness:
²⁷ And that he would overthrow their seed also among
      the nations,
    And to scatter them in the lands.
²⁸ They joined themselves also unto ²Baal-peor,
    And ate the sacrifices of the dead.
²⁹ Thus they provoked him to anger with their
      doings;
    And the plague brake in upon them.
³⁰ Then stood up Phinehas, and executed judgement:
    And so the plague was stayed.
³¹ And that was counted unto him for righteousness,
    Unto all generations for evermore.
³² They angered him also at the waters of ³Meribah,
    So that it went ill with Moses for their sakes:
³³ Because they were rebellious against his spirit,
    And so that he spake unadvisedly with his lips.

R.V. ¹ Heb. *make them fall.*   ² See Num. 25. 3.   ³ Or, *strife*

³⁴ They did not destroy the _{nations,}^{peoples,}
_{concerning}^{As} whom the LORD commanded _{them:}^{them:}
³⁵ But _{were mingled among}^{mingled themselves with} the _{heathen,}^{nations,}
And learned their _{works.}^{works:}
³⁶ And they served their _{idols:}^{idols:}
Which _{were}^{became} a snare unto _{them.}^{them:}
³⁷ Yea, they sacrificed their sons and their
daughters unto _{devils,}^{demons,}
³⁸ And shed innocent blood, even the blood of
their sons and of their daughters,
Whom they sacrificed unto the idols of _{Canaan:}^{Canaan:}
And the land was polluted with blood.
³⁹ Thus were they defiled with their _{own} works,
And went a whoring _{with}ⁱⁿ their _{own inventions.}^{doings.}
⁴⁰ Therefore was the wrath of the LORD kindled
against his people,
_{Insomuch that}^{And} he abhorred his _{own} inheritance.
⁴¹ And he gave them into the hand of the
_{heathen;}^{nations:}
And they that hated them ruled over them.
⁴² Their enemies also oppressed them,
And they were brought into subjection under
their hand.
⁴³ Many times did he deliver them ;
But they _{provoked *him* with}^{were rebellious in} their counsel,
And were brought low _{for}ⁱⁿ their iniquity.
⁴⁴ Nevertheless he regarded their _{affliction,}^{distress,}
When he heard their cry :
⁴⁵ And he remembered for them his covenant,

And repented according to the multitude of
his mercies.
⁴⁶ He made them also to be pitied
Of all those that carried them captives.

⁴⁷ Save us, O LORD our God,
And gather us from among the ⁿᵃᵗⁱᵒⁿˢ,
ₕₑₐₜₕₑₙ.
To give thanks unto thy holy name,
And to triumph in thy praise.

⁴⁸ Blessed be the ᴸᴼᴿᴰ, ᵗʰᵉ God of ᴵˢʳᵃᵉˡ.
ₗₒᵣ𝒹   ᵢₛᵣₐₑₗ
From everlasting ᵉᵛᵉⁿ to ᵉᵛᵉʳˡᵃˢᵗⁱⁿᵍ.
ₑᵥₑᵣₗₐₛₜᵢₙ𝓰:
And let all the people say, Amen.
¹Praise ye the LORD.

BOOK V

107 ¹ O give thanks unto the ᴸᴼᴿᴰ; for he is
ₗₒᵣ𝒹
good:
For his mercy *endureth* for ever.
² Let the redeemed of the LORD say *so*,
Whom he hath redeemed from the hand of the
ᵃᵈᵛᵉʳˢᵃʳʸ ;
ₑₙₑₘᵧ
³ And gathered them out of the lands,
From the ᵉᵃˢᵗ, and from the west,
ₑₐₛₜ,
From the ⁿᵒʳᵗʰ and ²from the south.
ₙₒᵣₜₕ,

⁴ They wandered in the wilderness in a ᵈᵉˢᵉʳᵗ way;
ₛₒₗᵢₜₐᵣᵧ

R.V.   ¹ Heb. *Hallelujah.*   ² Heb. *from the sea.*

They found no city ^{of habitation.}_{to dwell in.}

⁵ Hungry and thirsty,
 Their soul fainted in them.
⁶ Then they cried unto the LORD in their trouble,
 And he delivered them out of their distresses.
⁷ _{And he}^{He} led them _{forth}^{also} by ^{a straight}_{the right} way,
 That they might go to a city of habitation.
⁸ Oh that men would praise the LORD for his
   goodness,
 And for his wonderful works to the children of
   men !
⁹ For he satisfieth the longing soul,
 And _{filleth} the hungry soul ^{he filleth with good.}_{with goodness.}

¹⁰ Such as ^{sat}_{sit} in darkness and in the shadow of
    death,
  Being bound in affliction and iron ;
¹¹ Because they rebelled against the words of
    God,
  And contemned the counsel of the ^{Most}_{most} High :
¹² Therefore he brought down their heart with
    labour ;
  They fell down, and there was none to help.
¹³ Then they cried unto the LORD in their trouble,
  And he saved them out of their distresses.
¹⁴ He brought them out of darkness and the
    shadow of death,
  And brake their bands in sunder.
¹⁵ Oh that men would praise the LORD for his
    goodness,

And for his wonderful works to the children of
men!
¹⁶ For he hath broken the gates of brass,
And cut the bars of iron in sunder.

¹⁷ Fools because of ¹their transgression,
And because of their iniquities, are afflicted.
¹⁸ Their soul abhorreth all manner of meat;
And they draw near unto the gates of death.
¹⁹ Then they cry unto the LORD in their trouble,
And he saveth them out of their distresses.
²⁰ He ^{sendeth}/_{sent} his word, and ^{healeth}/_{healed} them,
And ^{delivereth}/_{delivered} *them* from their ²destructions.
²¹ Oh that men would praise the LORD for his
goodness,
And for his wonderful works to the children of
men!
²² And let them ^{offer}/_{sacrifice} the sacrifices of thanks-
giving,
And declare his works with ^{singing.}/_{rejoicing.}

²³ They that go down to the sea in ships,
That do business in great waters;
²⁴ These see the works of the LORD,
And his wonders in the deep.
²⁵ For he commandeth, and raiseth the stormy
wind,
Which lifteth up the waves thereof.

R.V.   ¹ Heb. *the way of their transgression.*   ² Heb. *pits.*

²⁶ They mount up to the heaven, they go down
  again to the depths:
 Their soul ^{melteth away}_{is melted} because of trouble.
²⁷ They reel to and fro, and stagger like a drunken
  man,
 And ¹are at their wits' end.
²⁸ Then they cry unto the LORD in their
  trouble,
 And he bringeth them out of their distresses.
²⁹ He maketh the storm a calm,
 So that the waves thereof are still.
³⁰ Then are they glad because they be quiet;
 So he bringeth them unto ^{2the haven where they would be.}_{their desired haven.}
³¹ Oh that men would praise the LORD for his
  goodness,
 And for his wonderful works to the children of
  men!
³² Let them exalt him also in the ^{assembly}_{congregation} of the
  people,
 And praise him in the ^{seat}_{assembly} of the elders.

³³ He turneth rivers into a wilderness,
 And _{the} watersprings into a ^{thirsty}_{dry} ground;
³⁴ A fruitful land into ^{a salt desert,}_{barrenness,}
 For the wickedness of them that dwell
  therein.
³⁵ He turneth ^a_{the} wilderness into a ^{pool of}_{standing} water,
 And ^{a dry land}_{dry ground} into watersprings.

R.V. ¹ Heb. *all their wisdom is swallowed up.* ² Heb. *the haven of their desire.*

197

³⁶ And there he maketh the hungry to dwell,
    That they may prepare a city ^{of}_{for} habitation;
³⁷ And sow _{the} fields, and plant vineyards,
    ^{And get them}_{which may yield} fruits of increase.
³⁸ He blesseth them also, so that they are multi-
    plied greatly;
    And ^{he} suffereth not their cattle to decrease.
³⁹ Again, they are minished and ^{bowed down}_{brought low}
    Through oppression, ^{trouble,}_{affliction,} and sorrow.
⁴⁰ He poureth contempt upon princes,
    And causeth them to wander in the ^{waste,}_{wilderness,}
    where there is no way.
⁴¹ Yet setteth he the ^{needy}_{poor} on high from affliction,
    And maketh *him* families like a flock.
⁴² The ^{upright}_{righteous} shall see it, and ^{be glad;}_{rejoice:}
    And all iniquity shall stop her mouth.
⁴³ Whoso is ^{wise shall give heed to}_{wise, and will observe} these things,
    ^{And}_{even} they shall ^{consider}_{understand} the ^{mercies}_{lovingkindness} of the
    Lord.

108

A ^{Song, a}_{Song or} Psalm of David.

¹ ¹My heart is fixed, O God,
    O God, my heart is fixed;
    I will ^{sing, yea, I will sing praises,}_{sing and give praise,} even with my glory.
² Awake, psaltery and harp:
    ²I myself will awake ^{right} early.
³ I will ^{give thanks unto}_{praise} thee, O Lord, among the
    ^{peoples}_{people} :

R.V. ¹ See Ps. 57. 7-11.   ² Or, *I will awake the dawn*

And I will sing praises unto thee among the
nations.
4 For thy mercy is great above the heavens [heavens,]:
And thy truth *reacheth* unto the skies [clouds].
5 Be thou exalted, O God, above the heavens:
And thy glory above all the earth [earth;].
6 [1]That thy beloved may be delivered [delivered:]
Save with thy right hand, and answer [2]us [me].
7 God hath spoken in his holiness; I will
exult [rejoice]:
I will divide Shechem, and mete out the valley
of Succoth.
8 Gilead is mine; Manasseh is mine;
Ephraim also is the defence [strength] of mine head;
Judah is my [3]sceptre [lawgiver];
9 Moab is my washpot;
[4]Upon [over] Edom will I cast out [over] my shoe [shoe;]:
Over Philistia will I shout [triumph].
10 Who will bring me into the fenced [strong] city?
[5]Who hath led [will lead] me unto [into] Edom?
11 [6]Hast not thou cast us off, O God [*Wilt* not *thou*, O God, *who* hast cast us off]?
And thou goest not forth, O God [wilt not thou, O God, go forth] with our hosts [hosts]?
12 Give us help against the adversary [from trouble]:
For vain is the [7]help of man.
13 Through God we shall do valiantly:
For he it is that shall tread down our adversaries [enemies].

R.V. 1 See Ps. 60. 5-12. 2 Another reading is, *me*. 3 Or,
lawgiver 4 Or, *Unto* 5 Or, *Who will lead me &c.*
6 Or, *Wilt not thou, O God, which hast cast us off, and goest...
hosts?* 7 Heb. *salvation.*

109

For the Chief Musician.
To the chief Musician,   A Psalm of David.

¹ Hold not thy peace, O God of my praise ;
² For the mouth of the wicked and the mouth
   of the deceitful are opened against me :
   They have spoken unto me with a lying tongue.
³ They compassed me about also with words of
   hatred,
   And fought against me without a cause.
⁴ For my love they are my adversaries :
   But I *give myself unto* prayer.
⁵ And they have ²rewarded me evil for good,
   And hatred for my love.
⁶ Set thou a wicked man over him :
   And let ³an adversary stand at his right hand.
⁷ When he shall be judged, let him come forth guilty,
   And let his prayer ⁴be turned into sin.
⁸ Let his days be few ;
   And let another take his office.
⁹ Let his children be fatherless,
   And his wife a widow.
¹⁰ Let his children be continually vagabonds, and beg :
   And let them seek *their bread* also ⁵out of their
   desolate places.
¹¹ Let the extortioner ⁶catch all that he hath ;
   And let the strangers make spoil of his labour.

R.V. ¹ Or, *against*   ² Heb. *laid upon me.*   ³ Or, *Satan*
Or. *an accuser*   ⁴ Or, *become*   ⁵ Or, *far from*   ⁶ Heb.
snare

¹² Let there be none to ¹extend mercy unto ^him:
    Neither let there be any to ^have ^pity ^on his father-
        less children.
¹³ Let his posterity be cut off;
    ^In ^and in the generation following let their name be
        blotted out.
¹⁴ Let the iniquity of his fathers be remembered
        with the LORD;
    And let not the sin of his mother be blotted out.
¹⁵ Let them be before the LORD continually,
    That he may cut off the memory of them from
        the earth.
¹⁶ Because that he remembered not to shew mercy,
    But persecuted the poor and needy man,
        And the broken in heart, to slay *them.*
        that he might even slay the broken in heart.
¹⁷ ^Yea, ^As he loved cursing, ^and ^it ^came ^so ^let ^it ^come unto ^him:
    ^And ^as he delighted not in blessing, ^and ^it ^was ^so ^let ^it ^be far
        from him.
¹⁸ ^He ^As ^he clothed himself ^also with cursing ^like as with
        his garment,
    ^And ^so ^let it ^came ^come into his ^inward ^parts ^bowels like water,
    And like oil into his bones.
¹⁹ Let it be unto him as the ^raiment ^wherewith ^he ^garment *which* cover-
        eth ^himself, ^him,
    And for ^the ^a girdle wherewith he is girded con-
        tinually.
²⁰ ^This ^is ^Let ^this *be* the reward of mine adversaries from
        the LORD,

And of them that speak evil against my soul.

21 But deal thou with me, O God the Lord, for thy
    name's sake:

Because thy mercy is good, deliver thou me.

22 For I am poor and needy,
    And my heart is wounded within me.

23 I am gone like the shadow when it [1]declineth:
    I am tossed up and down as the locust.

24 My knees [2]are weak through fasting;
    And my flesh faileth of fatness.

25 I am become also a reproach unto them:
    When they see me they shake their head.

26 Help me, O Lord my God:
    O save me according to thy mercy:

27 That they may know that this is thy hand;
    That thou, Lord, hast done it.

28 Let them curse, but bless thou:
    When they arise, they shall be ashamed; but thy servant
    shall rejoice.

29 [3]Let mine adversaries be clothed with dishonour,
    And let them cover themselves with their own
    shame, as with a mantle.

30 I will give great thanks unto the Lord with my mouth;
    Yea, I will praise him among the multitude.

31 For he shall stand at the right hand of the
    needy,
    To save him from them that judge his soul.

R.V. [1] Or, *is stretched out* [2] Or, *totter* [3] Or, *Mine
adversaries shall be clothed...and they shall cover &c.*

110
A Psalm of David.

¹ The Lord ˢᵃⁱᵈʰ unto my ˡᵒʳᵈ, Sit thou at my
right hand,
Until I make thine enemies thy footstool.
² The Lord shall ¹send ᶠᵒʳᵗʰ the rod of thy
strength out of Zion :
Rule thou in the midst of thine enemies.
³ Thy people ²offer themselves willingly ³in the day of thy
⁴power:
⁵In the beauties of ʰᵒˡⁱⁿᵉˢˢ, from the womb of
the ᵐᵒʳⁿⁱⁿᵍ:
⁶Thou hast the dew of thy youth.
⁴ The Lord hath sworn, and will not repent,
Thou art a priest for ever
After the ⁷order of Melchizedek.
⁵ The Lord at thy right hand
⁸Shall strike through kings in the day of his
wrath.
⁶ He shall judge among the ⁿᵃᵗⁱᵒⁿˢ,
⁹He ¹⁰shall fill *the places* with ₜₕₑ dead bodies ;
He ⁸shall strike through the head ¹¹in many countries.
⁷ He shall drink of the brook in the way :
Therefore shall he lift up the head.

R.V. ¹ Or, *stretch*   ² Heb. *are freewill offerings.*   ³ Or,
in the day of thy power, in the beauties of holiness: from &c.
⁴ Or, *army*   ⁵ Or, *In holy attire* According to another reading,
On the mountains of holiness.   ⁶ Or, *Thy youth are to thee
as the dew*   ⁷ Or, *manner*   ⁸ Or, *Hath stricken*   ⁹ Or,
The places are full of &c.   ¹⁰ Or, *hath filled*   ¹¹ Or, *over
a wide land*

III ¹ ¹Praise ye the LORD.

I will ^give thanks unto / praise the LORD with my whole heart,

In the ^council / assembly of the upright, and in the congregation.

² The works of the LORD are great,

Sought out of all them that have pleasure therein.

³ His work is ^honour and majesty / honourable and glorious :

And his righteousness endureth for ever.

⁴ He hath made his wonderful works to be remembered :

The LORD is gracious and full of compassion.

⁵ He hath given ²meat unto them that fear him :

He will ever be mindful of his covenant.

⁶ He hath shewed his people the power of his works,

^In giving that he may give them the heritage of the ^nations. / heathen.

⁷ The works of his hands are ^truth / verity and ^judgement / judgment ;

All his ^precepts / commandments are sure.

⁸ They ^are established / stand fast for ever and ever,

^They are and are ³done in truth and uprightness.

⁹ He ^hath sent redemption unto his ^people; / people:

He hath commanded his covenant for ever :

Holy and reverend is his name.

¹⁰ The fear of the LORD is the beginning of ^wisdom; / wisdom:

R.V.   ¹ Heb. *Hallelujah.*   ² Heb. *prey.*   ³ Or, *made*

204

¹A good understanding have all they that do
²thereafter
his commandments :
His praise endureth for ever.

¹ ³Praise ye the Lord.

112 Blessed is the man that feareth the
Lord,
That delighteth greatly in his commandments.
² His seed shall be mighty upon earth :
The generation of the upright shall be blessed.
³ Wealth and riches *are shall be* in his house :
And his righteousness endureth for ever.
⁴ Unto the upright there ariseth light in the
darkness :
He is gracious, and full of compassion, and
righteous.
5 Well is it with the man that dealeth graciously and lendeth;
A good man sheweth favour, lendeth:
He shall maintain his cause in judgement.
will guide his affairs with discretion.
6 For he shall never be moved;
Surely not be moved for ever:
The righteous shall be ʰᵃᵈ in everlasting remembrance.
⁷ He shall not be afraid of evil tidings :
His heart is fixed, trusting in the Lord.
⁸ His heart is established, he shall not be afraid,
Until he see *his desire* upon his adversaries.
enemies.
⁹ He hath dispersed, he hath given to the
needy ,
poor ;
His righteousness endureth for ever:
ever;

R.V. ¹ Or, *Good repute* ² Heb. *them.* ³ Heb. *Hallelujah.*

205

His horn shall be exalted with honour.
10 The wicked shall see it, and be grieved;
He shall gnash with his teeth, and melt
away:
The desire of the wicked shall perish.

113
¹ ¹Praise ye the LORD.
Praise, O ye servants of the LORD,
Praise the name of the LORD.
² Blessed be the name of the LORD
From this time forth and for evermore.
³ From the rising of the sun unto the going
down of the same
The LORD's name is to be praised.
⁴ The LORD is high above all nations,
And his glory above the heavens.
⁵ Who is like unto the LORD our God,
That hath his seat
who dwelleth on high,
⁶ That
Who humbleth himself ²to behold
The things that are in heaven
heaven, and in the earth?
earth!
⁷ He raiseth up the poor out of the dust,
And lifteth ᵘᵖ the needy from
out of the dunghill;
⁸ That he may set him with princes,
Even with the princes of his people.
⁹ He maketh the barren woman to keep house,
And to be a joyful mother of children.
¹Praise ye the LORD.

R.V. ¹ Heb. *Hallelujah.*   ² Or, *to regard the heavens and the earth.*

114
¹ When Israel went ^{forth} out of Egypt,
The house of Jacob from a people of
strange language;

² Judah ^{became}_{was} his sanctuary,
_{and} Israel his dominion.

³ The sea saw it, and ^{fled;}_{fled:}
Jordan was driven back.

⁴ The mountains skipped like rams,
_{and the}^{The} little hills like ^{young sheep.}_{lambs.}

⁵ What ^{aileth}_{ailed} thee, O thou sea, that thou ^{fleest}_{fleddest} ?
Thou Jordan, that thou _{wast driven}^{turnest} back ?

⁶ Ye mountains, that ye _{skipped}^{skip} like rams ;
_{and ye}^{Ye} little hills, like ^{young sheep}_{lambs} ?

⁷ Tremble, thou earth, at the presence of the
Lord,
At the presence of the God of Jacob ;

⁸ Which turned the rock into a ^{pool of}_{standing} water,
The flint into a fountain of waters.

115
¹ Not unto us, O Lᴏʀᴅ, not unto us,
But unto thy name give glory,
For thy mercy, and for thy truth's sake.

² Wherefore should the ^{nations}_{heathen} say,
Where is now their God ?

³ But our God is in the heavens :
He hath done whatsoever he _{hath} pleased.

⁴ Their idols are silver and gold,
The work of men's hands.

⁵ They have mouths, but they speak ^{not;}_{not:}

Eyes have they, but they see ᵏⁿᵒᵗ⁺:
⁶ They have ears, but they hear ⁿᵒᵗ⁺:
Noses have they, but they smell ⁿᵒᵗ⁺:
⁷ They have hands, but they handle ⁿᵒᵗ⁺:
Feet have they, but they walk ⁿᵒᵗ⁺:
Neither speak they through their throat.
⁸ They that make them ˢʰᵃˡˡ ᵇᵉ like unto them;
ʸᵉᵃ, every one that trusteth in them.
⁹ O Israel, trust thou in the LORD:
He is their help and their shield.
¹⁰ O house of Aaron, trust ʸᵉ in the LORD:
He is their help and their shield.
¹¹ Ye that fear the LORD, trust in the LORD:
He is their help and their shield.
¹² The LORD hath been mindful of ᵘˢ⁺: he will
bless ᵘˢ⁺;
He will bless the house of Israel;
He will bless the house of Aaron.
¹³ He will bless them that fear the LORD,
Both small and great.
¹⁴ The LORD ˢʰᵃˡˡ increase you more and more,
You and your children.
¹⁵ ᴮˡᵉˢˢᵉᵈ ᵃʳᵉ ʸᵉ of the ᴸᴼᴿᴰ,
ʸᵉ ᵃʳᵉ ᵇˡᵉˢˢᵉᵈ   ᴸᴼᴿᴰ
Which made heaven and earth.
¹⁶ The ʰᵉᵃᵛᵉⁿˢ ᵃʳᵉ ᵗʰᵉ ʰᵉᵃᵛᵉⁿˢ ᵒᶠ ᵗʰᵉ ᴸᴼᴿᴰ;
heaven, ᵉᵛᵉⁿ ᵗʰᵉ ʰᵉᵃᵛᵉⁿˢ, ᵃʳᵉ ᵗʰᵉ ᴸᴼᴿᴰ'ˢ:
But the earth hath he given to the children
of men.
¹⁷ The dead praise not ¹the LORD,

R.V.   ¹ Heb. *Jah.*

Neither any that go down into silence;

¹⁸ But we will bless ¹the Lord
From this time forth and for evermore.
²Praise ʸᵉ the Lord.

116 ¹ I love the Lord, because he hath heard
My voice and my supplications.
² Because he hath inclined his ear unto me,
Therefore will I call *upon him* as long as I live.
³ The sorrows of death compassed me,
And the pains of ³Sheol ⁴gat hold upon me:
I found trouble and sorrow.
⁴ Then called I upon the name of the Lord;
O Lord, I beseech thee, deliver my soul.
⁵ Gracious is the Lord, and righteous;
Yea, our God is merciful.
⁶ The Lord preserveth the simple:
I was brought low, and he helped me.
⁷ Return unto thy rest, O my soul;
For the Lord hath dealt bountifully with thee.
⁸ For thou hast delivered my soul from death,
Mine eyes from tears,
And my feet from falling.
⁹ I will walk before the Lord
In the ⁵land of the living.
¹⁰ ⁶I believe, for I will speak:

R.V. ¹ Heb. *Jah.*   ² Heb. *Hallelujah.*   ³ Or, *the grave*
⁴ Or, *found me*   ⁵ Heb. *lands*   ⁶ Or, *I believed, when I spake* thus

I was greatly afflicted:
11 I said in my ¹haste,
All men are ²ᵃ lie.
                liars.
12 What shall I render unto the LORD
For all his benefits toward me?
13 I will take the cup of salvation,
And call upon the name of the LORD.
14 I will pay my vows unto the LORD,
                                   LORD
Yea, in the presence of all his people.
now
15 Precious in the sight of the LORD
Is the death of his saints.
16 O LORD, truly I am thy servant:
                              servant;
I am thy servant, ₐₙ𝒹 the son of thine handmaid:
                                         handmaid:
Thou hast loosed my bonds.
17 I will offer to thee the sacrifice of thanksgiving,
And will call upon the name of the LORD.
18 I will pay my vows unto the LORD,
                                   LORD
Yea, in the presence of all his people;
now   people,
19 In the courts of the LORD's house,
In the midst of thee, O Jerusalem.
³Praise ye the LORD.

117 ¹ O praise the LORD, all ye nations:
                                      nations:
Laud him, all ye peoples.
praise   people.
² For his mercy   is great toward us:
          merciful kindness   us:
And the truth of the LORD *endureth* for ever.
³Praise ye the LORD.

R.V. ¹ Or, *alarm*   ² Heb. *liars*.   ³ Heb. *Hallelujah*.

118 ¹ O give thanks unto the LORD; for he is good:
For because his mercy *endureth* for ever.

² Let Israel now say,
That his mercy *endureth* for ever.

³ Let the house of Aaron now say,
That his mercy *endureth* for ever.

⁴ Let them now that fear the LORD say,
That his mercy *endureth* for ever.

5 Out of my distress I called upon ¹the LORD LORD in distress:
¹The LORD answered me me, *and set me* in a large place.

⁶ The LORD is on my side; I will not fear:
What can man do unto me?

⁷ The LORD is on taketh my side among part with them that help me:
Therefore shall I see *my desire* upon them that hate me.

⁸ It is better to trust in the LORD
Than to put confidence in man.

⁹ It is better to trust in the LORD
Than to put confidence in princes.

¹⁰ All nations compassed me about:
In but in the name of the LORD I will cut them off. will I destroy them.

¹¹ They compassed me about; yea, they compassed me about:
In but in the name of the LORD I will cut them off. destroy them.

¹² They compassed me about like bees; they are quenched as the fire of thorns:

R.V.　¹ Heb. *Jah.*

211

^{In}/for in the name of the LORD I will ^{cut them off.}/destroy them.

¹³ Thou ^{didst}/hast thrust sore at me that I might fall:
But the LORD helped me.

¹⁴ ¹The LORD is my strength and ^{song:}/song,
And ^{he} is become my salvation.

¹⁵ The voice of rejoicing and salvation is in the
^{tents}/tabernacles of the righteous:
The right hand of the LORD doeth valiantly

¹⁶ The right hand of the LORD is exalted:
The right hand of the LORD doeth valiantly.

¹⁷ I shall not die, but live,
And declare the works of ¹the LORD.

¹⁸ ¹The LORD hath chastened me sore:
But he hath not given me over unto death.

¹⁹ Open to me the gates of righteousness:
I will ^{enter}/go into them, _{and} I will ^{give thanks unto}/praise the ¹the LORD.
LORD:

²⁰ This ^{is the} gate of the ^{LORD;}/LORD,
^{The}/into which the righteous shall enter ^{into it}.

²¹ I will ^{give thanks unto thee,}/praise thee: for thou hast ^{answered}/heard me,
And art become my salvation.

²² The stone which the builders ^{rejected}/refused
Is become the head _{stone} of the corner.

²³ ²This is the LORD's doing;
It is marvellous in our eyes.

²⁴ This is the day which the LORD hath made;
We will rejoice and be glad in it.

²⁵ Save now, ^{we}/I beseech thee, O LORD:

R.V.   ¹ Heb. *Jah*.   ² Heb. *This is from the LORD.*

O Lord, $^{we}_{I}$ beseech thee, send now prosperity.
26 Blessed be he that ¹cometh in the name of the
Lord:
We have blessed you out of the house of the
Lord.
27 $^{The\ Lord\ is\ God,\ and\ he}_{God\ is\ the\ Lord,\ which}$ hath $^{given}_{shewed}$ us light:
Bind the sacrifice with cords, even unto the
horns of the altar.
28 Thou art my God, and I will $^{give\ thanks\ unto}_{praise}$ thee:
Thou art my God, I will exalt thee.
29 O give thanks unto the Lord; for he is good:
For his mercy *endureth* for ever.

119   א ALEPH.

¹ Blessed are $^{they\ that\ are\ ²perfect}_{the\ undefiled}$ in the way,
Who walk in the law of the Lord.
² Blessed are they that keep his testimonies,
$^{That}_{and\ that}$ seek him with the whole heart.
³ $^{Yea,\ they}_{They\ also}$ do no $^{unrighteousness;}_{iniquity:}$
They walk in his ways.
⁴ Thou hast commanded *us* $^{thy\ precepts,}$
$^{That\ we\ should\ observe\ them}_{to\ keep\ thy\ precepts}$ diligently.
⁵ $^{Oh}_{O}$ that my ways were $^{established}_{directed}$
To $^{observe}_{keep}$ thy statutes!
⁶ Then shall I not be ashamed,
When I have respect unto all thy commandments.
⁷ I will $^{give\ thanks\ unto}_{praise}$ thee with uprightness of heart,

R.V.   ¹ Or, *entereth*   ² Or, *upright in way*

When I _{shall have learned}^{learn} thy righteous ^{judgements.}_{judgments.}
⁸ I will ^{observe}_{keep} thy statutes:
O forsake me not utterly.

ב BETH.

⁹ Wherewithal shall a young man cleanse his
   way?
   By taking heed *thereto* according to thy word.
¹⁰ With my whole heart have I sought thee:
   O let me not wander from thy commandments.
¹¹ Thy word have I ^{laid up}_{hid} in mine heart,
   That I might not sin against thee.
¹² Blessed art thou, O LORD:
   Teach me thy statutes.
¹³ With my lips have I declared
   All the ^{judgements}_{judgments} of thy mouth.
¹⁴ I have rejoiced in the way of thy testimonies,
   As much as in all riches.
¹⁵ I will meditate in thy precepts,
   And have respect unto thy ways.
¹⁶ I will delight myself in thy statutes:
   I will not forget thy word.

ג GIMEL.

¹⁷ Deal bountifully with thy servant, that I may
   _{live;}
   live,
   So will I observe
   and keep thy word.
¹⁸ Open thou mine eyes, that I may behold
   Wondrous things out of thy law.

¹⁹ I am a ᵉᵒʲᵒᵘʳⁿᵉʳ/ₛₜᵣₐₙgₑᵣ in the earth:
Hide not thy commandments from me.

²⁰ My soul breaketh for the longing
That it hath unto thy ʲᵘᵈgᵉᵐᵉⁿᵗˢ/ⱼᵤdgₘₑₙₜₛ at all times.

²¹ Thou hast rebuked the proud ¹that are cursed,
Which do ʷᵃⁿᵈᵉʳ/ₑᵣᵣ from thy commandments.

²² ᵀᵃᵏᵉ ᵃʷᵃʸ/ᵣₑₘₒᵥₑ from me reproach and contempt;
For I have kept thy testimonies.

²³ Princes also ᵈᶦᵈ ₛₐₜ sit and ᵗᵃˡᵏᵉᵈ/ₛₚₑₐₖ against me:
But thy servant did meditate in thy statutes.

²⁴ Thy testimonies also are my delight
And ²my ᶜᵒᵘⁿˢᵉˡˡᵒʳˢ./꜀ₒᵤₙₛₑₗₗₑᵣₛ.

ד DALETH.

²⁵ My soul cleaveth unto the dust:
Quicken thou me according to thy word.

²⁶ I ₕₐᵥₑ declared my ways, and thou ᵃⁿˢʷᵉʳᵉᵈˢᵗ/ₕₑₐᵣdₑₛₜ me:
Teach me thy statutes.

²⁷ Make me to understand the way of thy
precepts:
So shall I ᵐᵉᵈᶦᵗᵃᵗᵉ/ₜₐₗₖ of thy wondrous works.

²⁸ My soul ³melteth for heaviness:
Strengthen thou me according unto thy word.

²⁹ Remove from me the way of ᶠᵃˡˢᵉʰᵒᵒᵈ/ₗyᵢₙg:
And grant me thy law graciously.

³⁰ I have chosen the way of ᶠᵃᶦᵗʰᶠᵘˡⁿᵉˢˢ/ₜᵣᵤₜₕ:
Thy ʲᵘᵈgᵉᵐᵉⁿᵗˢ/ⱼᵤdgₘₑₙₜₛ have I ₛₑₜ/ₗₐᵢd *before me.*

R.V. ¹ Or, *Cursed are they which &c.*   ² Heb. *the men of*
my counsel.   ³ Heb. *droppeth.*

³¹ I ^{cleave}_{have stuck} unto thy testimonies:
O Lord, put me not to shame.
³² I will run the way of thy commandments,
When thou shalt enlarge my heart.

ה HE.

³³ Teach me, O Lord, the way of thy statutes;
And I shall keep it unto the end.
³⁴ Give me understanding, and I shall keep thy
law;
Yea, I shall observe it with my whole heart.
³⁵ Make me to go in the path of thy command-
ments;
For therein do I delight.
³⁶ Incline my heart unto thy testimonies,
And not to covetousness.
³⁷ Turn away mine eyes from beholding ^{vanity,}_{vanity;}
And quicken _{thou} me in thy ^{ways.}_{way.}
³⁸ ^{Confirm}_{Stablish} thy word unto thy servant,
¹Which *belongeth* unto the fear of thee.
who *is devoted* to thy fear.
³⁹ Turn away my reproach ^{whereof I am afraid;}_{which I fear:}
For thy ^{judgements}_{judgments} are good.
⁴⁰ Behold, I have longed after thy precepts:
Quicken me in thy righteousness.

ו VAU.

⁴¹ Let thy mercies ^{also come}_{come also} unto me, O Lord,
Even thy salvation, according to thy word.

R.V.   ¹ Or, *Who* is devoted *to*

⁴² So shall I have ^{an answer for}_{wherewith to answer} him that reproacheth ^{me;}_{me:}
For I trust in thy word.
⁴³ And take not the word of truth utterly out of
my mouth;
For I have hoped in thy ^{judgements.}_{judgments.}
⁴⁴ So shall I ^{observe}_{keep} thy law continually
For ever and ever.
⁴⁵ And I will walk at ^{liberty;}_{liberty:}
For I ^{have sought}_{seek} thy precepts.
⁴⁶ I will ^{also} speak of thy testimonies _{also} before
kings,
And will not be ashamed.
⁴⁷ And I will delight myself in thy commandments,
Which I have loved.
⁴⁸ ^{I will lift up my hands also}_{My hands also will I lift up} unto thy commandments,
which I have loved;
And I will meditate in thy statutes.

ז ZAIN.

⁴⁹ Remember the word unto thy servant,
¹^{Because}_{upon which} thou hast ^{made}_{caused} me to hope.
⁵⁰ This is my comfort in my affliction:
²For thy word hath quickened me.
⁵¹ The proud have had me greatly in derision:
Yet have I not ^{swerved}_{declined} from thy law.
⁵² I ^{have} remembered thy ^{judgements}_{judgments} of old, O ^{LORD,}_{LORD;}

R.V. ¹ Or, *Wherein*   ² Or, *That*

And have comforted myself.
53 ¹Hot indignation / Horror hath taken hold upon me, / me,
   Because of the wicked that forsake thy law.
54 Thy statutes have been my songs
   In the house of my pilgrimage.
55 I have remembered thy name, O LORD, in the
      night,
   And have observed / kept thy law.
56 This I have had,
   ²Because I kept thy precepts.

ח CHETH.

57   ³The LORD is my portion
   Thou art my portion, O LORD :
   I have said that I would observe / keep thy words.
58 I intreated thy favour with my whole heart :
   Be merciful unto me according to thy word.
59 I thought on my ways,
   And turned my feet unto thy testimonies.
60 I made haste, and delayed not, / not,
   To observe / keep thy commandments.
61 The cords / bands of the wicked have wrapped me round: / robbed me:
   But I have not forgotten thy law.
62 At midnight I will rise to give thanks unto
      thee
   Because of thy righteous judgements. / judgments.
63 I am a companion of all them that fear thee,
   And of them that observe / keep thy precepts.

R.V. ¹ Or, *Horror*   ² Or, *That I have kept*   ³ Or, *The*
LORD *is my portion, have I said : that I may observe &c.*

⁶⁴ The earth, O Lord, is full of thy mercy :
   Teach me thy statutes.

ט TETH.

⁶⁵ Thou hast dealt well with thy servant,
   O Lord, according unto thy word.
⁶⁶ Teach me good ^judgement_judgment and ^knowledge:_knowledge:
   For I have believed ^in thy commandments.
⁶⁷ Before I was afflicted I went ^astray;_astray:
   But now ^I observe_have I kept thy word.
⁶⁸ Thou art good, and doest good ;
   Teach me thy statutes.
⁶⁹ The proud have forged a lie against me :
   With my whole heart will I keep thy precepts.
   but I will keep thy precepts with my whole heart.
⁷⁰ Their heart is as fat as grease ;
   But I delight in thy law.
⁷¹ It is good for me that I have been afflicted ;
   That I might learn thy statutes.
⁷² The law of thy mouth is better unto me
   Than thousands of gold and silver.

י JOD.

⁷³ Thy hands have made me and ¹fashioned me :
   Give me understanding, that I may learn thy
   commandments.
⁷⁴ They that fear thee ^shall see me and be glad_will be glad when they see me ;
   Because I have hoped in thy word.
⁷⁵ I know, O Lord, that thy ^judgements_judgments are ^righteous,_right,

R.V.   ¹ Or, *established*

219

And that _{thou in faithfulness} hast afflicted me.

⁷⁶ Let, I pray thee, thy _{merciful kindness} be for my comfort,

According to thy word unto thy servant.

⁷⁷ Let thy tender mercies come unto me, that I may live :

For thy law is my delight.

⁷⁸ Let the proud be ashamed ; for they _{dealt} _{overthrown} ¹wrongfully _{perversely with} me _{without a cause} :

But I will meditate in thy precepts.

⁷⁹ Let those that fear thee turn unto me,

²And _{those that have known} thy testimonies.

⁸⁰ Let my heart be _{sound} in thy statutes ;

That I be not ashamed.

כ CAPH.

⁸¹ My soul fainteth for thy salvation :

But I hope in thy word.

⁸² Mine eyes fail for thy word,

_{saying,} When wilt thou comfort me ?

⁸³ For I am become like a ³bottle in the smoke ;

Yet do I not forget thy statutes.

⁸⁴ How many are the days of thy servant ?

When wilt thou execute _{judgment} on them that persecute me ?

⁸⁵ The proud have digged pits for me,

_{which} are not after thy law.

R.V.   ¹ Or, *with falsehood*   ² Another reading is, *Even they that know.*   ³ Or, *wine-skin*

⁸⁶ All thy commandments are faithful:
They persecute me ¹wrongfully; help thou me.
⁸⁷ They had almost consumed me upon earth:
But I forsook not thy precepts.
⁸⁸ Quicken me after thy lovingkindness;
So shall I ^{observe}_{keep} the testimony of thy mouth.

ל LAMED.

⁸⁹ For ever, O Lord,
Thy word is settled in heaven.
⁹⁰ Thy faithfulness is unto all generations:
Thou hast established the earth, and it abideth.
⁹¹ ²They _{continue}^{abide} this day according to thine ^{ordinances;}_{ordinances:}
For all ^{things} are thy servants.
⁹² Unless thy law had been my ^{delight,}_{delights,}
I should then have perished in mine affliction.
⁹³ I will never forget thy ^{precepts:}_{precepts:}
For with them thou hast quickened me.
⁹⁴ I am thine, save me;
For I have sought thy precepts.
⁹⁵ The wicked have waited for me to destroy ^{me;}_{me:}
But I will consider thy testimonies.
⁹⁶ I have seen an end of all ^{perfection;}_{perfection:}
But thy commandment is exceeding broad.

מ MEM.

⁹⁷ ^{Oh}_O how love I thy law!
It is my meditation all the day.

R.V. ¹ Or, *with falsehood* ² Or, *As for thy judgements,*
they abide this day

⁹⁸ Thou through thy [¹Thy] commandments hast made [make] me wiser
  than mine enemies: [enemies;]
  For they are ever with me.
⁹⁹ I have more understanding than all my teachers: [teachers:]
  For thy testimonies are my meditation.
¹⁰⁰ I understand more than the ancients, [aged.]
  Because I have kept [keep] thy precepts.
¹⁰¹ I have refrained my feet from every evil way,
  That I might observe [keep] thy word.
¹⁰² I have not turned aside [departed] from thy judgements: [judgments:]
  For thou hast taught me.
¹⁰³ How sweet are thy words unto my ²taste!
  Yea, sweeter than honey to my mouth!
¹⁰⁴ Through thy precepts I get understanding:
  Therefore I hate every false way.

) NUN.

¹⁰⁵ Thy word is a lamp unto my feet,
  And a light [light] unto my path.
¹⁰⁶ I have sworn, and I will perform [have confirmed] it,
  That I will observe [keep] thy righteous judgements. [judgments.]
¹⁰⁷ I am afflicted very much:
  Quicken me, O Lᴏʀᴅ, according unto thy
  word.
¹⁰⁸ Accept, I beseech thee, the freewill offerings
  of my mouth, O Lᴏʀᴅ,
  And teach me thy judgements. [judgments.]

R.V. ¹ Or, *Thou through thy commandments makest*   ² Heb.
palate.

¹⁰⁹ My soul is continually in my ᴴᵃⁿᵈ: (hand:)
  Yet do I not forget thy law.
¹¹⁰ The wicked have laid a snare for ᵐᵉ: (me:)
  Yet ᵂᵉⁿᵗ ᴵ ⁿᵒᵗ ᵃˢᵗʳᵃʸ (I erred not) from thy precepts.
¹¹¹ Thy testimonies have I taken as an heritage
      for ᵉᵛᵉʳ: (ever:)
  For they are the rejoicing of my heart.
¹¹² I have inclined mine heart to perform thy ˢᵗᵃᵗᵘᵗᵉˢ, (statutes)
  ᶠᵒʳ ᵉᵛᵉʳ, (alway,) even unto the end.

ב SAMECH.

¹¹³ I hate ᵗʰᵉᵐ ᵗʰᵃᵗ ᵃʳᵉ ᵒᶠ ᵃ ᵈᵒᵘᵇˡᵉ ᵐⁱⁿᵈ; (*vain* thoughts:)
  But thy law do I love.
¹¹⁴ Thou art my hiding place and my shield:
  I hope in thy word.
¹¹⁵ Depart from me, ye ᵉᵛⁱˡ-ᵈᵒᵉʳˢ; (evildoers:)
  ᵀʰᵃᵗ ᴵ ᵐᵃʸ (for I will) keep the commandments of my God.
¹¹⁶ Uphold me according unto thy word, that I
      may ˡⁱᵛᵉ; (live:)
  And let me not be ashamed of my hope.
¹¹⁷ Hold thou me up, and I shall be ˢᵃᶠᵉ. (safe:)
  And ˢʰᵃˡˡ (I will) have respect unto thy statutes con-
      tinually.
¹¹⁸ Thou hast ˢᵉᵗ ᵃᵗ ⁿᵒᵘᵍʰᵗ (trodden down) all them that err from thy
      ˢᵗᵃᵗᵘᵗᵉˢ; (statutes:)
  For their deceit is ¹falsehood.
¹¹⁹ Thou ²puttest away all the wicked of the earth
      like dross:

R.V.   ¹ Or, *vain*   ² Heb. *causest to cease.*

Therefore I love thy testimonies.
¹²⁰ My flesh trembleth for fear of thee ;
And I am afraid of thy ^{judgements.}_{judgments.}

ע AIN.

¹²¹ I have done ^{judgement}_{judgment} and justice :
Leave me not to mine oppressors.
¹²² Be surety for thy servant for good :
Let not the proud oppress me.
¹²³ Mine eyes fail for thy salvation,
And for ^{thy righteous word.}_{the word of thy righteousness.}
¹²⁴ Deal with thy servant according unto thy
mercy,
And teach me thy statutes.
¹²⁵ I am thy ^{servant,}_{servant;} give me ^{understanding;}_{understanding,}
That I may know thy testimonies.
¹²⁶ It is time for ^{the LORD to work;}_{*thee*, LORD, to work:}
For they have made void thy law.
¹²⁷ Therefore I love thy commandments
Above ^{gold;}_{gold;} yea, above fine gold.
¹²⁸ Therefore I esteem ¹all *thy* precepts concern-
ing all *things* to be right ;
And I hate every false way.

פ PE.

¹²⁹ Thy testimonies are wonderful :
Therefore doth my soul keep them.

R.V.   ¹ Or, as read by the Sept., Syr. and Vulg., *all thy precepts
to be right*

130 The ^{opening}_{entrance} of thy words giveth light ;
    It giveth understanding unto the simple.
131 I opened ^{wide} my mouth, and ^{panted;}_{panted:}
    For I longed for thy commandments.
132 ^{Turn thee unto}_{Look thou upon} me, and ^{have mercy upon}_{be merciful unto} me,
    As thou usest to do unto those that love thy
    name.
133 Order my ^{footsteps}_{steps} in thy ^{word;}_{word:}
    And let not any iniquity have dominion over
    me.
134 ^{Redeem}_{Deliver} me from the oppression of man :
    So will I ^{observe}_{keep} thy precepts.
135 Make thy face to shine upon thy servant ;
    And teach me thy statutes.
136 ^{Mine eyes}_{Rivers of waters} run down ^{with rivers of water,}_{mine eyes,}
    Because they ^{observe}_{keep} not thy law.

צ   TZADE.
    TZADDI.

137 Righteous art thou, O LORD,
    And upright ¹are thy ^{judgements.}_{judgments.}
138 Thou hast commanded thy testimonies in righteousness
    Thy testimonies *that* thou hast commanded *are* righteous
    And very ^{faithfulness.}_{faithful.}
139 My zeal hath ²consumed me,
    Because mine ^{adversaries}_{enemies} have forgotten thy words.
140 Thy word is very ³^{pure;}_{pure:}
    Therefore thy servant loveth it.
141 I am small and despised :

R.V. ¹ Or, *in thy judgements*   ² Heb. *cut me off.*   ³ Heb.
tried, or, *refined.*

Yet do not I forget thy precepts.

¹⁴² Thy righteousness is an everlasting righteousness,

And thy law is _{the} truth.

¹⁴³ Trouble and anguish have ¹taken hold on me:

Yet thy commandments are my ^{delight.}_{delights.}

¹⁴⁴ ^{Thy testimonies are righteous for ever}
_{The righteousness of thy testimonies *is* everlasting :}

Give me understanding, and I shall live.

פ KOPH.

¹⁴⁵ I ^{have called}_{cried} with my whole heart; ^{answer}_{hear} me, O
LORD :

I will keep thy statutes.

¹⁴⁶ I ^{have called}_{cried} unto thee; save me,

And I shall ^{observe}_{keep} thy testimonies.

¹⁴⁷ I prevented the dawning of the morning, and
cried :

I hoped in thy ^{words.}_{word.}

¹⁴⁸ Mine eyes ^{prevented}_{prevent} the night watches,

That I might meditate in thy word.

¹⁴⁹ Hear my voice according unto thy lovingkindness :

^{Quicken me, O LORD,}_{O LORD, quicken me} ²according to thy ^{judgements.}_{judgment.}

¹⁵⁰ They draw nigh ³that follow after ^{wickedness;}_{mischief:}

They are far from thy law.

¹⁵¹ Thou art ^{nigh,}_{near,} O LORD;

And all thy commandments are truth.

R.V. ¹ Or, *found me*   ² Or, *as thou art wont*   ³ Or,
that persecute me *with wickedness*

152   Of old have I known from thy testimonies,
       Concerning thy testimonies, I have known of old,
       That thou hast founded them for ever.

ר RESH.

153 Consider mine affliction, and deliver me;
       For I do not forget thy law.
154 Plead thou my cause, and redeem me:
       Quicken me according to thy word.
155 Salvation is far from the wicked:
       For they seek not thy statutes.
156 Great are thy tender mercies, O LORD:
       Quicken me according to thy judgements.
157 Many are my persecutors and mine adversaries;
       Yet have I not swerved from thy testimonies.
158 I beheld the treacherous dealers, and ¹was grieved ;
       Because they observe not thy word.
159 Consider how I love thy precepts :
       Quicken me, O LORD, according to thy loving-
          kindness.
160   The sum of thy word is truth;
       Thy word *is* true *from* the beginning:
       And every one of thy righteous judgements en-
          dureth for ever.

שׁ SHIN.
    SCHIN.

161 Princes have persecuted me without a cause:
       But my heart standeth in awe of thy words.
162 I rejoice at thy word,

R.V.   ¹ Or, *loathed* them
227   H 2

As one that findeth great spoil.
163 I hate and abhor ^{falsehood:}_{lying:}
But thy law do I love.
164 Seven times a day do I praise ^{thee,}_{thee}
Because of thy righteous ^{judgements.}_{judgments.}
165 Great peace have they which love thy ^{law:}_{law:}
And ^{they have none occasion of stumbling.}_{nothing shall offend them.}
166 _{LORD,} I have hoped for thy salvation, ^{O LORD,}
And ^{have} done thy commandments.
167 My soul hath ^{observed}_{kept} thy testimonies;
And I love them exceedingly.
168 I have ^{observed}_{kept} thy precepts and thy ^{testimonies:}_{testimonies:}
For all my ways are before thee.

ת TAU.

169 Let my cry come near before thee, O LORD :
Give me understanding according to thy word.
170 Let my supplication come before thee :
Deliver me according to thy word.
171 ^{Let my lips}_{My lips shall} utter ^{praise:}_{praise,}
^{For}_{when} thou ^{teachest}_{hast taught} me thy statutes.
172 ^{Let my}_{My} tongue ^{sing}_{shall speak} of thy ^{word:}_{word:}
For all thy commandments are righteousness.
173 Let thine hand ^{be ready to} help me ;
For I have chosen thy precepts.
174 I have longed for thy salvation, O LORD ;
And thy law is my delight.
175 Let my soul live, and it shall praise thee ;
And let thy ^{judgements}_{judgments} help me.

228

¹⁷⁶ I have gone astray like a lost sheep; seek thy
    servant;
  For I do not forget thy commandments.

120
A Song of ^{Ascents.}/degrees.

¹ In my distress I cried unto the LORD,
  And he ^{answered}/heard me.
² Deliver my soul, O LORD, from lying lips,
  And from a deceitful tongue.
³ What shall be given unto ^{thee, and}/thee? or what shall be
    done ^{more} unto thee,
  Thou ^{deceitful}/false tongue?
⁴ ¹Sharp arrows of the mighty,
  With coals of ²juniper.
⁵ Woe is me, that I sojourn in ^{Meshech,}/Mesech,
  That I dwell ^{among}/in the tents of Kedar!
⁶ My soul hath long ^{had her dwelling}/dwelt
  With him that hateth peace.
⁷ I am *for* peace:
  But when I speak, they are for war.

121
A Song of ^{Ascents.}/degrees.

¹ I will lift up mine eyes unto the ^{mountains:}/hills,
  From whence ^{shall my help come?}/cometh my help.
² My help *cometh* from the LORD,

R.V. ¹ Or, It is as *the sharp arrows of the mighty* man
² Or, *broom*

229

Which made heaven and earth.

3 [1]He will not suffer thy foot to be moved:
He that keepeth thee will not slumber.
4 Behold, he that keepeth Israel
Shall neither slumber nor sleep.
5 The LORD is thy keeper:
The LORD is thy shade upon thy right hand.
6 The sun shall not smite thee by day,
Nor the moon by night.
7 The LORD shall keep/preserve thee from all evil;/evil:
He shall keep/preserve thy soul.
8 The LORD shall keep/preserve thy going out and thy
coming in,/in
From this time forth/forth, and even for evermore.

122

A Song of Ascents;/degrees of David.

1 I was glad when they said unto me,
Let us go unto/into the house of the LORD.
2 Our feet [2]are standing/shall stand
Within thy gates, O Jerusalem;/Jerusalem.
3 Jerusalem, that art/Jerusalem is builded
As a city that is compact together:
4 Whither the tribes go up, even the tribes of [3]the
LORD,
For a/unto the testimony unto/of Israel,
To give thanks unto the name of the LORD.

R.V. [1] Or, *Let him not suffer...let him not slumber that &c.*
[2] Or, *have stood*   [3] Heb. *Jah.*

⁵ For there ¹are set thrones ^{for judgement,}_{of judgment,}
　The thrones of the house of David.
⁶ ²Pray for the peace of Jerusalem : .
　³They shall prosper that love thee.
⁷ Peace be within thy walls,
　And prosperity within thy palaces.
⁸ For my brethren and companions' sakes,
　I will now ⁴say, Peace be within thee.
⁹ ^{For the sake}_{Because} of the house of the Lord our God
　I will seek thy good.

123　　　A Song of ^{Ascents.}_{degrees.}

¹ Unto thee ^{do I lift}_{lift I} up mine eyes,
　O thou that ^{sittest}_{dwellest} in the heavens.
² Behold, as the eyes of servants *look* unto the
　hand of their ^{master,}_{masters,}
　_{and} ^{As}_{as} the eyes of a maiden unto the hand of
　her mistress ;
　So our eyes ^{look unto}_{wait upon} the Lord our God,
　Until _{that} he have mercy upon us.
³ Have mercy upon us, O Lord, have mercy
　upon us :
　For we are exceedingly filled with contempt.
⁴ Our soul is exceedingly filled
　With the scorning of those that are at ease,
　And with the contempt of the proud.

R.V. ¹ Or, *were*　² Or, *Salute ye Jerusalem*　　³ Or, *May*
they　⁴ Or, *speak peace concerning thee*

231

124
A Song of $^{\text{Ascents};}_{\text{degrees}}$ of David.

1 If it had not been the LORD who was on our
side,
$^{\text{Let Israel now}}_{\text{now may Israel}}$ say;
2 If it had not been the LORD who was on our
side,
When men rose up against us:
3 Then they had swallowed us up $^{\text{alive,}}_{\text{quick,}}$
When their wrath was kindled against us:
4 Then the waters had overwhelmed us,
The stream had gone over our soul:
5 Then the proud waters had gone over our
soul.
6 Blessed be the LORD,
Who hath not given us as a prey to their
teeth.
7 Our soul is escaped as a bird out of the snare
of the fowlers:
The snare is broken, and we are escaped.
8 Our help is in the name of the LORD,
Who made heaven and earth.

125
A Song of $^{\text{Ascents.}}_{\text{degrees.}}$

1 They that trust in the LORD
$^{\text{Are}}_{\text{shall be}}$ as mount Zion, which cannot be $^{\text{moved,}}_{\text{removed,}}$
but abideth for ever.
2 As the mountains are round about Jerusalem,

So the LORD is round about his people,
From this time forth and for evermore.

³ For the sceptre of wickedness shall not rest upon the
lot of the righteous;
That the righteous put not forth their hands unto
iniquity.

⁴ Do good, O LORD, unto those that be good,
And to them that are upright in their hearts.

⁵ But as for such as turn aside unto their crooked
ways,
The LORD shall lead them forth with the
workers of iniquity:
Peace be upon Israel.

126　　A Song of Ascents.

¹ When the LORD ¹turned again the captivity of
Zion,
We were like unto them that dream.

² Then was our mouth filled with laughter,
And our tongue with singing:
Then said they among the nations,
The LORD hath done great things for them.

³ The LORD hath done great things for us;
Whereof we are glad.

⁴ Turn again our captivity, O LORD,
As the streams in the South.

⁵ They that sow in tears shall reap in joy.

R.V. ¹ Or, *brought back those that returned to Zion*

6 Though he ^{He that} goeth ^{on his way weeping,}_{forth and weepeth,} 1bearing ^{forth the seed;}_{precious seed,}
^{He shall}_{shall doubtless} come again with ^{joy,}_{rejoicing,} bringing his
sheaves *with him.*

127
A Song of ^{Ascents;}_{degrees} ^{of}_{for} Solomon.

¹ Except the LORD build the house,
They labour in vain that build it :
Except the LORD keep the city,
The watchman waketh but in vain.
² It is vain for you ^{that}_{to} ye rise up early, ^{and so late}_{to sit up}
_{take rest,}
_{late,}
^{And}_{to} eat the bread of _{sorrows}^{toil} :
For so he giveth ^{unto} his beloved ²sleep.
³ Lo, children are an heritage of the LORD :
And the fruit of the womb is *his* reward.
⁴ As arrows _{are} in the hand of a mighty ^{man,}_{man;}
So are ^{the} children of _{the} youth.
⁵ Happy is the man that hath his quiver full of
them :
They shall not be ashamed,
^{When they}_{but they shall} speak with ^{their}_{the} enemies in the gate.

128
A Song of ^{Ascents.}_{degrees.}

¹ Blessed is every one that feareth the ^{LORD,}_{LORD;}
That walketh in his ways.
² For thou shalt eat the labour of thine hands :

R.V. ¹ Or, *bearing the measure of seed*   ² Or, *in sleep*

Happy shalt thou be, and it shall be well with thee.

3 Thy wife shall be as a fruitful ^{vine, in the innermost parts} _{vine by the sides} of thine house:

Thy children like olive ^{plants,} _{plants} round about thy table.

4 Behold, that thus shall the man be blessed
That feareth the LORD.

5 The LORD ¹shall bless thee out of Zion:
And ²thou shalt see the good of Jerusalem all the days of thy life.

6 Yea, thou shalt see thy children's ^{children.} _{children,}
^{³Peace be} _{and peace} upon Israel.

129   A Song of ^{Ascents.} _{degrees.}

1 ⁴Many a time have they afflicted me from my ^{youth up,} _{youth,}
^{Let} _{may} Israel now ^{say:} _{say:}

2 ⁴Many a time have they afflicted me from my youth ^{up}:
Yet they have not prevailed against me.

3 The plowers plowed upon my ^{back:} _{back:}
They made long their furrows.

4 The LORD is righteous:
He hath cut asunder the cords of the wicked.

5 Let them _{all} be ^{ashamed} _{confounded} and turned ^{backward,} _{back}

^{All they} that hate Zion.

⁶ Let them be as the grass upon the housetops,
Which withereth afore it ¹groweth up:

⁷ Wherewith the ^{reaper}_{mower} filleth not his ^{hand,}_{hand;}
Nor he that bindeth sheaves his bosom.

⁸ Neither do they which go by say,
The blessing of the LORD be upon ^{you;}_{you:}
We bless you in the name of the LORD.

130   A Song of ^{Ascents.}_{degrees.}

¹ Out of the depths have I cried unto thee, O
LORD.

² Lord, hear my voice:
Let thine ears be attentive
To the voice of my supplications.

³ If thou, ²LORD, shouldest mark iniquities,
O Lord, who shall stand?

⁴ But there is forgiveness with thee,
That thou mayest be feared.

⁵ I wait for the LORD, my soul doth wait,
And in his word do I hope.

⁶ My soul ^{looketh}_{waiteth} for the ^{Lord,}_{Lord}
More than ^{watchmen look}_{they that watch} for the ^{morning:}_{morning:}
^{Yea,}_{I say,} *more than* _{they that watch}^{watchmen} for the morning.

⁷ ^{O Israel,}_{Let Israel} hope in the ^{LORD;}_{LORD:}
For with the LORD there is mercy,
And with him is plenteous redemption.

R.V.   ¹ Or, *be plucked up*   ² Heb. *Jah.*

⁸ And he shall redeem Israel
From all his iniquities.

131

A Song of Ascents; of David.
degrees

¹ LORD, my heart is not haughty, nor mine eyes
lofty;
lofty:
Neither do I ¹exercise myself in great matters,
Or in things too wonderful for me.
high
² Surely I have stilled and quieted my soul;
behaved myself,
Like a weaned child that is weaned of his mother,
as a with mother:
My soul is with me like a weaned child.
even as
³ O Israel, hope in the LORD
Let Israel
From this time forth and for evermore.
henceforth ever.

132

A Song of Ascents.
degrees.

¹ LORD, remember for David David,
All his affliction;
and all afflictions:
² How he sware unto the LORD,
And vowed unto the Mighty One of Jacob:
mighty God Jacob:
³ Surely I will not come into the ²tabernacle of
my house,
Nor go up into ³my bed;
⁴ I will not give sleep to mine eyes,
Or slumber to mine eyelids;
eyelids,
⁵ Until I find out a place for the LORD,

R.V. ¹ Heb. *walk*.   ² Heb. *tent*.   ³ Heb. *the couch of
my bed*.

¹A tabernacle / an habitation for the Mighty One / mighty *God* of Jacob.
6 Lo, we heard of it in ³Ephrathah / at Ephratah :
  We found it in the field / fields of ³the wood.
7 We will go into his tabernacles; / tabernacles:
  We will worship at his footstool.
8 Arise, O LORD, into thy resting place ; / rest
  Thou, and the ark of thy strength.
9 Let thy priests be clothed with righteousness ;
  And let thy saints shout for joy.
10 For thy servant David's sake
   Turn not away the face of thine anointed.
11 The LORD hath sworn unto David in truth / *in* truth unto David ;
   He will not turn from it: / it:
   Of the fruit of thy body will I set upon thy
     throne.
12 If thy children will keep my covenant
   And my testimony that I shall teach them,
   Their children also shall / shall also sit upon thy throne for
     evermore.
13 For the LORD hath chosen Zion ;
   He hath desired it for his habitation.
14 This is my resting place / rest for ever :
   Here will I dwell ; for I have desired it.
15 I will ⁴abundantly bless her provision :
   I will satisfy her poor with bread.
16 Her priests also will I clothe / I will also clothe her priests with salvation :
   And her saints shall shout aloud for joy.

R.V. ¹ Heb. *Tabernacles.*   ² Or, *Ephraim*   ³ Or, *Jaar*
See 1 Chr. 13. 5.   ⁴ Or, *surely*

¹⁷ There will I make ¹the horn of David to bud :
  I have ²ordained a lamp for mine anointed.
¹⁸ His enemies will I clothe with shame :
  But upon himself shall his crown flourish.

133
A Song of Ascents; of David.

¹ Behold, how good and how pleasant it is
  For brethren to dwell together in unity !
² It is like the precious ointment upon the head,
  That ran down upon the beard,
  Even Aaron's beard :
  That came down upon the skirt of his garments ;
³ Like the dew of Hermon,
  That cometh down and as the dew that descended upon the mountains of
      Zion :
  For there the LORD commanded the blessing,
  Even life for evermore.

134
A Song of Ascents.

¹ Behold, bless ye the LORD, all ye servants of
      the LORD,
  Which by night stand in the house of the
      LORD.
² Lift up your hands ⁴to the sanctuary,
  And bless ye the LORD.

R.V. ¹ Or, *a horn to spring forth unto David*   ² Or, *prepared*
³ Or, *collar*   ⁴ Or, *in holiness*

239

³ The Lord bless thee out of Zion:
that made heaven and earth
Even he that made heaven and earth,
bless thee out of Zion.

135

¹ ¹Praise ye the Lord.
Praise ye the name of the Lord;
Praise *him*, O ye servants of the Lord:

² Ye that stand in the house of the Lord,
In the courts of the house of our God.

³ Praise ʸᵉ the Lord; for the Lord is good:
Sing praises unto his name; for it is pleasant.

⁴ For ²the Lord hath chosen Jacob unto himself,
And Israel for his peculiar treasure.

⁵ For I know that the Lord is great,
And that our Lord is above all gods.

⁶ Whatsoever the Lord pleased, that hath he done,
did he
In heaven, and in earth, in the seas, and in all deeps.
all deep places.

⁷ He causeth the vapours to ascend from the
ends of the earth;
He maketh lightnings for the rain;
He bringeth ᶠᵒʳᵗʰ the wind out of his treasuries.

⁸ Who smote the firstborn of Egypt,
Both of man and beast.

⁹ He sent signs and wonders into the midst of
Who tokens
thee, O Egypt,
Upon Pharaoh, and upon all his servants.

¹⁰ Who smote ³many nations,
great
And slew mighty kings;

R.V. ¹ Heb. *Hallelujah.*   ² Heb. *Jah.*   ³ Or, *great*

¹¹ Sihon king of the Amorites,
And Og king of Bashan,
And all the kingdoms of Canaan:
¹² And gave their land for an heritage,
An heritage unto Israel his people.
¹³ Thy name, O Lord, *endureth* for ever;
Thy *and thy* memorial, O Lord, throughout all generations.
¹⁴ For the Lord shall *will* judge his people,
And he will repent himself concerning his
servants.

¹⁵ ¹The idols of the nations *heathen* are silver and gold,
The work of men's hands.
¹⁶ They have mouths, but they speak not;
Eyes have they, but they see not;
¹⁷ They have ears, but they hear not;
Neither is there any breath in their mouths.
¹⁸ They that make them shall be *are* like unto them *them*:
Yea, *so is* every one that trusteth in them.
19 O house of Israel, bless ye the Lord:
Bless the Lord, O house of Israel:
O house of Aaron, bless ye the Lord:
bless the Lord, O house of Aaron:
20 O house of Levi, bless ye the Lord:
Bless the Lord, O house of Levi:
Ye that fear the Lord, bless ye the Lord.
²¹ Blessed be the Lord out of Zion,
Who *which* dwelleth at Jerusalem.
²Praise ye the Lord.

R.V.   ¹ See Ps. 115. 4, &c.   ² Heb. *Hallelujah.*

136 ¹ O give thanks unto the Lord ; for he is good :
For his mercy *endureth* for ever.
² O give thanks unto the God of gods :
For his mercy *endureth* for ever.
³ O give thanks ᵘⁿᵗᵒ the Lord of lords :
For his mercy *endureth* for ever.
⁴ To him who alone doeth great wonders :
For his mercy *endureth* for ever.
⁵ To him that by ᵘⁿᵈᵉʳˢᵗᵃⁿᵈⁱⁿᵍ_wisdom made the heavens :
For his mercy *endureth* for ever.
⁶ To him that ˢᵖʳᵉᵃᵈ ᶠᵒʳᵗʰ_stretched out the earth above the waters :
For his mercy *endureth* for ever.
⁷ To him that made great lights :
For his mercy *endureth* for ever :
⁸ The sun to rule by day :
For his mercy *endureth* for ever :
⁹ The moon and stars to rule by night :
For his mercy *endureth* for ever.
¹⁰ To him that smote Egypt in their firstborn :
For his mercy *endureth* for ever :
¹¹ And brought out Israel from among them :
For his mercy *endureth* for ever :
¹² With a strong hand, and with a stretched out arm :
For his mercy *endureth* for ever.
¹³ To him which divided the Red Sea in sunder_sea into parts :
For his mercy *endureth* for ever :

[14] And made Israel to pass through the midst of it:
For his mercy *endureth* for ever:
[15] But [1]overthrew Pharaoh and his host in the
Red ^{Sea}_{sea}:
For his mercy *endureth* for ever.
[16] To him which led his people through the
wilderness:
For his mercy *endureth* for ever.
[17] To him which smote great kings:
For his mercy *endureth* for ever:
[18] And slew famous kings:
For his mercy *endureth* for ever:
[19] Sihon king of the Amorites:
For his mercy *endureth* for ever:
[20] And Og _{the} king of Bashan:
For his mercy *endureth* for ever:
[21] And gave their land for an heritage:
For his mercy *endureth* for ever:
[22] Even an heritage unto Israel his servant:
For his mercy *endureth* for ever.
[23] Who remembered us in our low estate:
For his mercy *endureth* for ever:
[24] And hath ^{delivered}_{redeemed} us from our ^{adversaries}_{enemies}:
For his mercy *endureth* for ever.
[25] ^{He}_{Who} giveth food to all flesh:
For his mercy *endureth* for ever.
[26] O give thanks unto the God of heaven:
For his mercy *endureth* for ever.

137 ¹ By the rivers of Babylon,
There we sat down, yea, we wept,
When we remembered Zion.

2 Upon the willows in the midst thereof
  We hanged our harps
We hanged up our harps,
  upon the willows in the midst thereof.

³ For there they that _{carried}^{led} us _{away} captive required
of us _{a song;}^{¹songs,}

And ²they that wasted us *required of us* mirth,
saying,

Sing us one of the songs of Zion.

⁴ How shall we sing the LORD's song
In a strange land?

⁵ If I forget thee, O Jerusalem,
Let my right hand forget *her cunning*.

6 Let my tongue cleave to the roof of my mouth,
      If I do not remember thee,
If I remember thee not;
  let my tongue cleave to the roof of my mouth;

If I prefer not Jerusalem
Above my chief joy.

⁷ Remember, O LORD, ^{against} the children of Edom
_{in the}^{The} day of Jerusalem;
Who said, Rase it, rase it,
Even to the foundation thereof.

⁸ O daughter of Babylon, _{who}^{³that} art to be destroyed;
Happy shall he be, that rewardeth thee
As thou hast served us.

R.V.   ¹ Heb. *words of song.*   ² Or, *our tormentors*   ³ Or,
that art laid waste

⁹ Happy shall he be, that taketh and dasheth
　　thy little ones
　　Against the _{stones.}^{rock.}

138   *A Psalm* of David.

¹ I will ^{give thee thanks}_{praise thee} with my whole heart:
　　Before the gods will I sing ^{praises}_{praise} unto thee.
² I will worship toward thy holy temple,
　　And ^{give thanks unto}_{praise} thy name for thy lovingkindness
　　　and for thy truth:
　　For thou hast magnified thy word above all
　　　thy name.
³ In the day ^{that I called}_{when I cried} thou answeredst me,
　　^{Thou didst encourage}_{and strengthenedst} me with strength in my soul.
⁴ All the kings of the earth shall ^{give thee thanks,}_{praise thee,} O
　　LORD,
　　^{For}_{when} they ^{have heard}_{hear} the words of thy mouth.
⁵ Yea, they shall sing ^{of}_{in} the ways of the
　　^{LORD;}_{LORD:}
　　For great is the glory of the LORD.
⁶ ^{For though}_{Though} the LORD be high, yet hath he respect
　　unto the lowly:
　　But the ^{haughty}_{proud} he knoweth ^{from afar.}_{afar off.}
⁷ Though I walk in the midst of trouble, thou
　　wilt revive ^{me;}_{me:}
　　Thou shalt stretch forth thine hand against the
　　　wrath of mine enemies,
　　And thy right hand shall save me.

⁸ The LORD will perfect that which concerneth
　　me :
　　Thy mercy, O LORD, *endureth* for ever:
　　Forsake not the works of thine own hands.

139　　For the Chief Musician.
　　　　　To the chief Musician,　A Psalm of David.

¹ O LORD, thou hast searched me, and known
　　me.
² Thou knowest my downsitting and mine up-
　　rising,
　　Thou understandest my thought afar off.
³ Thou ¹searchest out my path and my lying down,
　　　compassest
　　And art acquainted with all my ways.
⁴ For there is not a word in my tongue,
　　But, lo, O LORD, thou knowest it altogether.
⁵ Thou hast beset me behind and before,
　　And laid thine hand upon me.
⁶ *Such* knowledge is too wonderful for me ;
　　It is high, I cannot attain unto it.
⁷ Whither shall I go from thy spirit ?
　　Or whither shall I flee from thy presence ?
⁸ If I ascend up into heaven, thou art there :
　　If I make my bed in Sheol, behold, thou art
　　　　　　　　　　　　　hell,
　　there.
⁹ If I take the wings of the morning,
　　And dwell in the uttermost parts of the sea ;
¹⁰ Even there shall thy hand lead me,

R.V.　¹ Or, *winnowest*

And thy right hand shall hold me.

11 If I say, Surely the darkness shall [1]overwhelm me, cover me;

    [2]And the light about me shall be night; even the night shall be light about me.

12 Even Yea, the darkness hideth not from thee, thee;

    But the night shineth as the day:

    The darkness and the light are both alike *to thee.*

13 For thou hast [3]possessed my reins:

    Thou hast [4]covered me in my mother's womb.

14 I will give thanks unto praise thee; for I am fearfully and wonderfully made:

    Wonderful marvellous are thy works;

    And that my soul knoweth right well.

15 My frame substance was not hidden hid from thee,

    When I was made in secret,

    And curiously wrought in the lowest parts of the earth.

16 Thine eyes did see my mine unperfect substance, substance, yet being unperfect;

    And in thy book [5]were all *my members* all *my members* were written,

    Which day by day in continuance were fashioned,

    When as yet there was none of them.

17 How precious also are thy thoughts unto me, O God!

    How great is the sum of them!

18 If I should count them, they are more in number than the sand:

R.V. [1] Or, *cover me* [2] Or, *Then the night shall be light about me* [3] Or, *formed* [4] Or, *knit me together* [5] Or, *they were all written,* even *the days that were ordained*

247

When I awake, I am still with thee.
¹⁹ ¹Surely thou wilt slay the wicked, O God:
Depart from me therefore, ye ^{bloodthirsty}_{bloody} men.
²⁰ For they ²speak against thee wickedly,
And thine enemies ³take *thy name* in vain.
²¹ Do not I hate them, O Lord, that hate thee?
And ⁴am not I grieved with those that rise up
against thee?
²² I hate them with perfect hatred:
I count them mine enemies.
²³ Search me, O God, and know my heart:
Try me, and know my thoughts:
²⁴ And see if there be any ^{way of 5wickedness}_{wicked way} in me,
And lead me in the way everlasting.

140   For the Chief Musician.   A Psalm of David.
To the chief Musician,

¹ Deliver me, O Lord, from the evil ^{man:}_{man:}
Preserve me from the violent ^{man:}_{man;}
² Which imagine mischiefs in their heart;
Continually ^{do they 6gather themselves}_{are they gathered} together for war.
³ They have sharpened their ^{tongue}_{tongues} like a serpent;
Adders' poison is under their lips. _{Selah.}   [Selah
⁴ Keep me, O Lord, from the hands of the
wicked;
Preserve me from the violent ^{man:}_{man;}

R.V. ¹ Or, *Oh that thou wouldest slay*   ² Or, *utter thy
name* (Heb. *thee*) Or, as otherwise read, *rebel against thee*   ³ Or,
lift themselves up against thee *for vanity*   ⁴ Or, *do not I loathe*
⁵ Or, *grief*   ⁶ Or, *stir up wars*

Who have purposed to ^{thrust aside}_{overthrow} my ^{steps.}_{goings.}

⁵ The proud have hid a snare for me, and cords;
They have spread a net by the ^{way side}_{wayside};
They have set gins for me.   Selah.   [Selah

⁶ I said unto the LORD, Thou art my God:
^{Give ear unto}_{hear} the voice of my supplications, O
LORD.

⁷ O GOD the Lord, the strength of my salvation,
Thou hast covered my head in the day of
battle.

⁸ Grant not, O LORD, the desires of the ^{wicked:}_{wicked:}
Further not his _{wicked}^{evil} device; *lest* they exalt
themselves.   Selah.   [Selah

⁹ As for the head of those that compass me about,
Let the mischief of their own lips cover them.

¹⁰ Let burning coals fall upon them:
Let them be cast into the fire;
Into ¹deep pits, that they rise not up again.

¹¹ ²An evil speaker shall not be established in the earth:
_{Let not an evil speaker}
Evil shall hunt the violent man to overthrow
him.

¹² I know that the LORD will maintain the cause
of the afflicted,
And the right of the ^{needy.}_{poor.}

¹³ Surely the righteous shall give thanks unto thy
name:
The upright shall dwell in thy presence.

R.V.   ¹ Or, *floods*   ² Heb. *A man of tongue.*

249

141   A Psalm of David.

1 LORD, I ^{have called upon thee;} make haste unto ^{me:}_{me;}
   _{cry unto thee:}
   Give ear unto my voice, when I ^{call} unto thee.
   _{cry}

2 Let my prayer be set forth ^{as incense before thee.}
   _{before thee *as* incense ;}
   ^{The} lifting up of my hands as the evening
   _{*and* the}
         ¹sacrifice.

3 Set a watch, O LORD, before my mouth;
   Keep the door of my lips.

4 Incline not my heart to any evil thing,
   To ^{be occupied in deeds of wickedness}
      _{practise wicked works}
   With men that work iniquity:
   And let me not eat of their dainties.

5 Let the righteous smite ^{me,} *it shall be* a ^{kindness;}
                            _{me;}   _{kindness:}
   And let him reprove ^{me,} *it shall be* ^{as} oil upon the head;
                        _{me;}   _{an excellent oil,}
   _{Let not my head refuse it:}
   which shall not break my head:
      ²For ^{even in their ³wickedness shall my prayer continue.}
            _{yet my prayer also *shall be* in their calamities.}

6   ^{Their} judges are ^{thrown down by the sides of the rock;}
   _{When their}   _{overthrown in stony places,}
   ^{And} they shall hear my words; for they are
         sweet.

7 As when one ploweth and cleaveth the earth,
      Our bones are scattered at the grave's mouth,
   ⁴Our bones are scattered at ⁵the grave's mouth..
      as when one cutteth and cleaveth *wood* upon the earth.

8 ^{For} mine eyes are unto thee, O GOD the Lord:
   _{But}
   In thee ^{do I put} my trust; ⁶leave not my soul
           _{is}
         destitute.

R.V. ¹ Or, *oblation*   ² Or, *For still is my prayer against
their wickedness*   ³ Or, *calamities*   ⁴ According to some
ancient authorities, *Their.*   ⁵ Heb. *the mouth of Sheol.*   ⁶ Or,
pour thou not out my life

⁹ Keep me from the ₛₙₐᵣₑₛ^snare which they have laid for me,
And ᶠʳᵒᵐ the gins of the workers of iniquity.
¹⁰ Let the wicked fall into their own nets,
Whilst that I withal ¹escape.

142 Maschil of ᴅₐᵥᵢ𝑑^David, David; A Prayer when he was in the cave; a Prayer. cave.

¹ I ꜀ᵣᵢₑ𝑑^cry with my voice unto the LORD .
 ᴄᵣᵢₑ𝑑 unto the LORD with my voice;
With my voice unto the LORD 𝑑ᵢ𝑑^do I make ₘy supplication.
² I ₚₒᵤᵣₑ𝑑^pour out my complaint before him;
I ₛₕₑwₑ𝑑^shew before him my trouble.
³ When my spirit ²was overwhelmed within me,
 ₜₕₑₙ thou knewest my path.
In the way wherein I wₐₗₖₑ𝑑^walk have they ₚᵣᵢᵥᵢₗy ₗₐᵢ𝑑^hidden a snare for me.
⁴ ᵢ ₗₒₒₖₑ𝑑^³Look on *my* right hand, and ᵦₑₕₑₗ𝑑, ᵦᵤₜ ₜₕₑᵣₑ wₐₛ^see; for there is no man that wₒᵤₗ𝑑 ₖₙₒw^knoweth me:
Refuge ʰᵃᵗʰ failed me; no man ꜀ₐᵣₑ𝑑^careth for my soul.
⁵ I cried unto thee, O ᴸᴼᴿᴰ:^LORD:
I said, Thou art my ᵣₑfᵤgₑ^refuge,
 ₐₙ𝑑 ₘy^My portion in the land of the living.
⁶ Attend unto my cry; for I am brought very low:

R.V. ¹ Heb. *pass over*.   ² Or, *fainted*   ³ According to some ancient versions, *I looked...and saw &c.*

251

Deliver me from my persecutors; for they are stronger than I.

7 Bring my soul out of prison, that I may ^{give thanks unto} praise thy name:

The righteous shall ¹compass me about;

For thou shalt deal bountifully with me.

143   A Psalm of David.

1 Hear my prayer, O LORD; give ear to my supplications:

In thy faithfulness answer me, *and* in thy righteousness.

2 And enter not into judgement with thy servant:

For in thy sight shall no man living be justified.

3 For the enemy hath persecuted my soul;

He hath smitten my life down to the ground:

He hath made me to dwell in dark places, as those that have been long dead.

4 Therefore ²is my spirit overwhelmed within me;

My heart within me is desolate.

5 I remember the days of old;

I meditate on all thy doings;

I muse on the work of thy hands.

6 I spread forth my hands unto thee:

R.V. ¹ Or, *crown themselves because of me*   ² Or, *my spirit fainteth*

My soul *thirsteth* after thee, as a ^{weary} thirsty land.
[Selah

Selah.
7 Make haste to answer me, O Lord: my spirit faileth:
Hear me speedily,
Hide not thy face from me;
me,
Lest I become like them that go down into the pit.
be like unto
8 Cause me to hear thy lovingkindness in the
morning;
For in thee do I trust:
Cause me to know the way wherein I should
walk;
For I lift up my soul unto thee.
9 Deliver me, O Lord, from mine enemies:
¹I flee unto thee to hide me.
10 Teach me to do thy will; for thou art my God:
²Thy spirit is good; lead me into ²the land of
in
uprightness.
11 Quicken me, O Lord, for thy name's sake:
In thy righteousness bring my soul out of trouble.
for righteousness' sake
12 And in thy lovingkindness cut off mine enemies,
of mercy
And destroy all them that afflict my soul;
soul:
For I am thy servant.

144

A Psalm of David.

1 Blessed be the Lord my rock,
strength,
Which teacheth my hands to war,
And my fingers to fight:

R.V. ¹ Heb. *Unto thee have I hidden.* ² Or, *Let thy good*
spirit lead me ³ Or, *a plain country*

2 My ^{lovingkindness,}_{goodness,} and my ^{fortress,}_{fortress;}
　My high tower, and my deliverer ;
　My shield, and he in whom I trust ;
　Who subdueth my people under me.
3 LORD, what is man, that thou takest knowledge
　of ^{him?}_{him !}
　Or the son of man, that thou makest account
　of ^{him?}_{him !}
4 Man is like to ¹vanity :
　His days are as a shadow that passeth away.
5 Bow thy heavens, O LORD, and come down :
　Touch the mountains, and they shall smoke.
6 Cast forth lightning, and scatter ^{them ;}_{them !}
　^{Send}_{shoot} out thine arrows, and ^{discomfit}_{destroy} them.
7 ^{Stretch forth}_{Send} thine hand from above ;
　^{Rescue}_{rid} me, and deliver me out of great waters,
　^{Out of}_{from} the hand of ^{strangers}_{strange children} ;
8 Whose mouth speaketh vanity,
　And their right hand is a right hand of false-
　　hood.
9 I will sing a new song unto thee, O God :
　Upon a psaltery *and* an instrument of ten strings will
　　I sing praises unto thee.
10 It is he that giveth salvation unto kings :
　Who ^{rescueth}_{delivereth} David his servant from the hurtful
　　sword.
11 ^{Rescue}_{Rid} me, and deliver me ^{out}_{from} of the hand of
　　^{strangers,}_{strange children,}

R.V.　¹ Heb. *a breath.*

Whose mouth speaketh vanity,
And their right hand is a right hand of ^{falsehood.}_{falsehood:}

12 ^{When}_{That} our sons ^{shall be}_{may be} as plants grown up in their
   youth;
   ^{And}_{that} our daughters _{may be} as corner ^{stones hewn}_{stones, polished}
   after the _{similitude}^{fashion} of a _{palace:}^{palace;}
13 ^{When}_{That} our garners _{may be}^{are} full, affording all manner
   of ^{store;}_{store:}
   ^{And}_{that} our sheep _{may} bring forth thousands and ten
   thousands in our _{streets:}^{fields;}
14 ^{When}_{That} our oxen _{may be} ^{are well laden} strong to labour;
   ^{When}_{That} *there* ^{is}_{be} no breaking in, ^{and no}_{nor} ¹going ^{forth,}_{out;}
   ^{And}_{that *there be*} no ^{outcry}_{complaining} in our ^{streets;}_{streets.}
15 Happy ^{is the}_{*is that*} people, that is in such a case:
   Yea, happy ^{is the}_{*is that*} people, whose God is the
   Lord.

145   *A Psalm of* praise; of David.
         David's *Psalm* of praise.

¹ I will extol thee, my God, O ^{King;}_{king;}
  And I will bless thy name for ever and ever.
² Every day will I bless thee;
  And I will praise thy name for ever and ever.
³ Great is the Lord, and ^{highly}_{greatly} to be praised;
  And his greatness is unsearchable.
⁴ One generation shall _{praise}^{laud} thy works to another,
  And shall declare thy mighty acts.

R.V.   ¹ Or, *sallying*

⁵ I will speak ^{Of} of the glorious ^{majesty}_{honour} of ^{thine honour,}_{thy majesty,}
And of thy wondrous ^{works, will I meditate.}_{works.}

⁶ And men shall speak of the might of thy
terrible ^{acts;}_{acts:}
And I will declare thy greatness.

⁷ They shall _{abundantly} utter the memory of thy
great goodness,
And shall sing of thy righteousness.

⁸ The LORD is gracious, and full of compassion;
Slow to anger, and of great mercy.

⁹ The LORD is good to ^{all;}_{all:}
And his tender mercies are over all his works.

¹⁰ All thy works shall ^{give thanks unto}_{praise} thee, O LORD;
And thy saints shall bless thee.

¹¹ They shall speak of the glory of thy kingdom,
And talk of thy power;

¹² To make known to the sons of men his mighty
acts,
And the ^{glory of the}_{glorious} majesty of his kingdom.

¹³ Thy kingdom is an everlasting kingdom,
And thy dominion *endureth* throughout all
generations.

¹⁴ The LORD upholdeth all that fall,
And raiseth up all those that be bowed down.

¹⁵ The eyes of all wait upon thee;
And thou givest them their meat in due season.

¹⁶ Thou openest thine hand,
And [1]satisfiest the desire of every living thing.

R.V.   [1] Or, *satisfiest every living thing with favour*

¹⁷ The LORD is righteous in all his ways,
And ^{gracious}_{holy} in all his works.
¹⁸ The LORD is nigh unto all them that call upon
him,
To all that call upon him in truth.
¹⁹ He will fulfil the desire of them that fear ^{him}_{him};
He also will hear their cry, and will save them.
²⁰ The LORD preserveth all them that love ^{him}_{him};
But all the wicked will he destroy.
²¹ My mouth shall speak the praise of the ^{LORD}_{LORD};
And let all flesh bless his holy name for ever
and ever.

146 ¹ ¹Praise ye the LORD.
Praise the LORD, O my soul.
² While I live will I praise the LORD:
I will sing praises unto my God while I have
any being.
³ Put not your trust in princes,
Nor in the son of man, in whom there is no
help.
⁴ His breath goeth forth, he returneth to his
earth;
In that very day his ²thoughts perish.
⁵ Happy is he that hath the God of Jacob for
his help,
Whose hope is in the LORD his God:
⁶ Which made ^{heaven}_{heaven} and earth,

R.V.   ¹ Heb. *Hallelujah.*   ² Or, *purposes*

257   I

The sea, and all that ^{in them is;}_{therein *is:*}
Which keepeth truth for ever:
⁷ Which executeth ^{judgement}_{judgment} for the ^{oppressed;}_{oppressed:}
Which giveth food to the ^{hungry:}_{hungry.}
The LORD looseth the ^{prisoners;}_{prisoners:}
⁸ The LORD openeth *the eyes of* the ^{blind;}_{blind:}
The LORD raiseth ^{up} them that are bowed ^{down;}_{down:}
The LORD loveth the ^{righteous;}_{righteous:}
⁹ The LORD preserveth the strangers;
He ^{upholdeth}_{relieveth} the fatherless and ^{widow;}_{widow:}
But the way of the wicked he ¹turneth upside
down.
¹⁰ The LORD shall reign for ever,
_{*even*} ^{Thy} thy God, O Zion, unto all generations.
²Praise ye the LORD.

¹ ²Praise ye the ^{LORD;}_{LORD:}

147 ³For it is good to sing praises unto our
God;
For it is ^{pleasant;}_{pleasant:} *and* praise is comely.
² The LORD doth build up ^{Jerusalem;}_{Jerusalem:}
He gathereth together the outcasts of Israel.
³ He healeth the broken in heart,
And bindeth up their ⁴wounds.
⁴ He telleth the number of the stars;
He ^{giveth}_{calleth} them all _{by} ^{their} *their* names.
⁵ Great is our Lord, and ^{mighty in power;}_{of great power:}

R.V. ¹ Or, *maketh crooked*   ² Heb. *Hallelujah.*   ³ Or,
For he is good: sing praises unto our God, for he is gracious
⁴ Heb. *sorrows.*

His understanding is infinite.

6 The LORD ^{upholdeth} the meek:

He ^{bringeth} the wicked down to the ground.

7 Sing unto the LORD with thanksgiving;

Sing ^{praises} upon the harp unto our God:

8 Who covereth the heaven with clouds,

Who prepareth rain for the earth,

Who maketh grass to grow upon the mountains.

9 He giveth to the beast his food,

And to the young ravens which cry.

10 He delighteth not in the strength of the horse:

He taketh ^{no} pleasure in the legs of a man.

11 The LORD taketh pleasure in them that fear
     him,

In those that hope in his mercy.

12 Praise the LORD, O Jerusalem;

Praise thy God, O Zion.

13 For he hath strengthened the bars of thy gates;

He hath blessed thy children within thee.

14 ¹He maketh peace in thy ^{borders;}

^{He and} filleth thee with the ²finest of the wheat.

15 He sendeth ^{out} his commandment upon ^{earth;}

His word runneth very swiftly.

16 He giveth snow like ^{wool;}

He scattereth the ^{hoar frost} like ashes.

17 He casteth forth his ice like morsels:

Who can stand before his cold?

18 He sendeth out his word, and melteth them:

R.V.   ¹ Heb. *He maketh thy border peace.*   ² Heb. *fat of wheat.*

He causeth his wind to blow, and the waters flow.
19 He sheweth his word unto Jacob,
His statutes and his ^judgements_judgments unto Israel.
20 He hath not dealt so with any nation:
And as for his ^judgements,_judgments, they have not known
them.
¹Praise ye the LORD.

148

¹ ¹Praise ye the LORD.
Praise ye the LORD from the heavens:
Praise him in the heights.
2 Praise ye him, all his angels:
Praise ye him, all his ^host._hosts.
3 Praise ye him, sun and moon:
Praise him, all ye stars of light.
4 Praise him, ye heavens of heavens,
And ye waters that be above the heavens.
5 Let them praise the name of the LORD:
For he commanded, and they were created.
6 He hath also stablished them for ever and ever:
He hath made a decree ²which shall not pass ^away.
7 Praise the LORD from the earth,
Ye ³dragons, and all deeps:
8 ^Fire_Fire, and ^hail, snow,_hail; snow, and ^vapour;_vapours;
Stormy ^wind:_wind; fulfilling his word:
9 ^Mountains_Mountains, and all hills;
Fruitful ^trees_trees, and all cedars:

R.V. ¹ Heb. *Hallelujah.*   ² Or, *which none shall transgress*
³Or, *sea-monsters* Or, *waterspouts*
260

10 Beasts, and all cattle;
   Creeping things, and flying fowl:
11 Kings of the earth, and all peoples;
   Princes, and all judges of the earth:
12 Both young men, and maidens;
   Old men, and children:
13 Let them praise the name of the LORD:
   For his name alone is exalted:
   His glory is above the earth and heaven.
14 And he hath lifted up ¹the horn of his people,
   The praise of all his saints;
   Even of the children of Israel, a people near
      unto him.
   ²Praise ye the LORD.

                  ¹ ²Praise ye the LORD.
149   Sing unto the LORD a new song,
          And his praise in the assembly of the
             saints.
 2 Let Israel rejoice in him that made him:
   Let the children of Zion be joyful in their King.
 3 Let them praise his name in the dance:
   Let them sing praises unto him with the timbrel
      and harp.
 4 For the LORD taketh pleasure in his people:
   He will beautify the meek with ³salvation.
 5 Let the saints be joyful in glory:

R.V. ¹ Or, *a horn for his people, a praise for all his saints;
even for &c.*   ² Heb. *Hallelujah.*   ³ Or, *victory*

Let them sing ^{for joy}_{aloud} upon their beds.

⁶ *Let* the high praises of God *be* in their [1]mouth,
And a ^{two-edged}_{twoedged} sword in their hand;

⁷ To execute vengeance upon the ^{nations,}_{heathen,}
And punishments upon the ^{peoples}_{people};

⁸ To bind their kings with chains,
And their nobles with fetters of iron;

⁹ To execute upon them the ^{judgement}_{judgment} written:
[2]This honour have all his saints.
[3]Praise ye the LORD.

150   ¹ [3]Praise ye the LORD.
Praise God in his sanctuary:
Praise him in the firmament of his
power.

² Praise him for his mighty acts:
Praise him according to his excellent greatness.

³ Praise him with the sound of the trumpet:
Praise him with the psaltery and harp.

⁴ Praise him with the timbrel and dance:
Praise him with stringed instruments and ^{the pipe.}_{organs.}

⁵ Praise him upon the loud cymbals:
Praise him upon the high sounding cymbals.

⁶ Let every thing that hath breath praise [4]the
LORD.
[3]Praise ye the LORD.

R.V. [1] Heb. *throat.*   [2] Or, *He is the honour of all his saints*
[3] Heb. *Hallelujah.*   [4] Heb. *Jah.*

For EU product safety concerns, contact us at Calle de José Abascal, 56–1°,
28003 Madrid, Spain or eugpsr@cambridge.org.

www.ingramcontent.com/pod-product-compliance
Ingram Content Group UK Ltd.
Pitfield, Milton Keynes, MK11 3LW, UK
UKHW010850090126
466816UK00011B/140